The End of the City of Gold? Industry and Economic Crisis in an Italian Jewellery Town

The End of the City of Gold?
Industry and Economic Crisis in an Italian Jewellery Town

By

Michele Filippo Fontefrancesco

CAMBRIDGE
SCHOLARS
PUBLISHING

The End of the City of Gold?
Industry and Economic Crisis in an Italian Jewellery Town,
by Michele Filippo Fontefrancesco

This book first published 2013

Cambridge Scholars Publishing

12 Back Chapman Street, Newcastle upon Tyne, NE6 2XX, UK

British Library Cataloguing in Publication Data
A catalogue record for this book is available from the British Library

ISBN (10): 1-4438-4847-6, ISBN (13): 978-1-4438-4847-3

To Antonio and Lelia

TABLE OF CONTENTS

LIST OF ILLUSTRATIONS

Photos and Graphs

Maps

ACKNOWLEDGMENT

The help and support of many people were crucial to completing this work. First of all, I want to thank Matei Candea, Ben Campbell and Paul Sant-Cassia for the many things they taught me and helped me to learn during the work together. Special thanks Thomas Yarrow and Victoria Goddard for their suggestions and reflections.

Many friends sustained me during the months of fieldwork and writing-up. I want to thank Claudia Merli, Federico Schneider, Carlo Caruso, Federico Federici, Piercarlo Grimaldi, Davide Porporato, Paola Bassino, Hamza Hasan, Klara Capova, Steve Emery, Gianpiera Conti, Luca Visconti, Arianna Peracchio, Massimo Mensi, Renato Lopena, Laura Como, Antonio Ornato. There are many others who should be thanked, so I must beg their forgiveness that their names do not appear here.

While researching and writing this book I benefited greatly from the help of Gianluca Barbero: He is a friend and the person that first opened the world of jewellery making to me. I am indebted to him and to the other friends and informants who supported my research.

Finally, I owe much to Bona, Amalia, Roberto, Gigi, Rodolfo, Claudia and all the other members of my family that have been always with me, always ready to sustain me and push me to continue the work.

Grazie.

Declaration

A first version of Chapter 1 has been published in the article: Fontefrancesco, Michele Filippo. 2011. "The City of Goldsmiths." *Anthropological Notebooks* 17, no. 1: 21-59

A first version of Chapter 8 has been published in the article: Fontefrancesco, Michele Filippo. 2012. “The Spectacle of the Crisis: Local Perception of Economic and Social Change in Valenza”. *Issues in Ethnology and Anthropology* 7 (1): 65-83

Abiding by the current *Ethical Guidelines for Good Research Practice* of the Association of Social Anthropologist of the UK and Ireland, in this book, all names of firms and informants quoted in the article are anonymised.

Crisis in the City of Gold: An Introduction

Uncertainty defines the current European economy. While top-down approaches fail to provide solutions for the transformations that are jeopardizing welfare and future development of countries such as Greece, Portugal, Spain and Italy, it appears urgent to look at the grassroots level to find those elements that can help to fully understand the crisis and its impact, in order to identify positive remedies. From this perspective, this book looks at Italy and one of its most prestigious industries, jewelery production, to investigate structural changes triggered by the current economic crisis. The volume does so by exploring the effects of the downturn in one of the key cities for the industry, Valenza, between 2008 and 2010. In so doing, it questions how the relationship between a community and a form of economic activity is perceived, established and performed, and how a downturn can reverberate throughout this web of meanings and practices.

The recent history of Italy has been characterised by a critical economic conjuncture. Scholars (e.g. Di Quirico, 2010; Festa and Sapelli, 2009; Bianchi Renzo, 2009; Rabellotti et al., 2009) and journalists (e.g. Limes, 2011) identify high national debt, heavy taxation and widespread tax-evasion, together with an overall stagnant economy and recession of industrial production – once the driving sector of Italian economy – as the principal causes of the present economic crisis. While an international debate continues regarding the causes and possible solutions to the Italian economic crisis, in this book I intend to bring to the fore the effects of industrial recession at the local level. In so doing, I will consider the recent transformations that a city, Valenza, and its main industry, jewellery production, have experienced in the last years of the 2000s.

Valenza is a representative case of the Italian economy. Its jewellery is an emblematic example of a 'made in Italy' commodity: internationally known and marketed, innovative and high-quality products (Fortis, 1998; Cristofaro, 2011). Moreover, the structure of Valenza's industry, based on the networking of hundreds of small firms, has made the city a widely studied example (e.g. Magni, 1999; Gaggio, 2007; Gaibisso, 1995; Bassano,

2008; Garofoli, 2004) of an Industrial District [ID]: a particular production articulation characteristic of the entire Italian economy, which has been considered a fundamental model of flexible production (Sabel and Piore, 1984) in the scholarly debate about post-Taylorist industrialism.

While the literature about IDs, and specifically about Valenza, has thoroughly investigated the structure of the business, in presenting the downturn of this city, as well as explaining the articulation of jewellery production, I will explore the cultural linkage between the urban community and the industry; an aspect scarcely broached by current literature.

In this book, I argue that the jewellery industry is a fundamental element of the identity discourse of Valenza (Chapter 1), and of the city's articulation through time and space (Chapter 2). Its pervasive presence, moreover, blurs rigid distinctions between production and non-production, private and public spaces, so as to lead the community to perceive the entire city as a macro-jewellery factory. Throughout the 20th century, while jewellery-making developed into a lucrative business, production was automated to only a limited degree, and the industry developed as a network of small enterprises (Chapter 3). It emerged as a source of widespread wealth for the city, particularly for goldsmiths, and locally became the most valued work activity and provided an inclusive social context that did not present strong social contrast and distinction between entrepreneurs and workers (Chapters 3 and 4). In this context, craftsmanship has become the keyword to define the profession and the specificities of local production. Moreover, craftsmanship imbues an understanding of the goldsmith profession rooted in an individualistic model of success based on an individual's art and entrepreneurial ability (Chapter 4). I demonstrate that this understanding, although echoing the neoliberal model of self-made man widely discussed in the national political debate in the past twenty years has been an expression of the entrepreneurial model that had developed in Valenza since the 1920s, rather than being an example of the appropriation of the neoliberal discourse (Briziarelli, 2011) similar to the one documented by Stacul (2007).

The downturn of the late 2000s (Chapter 5), I point out, represents a profound rupture in this history, jeopardizing the foundations of the district economy. The precarisation of about half of the goldsmithing jobs resulted in a progressive erosion of the social body (Chapter 6 and 7), and triggered internal social tensions (Chapter 7). The downturn has, moreover, thrown into crisis the entrepreneurial model of small workshops and the practice of networking. On a larger scale, the downturn undermined the trust and the identity link that bound people in Valenza to the business and triggered a redefinition of the 'sense of place' (cf. Field and Basso, 1996) of the city that marginalises the role of the jewellery industry (Chapter 8).

Exploring the effects of the downturn, this book, thus, contributes to anthropological debates on three main levels. Firstly, it is a contribution to the anthropological analysis of Italy, through an exploration of an aspect of the more general economic recession that engulfed Italy in the late 2000s. Secondly, by pointing out the possible causes of an incipient dissolution of the Valenza district, it offers insights for the on-going discussion in economic anthropology concerning flexible industrialisation, by showing the fragility of the ID model of local development in the context of the present global economy. Finally, the book contributes to the anthropology of economic crises by showing that a downturn can be explained as a cultural change that passes through the traumatic renegotiation of symbols, landmarks, memories, and worldviews.

In this introduction, I present the context of this research, the history and characteristics of Italian industrialism and the particular case of Valenza, as well as its theoretical framework, the interdisciplinary research on industrial districts and the anthropological debate on economic crises. In so doing, I show how the case of Valenza relates to these strands of research and can contribute to them. I will conclude the introduction by outlining the structure of the book and the principal contents of its chapters.

Italy and industry

Italy has just reached its 150th year after its national unification, which happened in 1861. According to the World Economic Outlook, released in September 2011 by the International Monetary Fund, it is the 8th largest nation by GDP, mostly based on its manufacturing industry.

In contrast to countries such as the United Kingdom, France or Germany, Italian national industrialisation began mostly in the last decades of the 19th century (Amatori et al., 1999). In the years of its unification, the nation still based its economy mostly on agricultural production, an economic sector that produced about 80% of the GDI (Bravo, 2001: 90-91). Factories were mostly concentrated around the largest cities, such as Milan, Turin, Genoa, Rome and Naples and only a limited number of these enterprises employed modern production management and technology. It was actually one of the priorities of the new Kingdom of Italy to 'modernise' the national economy, mostly providing the country with infrastructures, such as new roads and railways, and expanding national industry. From the late 1870s, Italy started its industrial revolution. Large enterprises, mainly steel and textile industries, were opened, mostly in North-Western Italy, in the so called 'industrial triangle' described by the cities of Turin, Milan and Genoa. The growth of the national market and state subsidies accelerated the expansion of the secondary sector (Cohen et al., 2001: 46-69). In the wake of WWI, the three largest cities in the North had turned into international industrial centres, and new industries were developing in other cities in Northern and Central Italy along the lines of a model that had emerged in Europe and America after the second industrial revolution and culminated in the rational Taylorist factory (Taylor, 2004 [1911]).

From the 1920s, with the exception of the years of WWII (Malanima and Zamagni, 2010), the secondary sector experienced a steady growth in terms of turnover and employment. Particularly, in the years immediately after WWII, during reconstruction (late 1940s) and in the following decades (1950s-1960s), the country experienced a new phase of rapid industrial growth (Crainz, 1996; Crainz, 2003; Bini, 2005; Cohen et al., 2001: 87-106). The industry of Miracolo Economico [Economic Miracle] was still a heavy, Taylorist one (Romeo, 1988) exemplified by firms such as the FIAT car industry, the ITALSIDER steel industry, or the MONTEDISON chemical industry (Romeo, 1988: 225-99). However, in the shadow of these companies, another form of industrialism had been growing: one made up by local, industrial agglomerations of small firms all specialised in a similar production; a model of industrialisation currently known as ID.

Valenza

Of this form of agglomerations, Valenza represents a paradigmatic example (e.g. Magni, 1999; Gaibisso, 1995; Garofoli, 2004; Gaggio, 2007; Crestanello, 2009). It is one of the world's most important centres for jewellery production (Gereffi et al., 2010; Gereffi, 2007; Carcano, 2007b). In this city, internationally known brands, such as Damiani (www.damiani.it), and international companies such as Bulgari (www.bulgari.com), Gucci (www.gucci.com), Cartier (www.cartier.com), and Boucheron (www. boucheron.com) manufacture their jewellery together with dozens of other small and medium enterprises. It is this network of firms and the expertise of local goldsmiths that have made this city the principal Italian centre for the production of high-quality jewellery: a local reality of production that has marketed its product throughout the entire world.

In the mid-2000s, the industrial fabric of the city was made up of over 1,200 companies, employing approximately 7,000 employees (Benzi and Fugagnoli, 2004b). In an urban population of about 21,000, these figures are a good indication of the relevance of this industry to the entire city: Almost half of Valenza's working population was directly involved in this business. To portray this relevance, people in Valenza as well as scholars (Fondazione Cassa di Risparmio di Alessandria and The European House Ambrosetti, 2010: 71), often defined the city as a '*monocoltura orafa*' [jewellery monoculture], conveying the idea of a human and physical space dominated by this industry (Chapters 1 and 2).

Due to its international economic success, scholars have extensively studied Valenza's industry and compared it with other Italian centres of jewellery production (Gaibisso, 1995; Bassano, 2008; Crestanello, 2009; Gaggio, 2007). They analytically investigated specific social and economic characteristics, such as local entrepreneurship (Lenti, 1994; Garofoli, 2004), the structure of the network of firms (Gereffi, 2007; Gaggio, 2007), the interconnection between formal and informal economies (Gaggio, 2007; Pietrasanta, 1991), and goldsmiths' working conditions (Gaggio, 2007; Garofoli, 2004; Tinelli et al., 1990; Pietrasanta, 1991). Moreover, this scholarship provides a detailed account of the industry's development during its two centuries of history (Lenti, 1994, 2010; Gaggio 2007).

The jewellery industry developed throughout the 19th century, as a secondary economic vocation. Principally a rural settlement until the 19th century, Valenza began its industrialisation in the second half of the century, largely propelled by the success of the footwear industry. This industry boomed during the 1930s and 1940s, only to decline after WWII and almost completely disappear in the 1960s (Maggiora, 2010; Penna Ivaldi, 2008). In the same decades as the footwear industry's declined, the jewellery industry boomed (Gaggio, 2007; Lenti, 1994): from a situation of 296 firms and 1,809 employees in 1951, by 1968, it had reached 1,021 firms and 5,562 employees and was continuing to expand (Gaggio, 2007: 88). In addition to high quality local production and crafts, the growth of the industry was propelled by the booming of the domestic market in the 1950s and 1960s – the years of the Italian *Miracolo Economico* (Bini, 2005; Zamagni, 1993: 337-79). The gradual opening of markets worldwide since the 1950s, and a national currency whose weakness against major international currencies, such as the German Mark, Japanese Yen and American Dollar, increased the competitiveness of 'made in Italy' products abroad, in spite of strict customs regulations in foreign markets.

During the last fifty years, the city has developed into an industrial network, which encompasses the city and a few other neighbouring villages (Benzi and Fugagnoli, 2004b). The network has mostly been made up of small and micro firms of which the average scale is 6 employees. The industry specialises in high quality, craft-based jewellery: a production based on creativity and a low level of mechanisation (Gaibisso, 1995; Garofoli, 2004; Gereffi, 2007). Differently from other Italian industrial agglomeration studies by anthropologists, however, it has to be noted that the micro-firms in general do not fit the typical model of family businesses[1]. Moreover, while friction can be found between talented and non-talented artisans (Chapter 4) and between large, often international, outsourcing companies and supplying micro firms[2], within the social body of jewellery makers, there is no perceived opposition between employer and employee[3].

---

[1] IDs' entrepreneurship has often been described as based on family businesses (Yanagisako, 2002: 25-29). In its strictest definition, family business refers to a company whose activities are carried out only by the members of a family. More commonly, the term refers to companies where management activities and direction of production are carried out by the members of the same family (Sharma, 2004: 3-4). Moreover, this definition assumes that the continuation of the enterprise is mostly subordinated to a passage from father to son in the direction of the company. While compared to this model, Valenza shows its first peculiarity. In the second half of the 2000s, only a minority, around 20%, of these businesses had a similar profile (Paradiso, 2008a). In a local context where the average lifespan of companies does not exceed 10 years, and in which most companies have been opened in the last thirty years, the majority of jewellery firms do not exceed the average of 6 employees. These firms are often organised around one or two artisans, the firm-owners, and a small number of workers employed for administrative and production purposes. Although it is not uncommon for firm-owners' wives or partners to be employed in the company, it is rare that their children are employed as well. When the firms' owners are on the verge of retirement, the firms are more commonly bought by some of the firm's workers, rather than passed on to the firm-owners' children. Such a succession is more frequent in larger firms (over twenty employees). In this case, the succession follows the model proposed by Yanagisako, where the new generation succeeds the old one in administrative positions, often being barely aware of the actual techniques concerning production.

[2] In light of these peculiarities, which I also noticed during my fieldwork, I will not over-emphasise the role that family businesses play in the city. Instead considering goldsmiths as member of one social group and exploring the distinctions that they draw within the group. I will highlight the power structure implied in the network industry.

[3] This lack of opposition is mirrored in the marginality of the trade unions within the industry. Already in the early 1960s, only about 300 out of 4,000 goldsmiths

Although in a purely Marxist perspective, the dynamics of labour exploitation (Marx, 2010 [1867]: 147-50) are inevitably present in this model of an enterprise, as pointed out by numerous scholars (e.g. Benzi and Fugagnoli, 2004a; Lenti and Pugnetti, 1974; Barozzi, 1976; Lenti, 1994; Gaggio, 2007), at least since the 1960s, Valenza had not experienced an opposition between entrepreneurs and workers as other IDs experienced (e.g. Blim, 1990). To explain this alignment between workers and entrepreneurs it is important to point out the generally higher wages of goldsmiths: between the 1970s and 1990s they were estimated to have been at least 150% of the wage of a metal worker with similar seniority. Moreover, the experience of micro-industries, which proliferated after the 1960s, has been fundamental for this alignment since they represented the ideal space that bridged the possible social and economic gap between employees and the employers, between entrepreneurs and workers. Firstly, in those firms, firm-owners worked together with their workers on the shop floor so that there was no functional division between the two roles. Secondly, the widespread practice of outsourcing and the availability of work meant particular managerial knowledge was not a requirement; instead, the success of a firm was made possible thanks to goldsmiths' artisan crafts. Finally, since they provided opportunities for any worker to easily become an entrepreneur thanks to the low investment required to start them.

These above mentioned were the principal characteristics that the industry developed after WWII, over a period of almost fifty years of substantial unfettered growth[4] that had led a small town to become an

---

were members of the unions (Maggiora, 2010: 220-22). In the course of the next thirty years this figure declined. In the early 1990s, in a body of over 7,000 goldsmiths, unions counted no more than 200 goldsmiths among their members (Lerner, 1991). In the 2000s the number was unchanged. The unions occupied a marginal role in the public space of the city as well. From the early 1970s until July 2005 (Sg Valenza, 2005), in the media and official records there is no trace of strikes or public demonstrations organised by the unions in the city. This marginality can mainly be explained by considering the social and legal peculiarity of work in a small firm that tends to marginalise the role of the unions in the mediation of work disputes between entrepreneurs and workers. However, we must also consider those aspects concerning the access to the means of production and the peculiarity of this production that are characteristics of Valenza.

[4] Although this pattern of development did not exclude downturns. Valenzani particularly remember the one that occurred between 1973-74, a particularly difficult period for the jewellery industry due to the surge in the price of gold and the world economic crisis following the Yom Kippur War (Maggiora, 2010: 242-

internationally known centre of production (Gaggio, 2007; Maggiora, 2010) with annual revenues that exceeded €800 million in 2001 (Paradiso, 2008c; Paradiso, 2008d). Focusing on this particular locale, my research aims to explore the role of jewellery making, the lynchpin of the industrial monoculture, in the city; how it shapes the space and time of Valenza and influences the sense of belonging of the inhabitants of the city and the identity rhetoric associated with it; how it is perceived and experienced by the community. In so doing, it interrogates the structure of the trade in Valenza, studying the practices of production and models of entrepreneurship. For this reason, this work is intertwined with a thread of research on modern industrialism that has flourished in the past forty years: the study of IDs.

Industrial Districts

Valenza, in fact, appears as an exemplar of a model of industrial organisation that is spread throughout the country (ISTAT, 2001). Since the 1970s, IDs have been at the centre of a broader intellectual debate that involved Italian economists and sociologists, among whom Bagnasco (1977), Garofoli (1981) and Beccattini (1978; 1979) were the forerunners in addressing these particular experiences.

Scholars were interested in understanding the organisation of the local economy, the interconnection among firms' productions and the relationship between industry and community. From this perspective, they took insight for the interpretation of these agglomerations from the ID theory proposed by the English scholar Alfred Marshall in the late 19th and early 20th centuries (Becattini, 1978, 1979)

Taking the textile districts of Lancashire and Sheffield as examples, in his works *The Economics of Industry* (Marshall and Marshall, 1879), and the later *Principles of Economics* (Marshall, 1920: IV.X.1-IV.X.21), Marshall explored the economic relationship between individual firms and the industrial characteristics of the region in which they are established, by treading a research path overlooked by previous theories of industry, such as Marx's (Marx, 2010 [1867]: 216-354) and John Stuart Mills' (Stuart Mills, 2009 [1848]). In these areas, Marshall saw that firms experienced a positive effect on their economy by being located within the district. This trend originated in the extensive collaboration in production that resulted

45). However, as early as 1975, Valenza's jewellery industry resumed growing apace, reaching its peak in 2000 (Paradiso, 2008c).

from the interconnection – hence interdependence – of firms' cycles of productions and from:

> "The nature and quality of the local labour market, which is internal to the district and highly flexible. Individuals move from firm to firm, and owners as well as workers live in the same community, where they benefit from the fact that 'the secrets of industry are in the air'." (Markusen, 1996: 299)

On the basis of Marshall's theory (e.g. Hart, 2009; Loasby, 2009), Becattini produced a description of an ideal Marshallian ID.

> "A Marshallian ID is a local system; that is, an area where a community of people live and work, with a great deal of persistently overlapping experiences." (Becattini, 2006: 347)

> "[It is a particular type of locality] characterised by a certain degree of local economic dominance of an industry ('local specialisation'). This main industry includes a mix of horizontal (competitive), vertical (input-output), and diagonal (related services and instruments) specialised activities. Together with the main industry, other secondary industrial activities may be localised in the district, more or less related to the main one, as a result of various evolutionary adjustments and developments." (Becattini et al., 2009: XVIII)[5]

Employing this concept in the study of the success of industries in Tuscany, Beccatini indicated the success of industrial agglomerations of micro and small firms in the presence of an economic and social network of relations within the bounded space of the agglomeration. The importance of this relational network meant that the source of competitive advantage of a single firm was not simply found in its internal organisation, but was ascribed to a wider dimension that included the territory, the other companies and the community (Becattini, 1989).

Industrial districts and flexible industrialisation

While over the course of the last thirty years, the model of Marshallian ID gave rise to one of the principal lines of interpretation that scholars have used to interpret post-WWII Italian industrialism (for a history of the

[5] See also: (Markusen, 1996: 298).

studies: Bianchi Patrizio, 2009: 104)[6], in the 1980s, this model became the subject of an international debate about forms of industrialism alternative to the model of Taylorist firms; a debate that interwove with the discussion on the flexibilisation of industry (Triglia, 2009) triggered by the work of Piore and Sabel (1984).

The work of these two scholars analyses the 1970s economic crisis in Western countries and recognised it as the result of a saturation of the goods market. After twenty five years of intense demand for cars, appliances, clothes, and other goods to which entrepreneurs had responded through a mass-production-oriented industry, the possibilities for further growth appeared to have been exhausted (Piore and Sabel, 1984: 24). In an exhausted market, Schumpeter (1994 [1943]) had already pointed out that the only way to revive demand is a permanent innovation that shortens the period of obsolescence of a product through the constant creation of new models. An industry based on large plants designed to mass-produce (identical) goods was not fit to keep up the necessary pace of innovation. In the face of this new necessity, Piore and Sabel (1984) suggested that the 1970s marked a second industrial divide that coincided with the rise of a new model of industrial production:

> "[It] is based on flexible—multi-use—equipment; skilled workers; and the creation, through politics, of an industrial community that restricts the forms of competition to those favouring innovation. For these reasons the spread of flexible specialisation amounts to a revival of craft forms of production that were emarginated at the first industrial" (Piore and Sabel, 1984: 17)

Piore and Sabel, hence, identify four existing models of industrial development that embodied the new paradigm of flexibility. Firstly, the 'federated enterprises', inspired by Japanese pre-war *zaibatsu,* are groups of firms mutually interlocked through financial and management strategies, such as reciprocal ownership of shares, shared ownership of production structures, joint boards of directors. Secondly, the 'solar firms' are systems of firms hinging on the presence of a leading company that expands its production through a network of supplying firms, often financially controlled by the leading firm. Thirdly, the 'workshop firms' are small scale automated firms that do not produce long runs of standardised productions. Both solar firms and workshop firms were

---

[6] Among the many examples of Italian IDs, there is Valenza, currently one of the top 36 Italian IDs, the annual turnover of which exceeds €500 million (Servizio Studi e Ricerche, 2011: 6-7).

models inspired by Western Germany's post-war industrialism. Finally the 'regional conglomerations', inspired by Italian IDs[7].

The success of Piore and Sabel's analysis sparked the interest of the scientific community towards these forms of alternative industrial development, and in particular Italian IDs became a subject of international interest (Becattini et al., 2009; Markusen, 1996; Amin, 2002).

Ethnographies of IDs

In the debate on IDs that followed, anthropologists offered their contribution. In particular, anthropologists have engaged with it by exploring the network economy, and the social relations and struggles that underpin it. The body of research developed since the late 1980[8] (e.g. Yanagisako, 2002; Blim, 1990; Cento Bull and Corner, 1993; Ghezzi, 2007; Gaggio, 2007) offers a critical analysis of this model of industry, in contrast to the rosy picture proposed by Piore and Sabel.

Social capital

In their analysis, these works have often relied on the concept of social capital to explore the sociality of the network economy and its "dark side" (cf. Field, 2003: 71).

Introduced by Bourdieu (1985: 248), since the 1980s, the concept of social capital has often been employed in the social sciences to objectify and define the role played by interpersonal relationships and social networks in influencing individuals in their economic actions (a review of the history and academic debate of this concept is offered by: Field, 2003; Fine, 2001). From this perspective, relationships had been defined as economic resources that facilitate the individual in their enterprise (Coleman, 1988: 98; Field, 2003: 20) and personal success (Coleman,

---

[7] This model encompasses geographic areas with high industrial density, where the manufacturing sector is mostly specialised in a single trade or interconnected trades (shoe production and machines for shoe production). Unlike the case of 'solar firms', in IDs firms are not necessarily bound by stable ties of cooperation, but the proximity of such specialised firms tends to reinforce the economic performances of each firm. Moreover, the activities within these conglomerations are not attributable to the presence of one, leading firm but to a more diffuse and independent entrepreneurship linked together by strong social ties (Piore and Sabel, 1984: 267-68).

[8] Benton (1989) offers a comparative study of Spanish regional agglomerations. This is the first example I came across of an ethnographic study of IDs.

1990: 300). The role played by the affects, such as trust, that link the players in the networks has been especially studied. Particularly significant for ID studies have been the studies by Putnam (2000; Putnam et al., 1993). Analysing the interconnection between economic prosperity and political participation in Italy (Putnam et al., 1993) and in the USA (Putnam, 2000), he made a strong connection between the presence of a widespread network of social relations among local actors, namely a high social capital, local economic success, civic participation and legality by equating social capital to 'civic virtue' and trust towards other individuals to trust towards the State (Putnam, 2000: 19). In developing this widely debated model (a synopsis of this debate is provided by: Gaggio, 2007: 1-32), he used the cases of IDs as examples in which the presence of social capital turns into civic virtue, that is "civic involvement and social solidarity" (Putnam et al., 1993: 16).

While after almost twenty years the theories of Putnam still resonate in the scholarly debate on IDs (Bagnasco, 2009; De Blasio et al., 2009), anthropologists have contributed to showing the problematic nature of Putnam's alignment between the thickness of social relationships and 'civic virtues', and more specifically, legality[9]. In particular, Valenza,

[9] Already, the first ethnography of an Italian ID (Blim, 1990) had shown that the economic success of this form of industry does not only rely on the civic virtuousness of its actors. Instead, this study of a shoe-making specialised industry in the Marche region demonstrated that the commercial advantage of the ID was based on a production articulation that involved degrees of labour exploitation, and a general tendency to support formal economy with informal activities, such as the employment of undocumented labour, tax evasion and exploitation of women's and children's work.

A decade later, Yanagisako came back to the theme of social capital in the IDs. She focused her attention on the role played by kinship in the silk industry of Como's ID. In approaching kinship, the ethnography examines the role played by women in the firms. Although women's importance emerges from the interviews with informants and from official documents, such as agreements between siblings and testaments, Yanagisako noticed the erasure of the active and passive roles women played in the history of the firms from the principal narrative of family businesses in Como. Although this negation can be based on a factual tendency to exclude women from the business or at least from the leadership of firms – a practice that emerges from widespread tendencies such as making daughters take careers as teachers or public servants, rather than integrating them into the firms as clerks, accountants or managers – the scholar used this tendency to point out a broader cultural (or ideological) instance underpinning this exclusion. She explains that oblivion can be considered the effect of a cultural understanding of entrepreneurship as an almost exclusively masculine business. This does not only tend to marginalise or exclude female family members in the management of the

together with Arezzo and Vicenza, were used by Gaggio as significant examples to explain in a historical perspective how the economic success of these districts relied on what he terms a 'reversed mafia' (Gaggio, 2007: 321): secretive and informal relations and an unbalanced economic and social power between outsourcers (the strongest) and suppliers (the weaker). Thus, in these cities social capital was not allied to civic virtue; instead, the social capital of a community was the fundamental element in the spreading of informal activities and their regular employment in the business.

Although the literature on IDs has consistently relied on the concept of social capital to describe the nexus between sociality and industry, in this work I will depart from this tradition. In the 2000s, authors, such as Rankin (2004) and Fine (2001; 2010), pointed out particular limits to this concept. First of all, from its very name, this concept conveys an idea of economic activities as divorced and substantially different from the social actions (Fine, 2001: 141-42). Moreover, it also fosters the idea of a capital without a social dimension, which appears to have been turned into a model of conceptualizing all the other aspects of the lives of individuals as a particular form of 'capital' (Rankin, 2004: 23). Finally, although in econometric calculations such a concept can be employed as a strategic factor to remember that economy is embedded in and shaped by culture, it is arguable that the utility of the concept disappears in an anthropological discourse that starts from the assumption that the economy is social

---

company, but also fails to recognise the vital role they carry out for the continuation of production activities. Besides this interest in the gender issue, which Yanagisako (1991) had also showed in previous works, the author underlines the criticality of generational change at the top of the company. She points out the difficult agreements between siblings and the lack of preparation of the new generation in covering all those activities that were covered by the older generation. Exploring these different aspects of entrepreneurship in Como, Yanagisako is able to demonstrate how family businesses are a ground of mutual influence between the production and family.

More recently, Gaggio openly challenged Putman's assumption by focusing on four IDs: Valenza, Arezzo, Vicenza and Providence, MA (USA). The three Italian centres are the most important jewellery districts in Italy, and among the main centres for jewellery production in the world. Gaggio shows that in these three IDs, where jewellery production is based on a strong network of relationships and collaboration between companies, trust and non-contractual relationships were not only a principal driver of local capitalism, but where also entwined with the widespread employment of activities, such as the exploitation of undocumented work, smuggling, and tax evasion; activities that overtly go in the opposite direction of civic virtues.

(Rankin, 2004: 23). Agreeing with Fine's and Rankin's analyses, I will not employ the concept of social capital, although I will deal extensively with social relations and how they become central to the jewellery business. Instead, I prefer to talk about relations and affects as elements of a social life without implying their objectification into an economic resource, such as social capital.

The Problematisation of flexible industry

Since the work of Blim (1990), the body of ethnographies about Italian IDs has shown the ambiguity that lies behind the dense social network and sociality that propel and underpin the network industry. In so doing they laid the basis for a problematisation of the idea of flexibilisation of production and work and its effects on communities. In this respect, they addressed an inadequacy of the theoretical model particularly noted by the anthropological community and overtly voiced by Narotzky (1997). While only the most recent works, such as Ghezzi (2007), display the specific genealogical link between the literature on Italian IDs and Narotzky, this body of research follows a methodological approach to the study of the locales that echoes her suggestions, in particular in the use of historical analysis as a complement to ethnography to explore the structuring of the network and the role played by flexibilisation in shaping the locale. In so doing, these studies have traced the thread that ties present experiences of industrial production to past enterprises rooted in pre-industrial manufacturing and agricultural economies. IDs did not emerge from a break with the past, but they still bear traces of these ways of living and understanding production and life. This particularly emerges in the social practices that underpin businesses, in the family running of businesses (Yanagisako, 2002, Ghezzi, 2007), and in the relationships between firms (Ghezzi, 2007; Gaggio, 2007). Considering labour and capital, moreover, these studies have revealed the limits of small (often family) businesses. They express an innovative capacity less developed than the one described by Piore and Sabel, and an overall economic structural weakness, since the firms are often unable to survive beyond their founders, being profoundly centred on them. Anthropologists have also revealed the deep bond that ties formal activities to informal practices, such as tax evasion, the exploitation of undocumented labour, smuggling and counterfeiting (Blim, 1990, Gaggio, 2007). Thus, they contributed to demystify a business model by highlighting its historicity, specificity and critical aspects.

These studies, thus, have shown the potentiality of a methodology that combines ethnography with historical analysis. In this work I will employ a similar approach to the analysis of Valenza's ID, in particular, in the investigation of the structuring of the network (Chapter 3 and 5) and the genealogy of the artisan ethos that underpins it (Chapter 4).

Unexplored issues

While current literature has highlighted the embeddedness of economic practices in a wider fabric of social practices and relations by investigating the role of trust and kinship, it did not enquire into a further level of embeddedness of the role of industry, what Feld and Basso, writing more generally, defined as the 'sense of place' (cf. Field and Basso, 1996): the different ways in "which people encounter places, perceive them, [...] invest them with significance [, and] in which places naturalise different worlds of sense." (Feld and Basso, 1996: 8).

Thus, it appears that "the intricate strengths and fragilities that connect places to social imagination and practice, to memory and desire, dwelling and movement" (Feld and Basso, 1996: 8) and the role that an industry plays in "illuminating different ways in which place is voiced and experienced" (Feld and Basso, 1996: 8) is still unexplored in the case of IDs. Thus, the more profound role that economic activities can have in a community (being one of the pillars of individuals' understanding of the world, their community and place) remains to be investigated.

Moreover, being mostly based on research conducted between the 1980s and 1990s—the historical period in which IDs were established and achieved their international success (Malanima and Zamagni, 2010; Colli, 2010)—these ethnographies describe Italian IDs as dynamic realities, mostly in expansion. Thus, they do not explore the on-going changes in working conditions and business structure that have occurred in IDs since the early 2000s, which have been seen as a decline of this industrial model.

According to the IMF (2011), the Italian economy slowed down from 2001, reaching an overall stagnation: +0.16% annual growth between 2001 and 2010. In this context, historians and economists (Sforzi, 2009; Rabellotti et al., 2009; Bianchi Renzo, 2009; Ramazzotti, 2008; Dunford, 2006; Sabel, 2004) have pointed out that the momentum of the districts has weakened and dissipated. A neoliberal reform of the Italian market – which was until the early 1990s a sheltered area whose competitiveness was protected by national inflationary policies and a strong customs policy (Nesi, 2010) –, the institution of the Euro as the national currency (Brunetti et al., 2000), and the increasing competition in international markets due to the strengthening of Eastern European and Asian competitors were some of the principal reasons for the industrial transformation (Solinas, 2006). This transformation appears to lead in two directions: first of all ,towards a reduction of the entrepreneurial density of the districts, and consequentially to the shutdown of smaller workshops; secondly, towards a rapid process of redefinition from the acephalic networks described by Piore and Sabel to more centralised systems governed by large, often multinational, corporations (Rabellotti et al., 2009).

These profound economic transformations reveal social and cultural changes concerning the cohesion and structure of the social body of practitioners involved in the industry, the change in entrepreneurial models, the meaning of work, the relationship between population and industry and the ways in which the transformations are perceived, understood and narrated by the participants of this change, be they workers, entrepreneurs, relatives or just fellow townsmen in a "district on the move" (cf. Sabel, 2004). However, these issues were not explored by the current literature.

My work, thus, aims to address these issues, by exploring the recent past of Valenza and the downturn that started in 2008.

Valenza and the economic crisis

In the 2000s, Valenza's economy followed the general trend of Italian industry. After thirty years of success and growth, the jewellery economy faltered. Between 2002 and 2008, it experienced a phase of substantial stagnation: a two-year period (2002-2003) of a significant recession, mainly due to the instability of the markets after the 9/11 terrorist attacks and the military campaigns in Afghanistan and Iraq, and a new growth that, from 2004 to 2007, brought the local industry to reach sales volumes similar to those of 2001 (Paradiso, 2008d; Paradiso, 2007). Alongside this slowdown in sales, the industry stopped its expansion in terms of number of employees (Maggiora, 2010: 528-30).

Faced with this change, starting in 2006, goldsmiths and the local government opened a public debate on the future of the district (Raselli and Mensi, 2007): a debate that outlined a future of the city where, in Piore and Sabel's terms, the regional conglomeration would have developed into a solar system governed by multinational corporations. Some signs of this change could be seen in previous years, such as the decision of Bulgari to acquire its historical local supplier, Crova, and plan an establishment for over 500 employees on the outskirts of the city (Bulgari Group, 2006), and Damiani's project to build a new factory on a plot of about 20,000 m^2, in the western periphery of the city. In other words, the future of a flexible industry appeared to be enclosed in a Taylorist shift. While Valenza had been generally recognised as a significant example of network industry and ID (e.g. Magni, 1999; Gaibisso, 1995; Garofoli, 2004; Gaggio, 2007; Crestanello, 2009), the transformations revealed a structural change comparable to the broader trend described for Italian IDs. Due to this similarity, Valenza's change appeared to be a possible field of investigation to answer those questions about the relationship between community and industry still not addressed by existing scholars. Consequentially, my original plan was to conduct a study of this transformation, from the perspective of the change of production in Valenza and the 'sense of place' (cf. Field and Basso, 1996) and meaning that people in the city gave to jewellery making. However...

The bubble of subprime mortgage derivatives that burst in the early autumn of 2008 (Tett, 2009a, 2009b; Attali, 2009 [2008]) ushered in a deep recession for the Italian economy (in 2008, the Italian GDP shrank by 1.2% and in 2009, by 5.2%), and inaugurated a period of extreme uncertainty for the world jewellery market. Between 2008 and 2009, the world's demand for jewellery fell by 20% (Gereffi et al., 2010). For the Valenza industry, this led to a sudden plunge in exports, which halved between 2007 and 2009 (Gereffi et al., 2010), causing a wave of firm closures, and initiating a major redundancy as brutal as it was unexpected (2,000 people lost their jobs between 2009 and 2010). Moreover, the increase in national public debt in the face of the lack of an effective policy to revitalise the national economy between 2008 and 2011 has exacerbated the effects of the downturn at the local level (Di Quirico, 2010; Bianchi Renzo, 2009), in particular due to an erosion of public services and an increase in fiscal pressure.

After almost a decade of stagnation, 2008's Credit Crunch started a period of recession for Valenza: a new phase in its history that people in the city call simply *'la Crisi'* [the crisis]. My fieldwork, thus, resulted in the study of the downturn and its effects that led goldsmiths to rethink their work, their being goldsmiths. In face of *'la Crisi'*, all the community of Valenza problematize and the identity bond between the jewellery industry and Valenza. The study sought to question the meaning of an economic crisis for a local community in order to search for the socio-cultural effects caused by a rapid and deep global and local change, and to enquire into the present and possible future of IDs' flexible industry.

Economic crisis

Against this very specific background, this work addresses an apparently simple question: what is an economic crisis?

A first answer to this question comes from economics, the social science in which this concept was developed, during the 19th century, to define the slowdown of the exchange of goods. Particularly important in this theorisation were the works of Marx and Engels, who explained the concept of economic crisis in their *Manifesto of the Communist Party* (2000 [1848]: 7) and, more analytically, in Marx's *The Capital* (Marx, 2010 [1867]: 87-88, 2010 [1885]: 43-44) and Engels' *Socialism: Utopian and Scientific* (2010 [1880]).

They define 'economic crisis' as a feature of the market economy. In particular, working within a classical economic paradigm that describes the market economy as the result of the interaction between banks, firms and people, Marx argues that it is a cyclical process that passes through four phases: economic recovery, boom and prosperity, overproduction and slump, crisis and depression (Mandel, 1968: 347-49). Within this cycle, a crisis appears as a period of interruption of the process of accumulation of capital in the hands of the capitalists due to the blockage of goods consumption in the market (Marx, 2010 [1867]: 43). Hence, the term 'crisis' refers to a particular dynamic of the market; a precise configuration of its characteristics that brings the normal flow of exchanges to a halt.

Marx goes on to expand on an interpretation of the market already hinted at in his *Manifesto*. There, Marx and Engels explain the market economy as the complex set of exchanges that substantiates modern economic life and society. In such a conceptual framework, every market crash has a potentially profound social impact on society. In fact, in times of crisis, the material basis of human life becomes significantly reduced. Marx and Engels draw an analogy between economic crises and natural disasters for the devastating social and economic effects that these events can have on a society. In particular, they pointed out that economic crises, like famine, war and natural disasters in pre-capitalist societies, would lead not only to a precarisation of individuals' lives, but even to a return to barbarism (Marx and Engels, 2000 [1848]: 7). As Knight noticed:

> "One may not wholly agree that economic crisis, such as is currently being experienced internationally, is directly comparable to famine in sub-Saharan Africa, and the terms 'civilisation' and 'barbarism' do not sit so comfortably nowadays, but as an analogy of social change and when one considers a relativisation of normative circumstance, the concept becomes slightly less melodramatic." (2011: 168)

Despite the melodramatic tone of the description, in binding together (market) economic and social elements, and in emphasizing the severe consequences that can occur after an economic crisis, Marx and Engels on the one hand describe the critical nature of crises, and on the other point out how these moments also represent interruptions to the society's power system, so that they can potentially open the ground to social, political and economic change.

During the late nineteenth and early to mid-twentieth centuries, the debate about economic crises and market dynamics continued. Marx's ideas were influential on the works of the new generation of thinkers. However, we can trace a more general appropriation and reworking of his theory of the market within Economics. In this sense, Schumpeter's work is particularly significant. Influenced by Kontradiev (1981 [1925]), in his *Business Cycles* (2008 [1939]), the Austrian economist expands Marx's analysis of economic cycles and interprets it from a novel, liberal perspective, exploring the historical succession of phases from 1786 to 1929 with a focus on the transformation of social aspects "such as changes in tastes, changes in quantity (or quality) of factors of production, changes in methods of Supplying Commodities." (Schumpeter, 2008 [1939]: 66)

In particular, Schumpeter lays the foundation of his theory of innovation and destructive creativity, which he developed in more detail in his later *Capitalism, Socialism and Democracy* (1994 [1943]). In contrast to Marx, Schumpeter suggests the overall positivity of economic crises. Despite the momentary distress in exchanges and their social costs (an aspect that Schumpeter did not particularly explore), crises are seen as a generative force in the market economy. He argues that they lead individuals to explore new forms of production and products, and result in an overall betterment of the market and an expansion of the possibilities for individuals.

From the writings of Marx and Schumpeter emerges an understanding of economic crises as recurrent phases in the market economy. Moreover, the scholars' works bring to the foreground a profound relationship between the status of the exchanges, that is, the market economy (but more broadly, any structure of the economy), and other aspects of individuals' lives, which include not only the material quality of life, but also the political and social structure of communities. While these collateral effects are rarely investigated by economic theory, they have been the grounds for an anthropological analysis since the mid-20th century.

Anthropology and economic crises

Since the 1950s, economic downturns have often been the spatial-temporal contexts, although not the main subjects, of anthropological analyses that explored themes such as poverty (e.g. Lewis, 1963), industrial work (Burawoy, 1979; Richardson, 1979; Applebaum, 1986a, 1986b), migration (Brettel, 2000), territorial belonging (Ferguson, 1999; Stewart, 1996), and globalisation (Tsing, 2005; Appadurai, 1996; Inda and Prosaldo, 2002). More recently, the theme of economic crisis, and specifically the current global crisis, has come back to the attention of the anthropological community as a particularly urgent subject of exploration (Hart and Ortiz, 2008: 1). While the social sciences, including anthropology, economic crises are commonly simply interpreted as events limited to the sphere of trade and capital flows (Clarke, 2006), this interpretation has been openly challenged to include the social effects that these events have in the market, and more broadly, in present societies. At stake, in this new wave of studies, is the possibility of gaining an insight into the structure of global finance (Schwegler, 2009: 9; Schwittay, 2009), and more broadly the global economy (Hart and Ortiz, 2008: 2; Robbins, 2009; Røyrvik, 2011).

As a result, economic crises have become the context of ethnographic analyses of the process of definition and development of financial tools (e.g. Ouroussoff, 2010, Leins, 2011), while the upsurge of insecurity in market flows, and the reverberation of instability from global finance out to everyday economic practices, became the "geological window" (cf. Lévi-Strauss, 1971: 56) to explore this structure of the world's economy (Gudeman, 2010; Hart et al., 2010), often described by the media as a complex system governed by impersonal principles and supranational bodies. In particular, following a heuristic path opened by Malinowski (1932 [1922]) and Mauss (1967 [1925]), and established during the heated debate between formalists and substantivists ignited by the late works of Polanyi (1971, see also Polanyi et al., 1957), anthropological enquiring has reconsidered the role played by people, their way of living and perceiving the economy. In so doing, it has fostered an understanding of economies that takes into account the specificities of local cultures in economic actions and reintroduces people into an economic framework of impersonal bodies and universal laws (Hann and Hart, 2011: 72-99).

It is in this heuristic tableau that the question "what is an economic crisis?" is to be framed. In recent years, some scholars have answered this question by pointing out the impoverishment of conditions of life and the erosion of the social fabric of local communities (e.g. Gudeman, 2010).

Together with this answer, scholars (e.g. Loftsdóttir, 2010; Herzfeld, 2011) went beyond a materialist approach and pointed out that an economic crisis represents a transformation in the perception and symbolic meaning of a form of economy and production, and of the locale, the geographical and social space that an individual and a community inhabit.

Back in the 1990s, two ethnographies had moved in the same direction, creating the bedrock of this cultural interpretation. I am referring specifically to Ferguson's *Expectations of Modernity* (1999) and Stewart's *A Space on the Side of the Road* (1996).

In Ferguson, this analysis is framed within a broader reflection on globalisation. Whereas globalisation had commonly been described as the result of a world made up of connected communities (e.g. Castells; 1996, Bauman, 1998), Ferguson built his argument on an opposite assumption, that is that the 'natural' condition of each local community is to be disconnected from the others, and in so doing he emphasises the symbolic and socio-economic processes through which connections are made (see also: Ferguson, 2002). In Zambia, the main instrument had been the mining industry. Thanks to the abundant income from this activity, the state could establish a strong link with the Western idea of social success. The city-dwellers, as well as those people who migrated to the urban centres from rural areas, embraced the new, modern way of life by repudiating their past models of living and cutting ties with their native communities. In this sense, the mining industry represented a fundamental element through which individuals made sense of the world.

This economy, however, after decades of growth, experienced a profound slump in the late 1980s and early 1990s, the period of Ferguson's fieldwork. In the face of this downturn, the anthropologist concluded that:

> "Zambia's recent crisis is not only an economic crisis but a crisis of meaning, in which the way that people are able to understand their experience and to imbue it with significance and dignity has (for many) been dramatically eroded. Yet people are never passive in the face of such changes; mineworkers on the Copperbelt today are struggling to make sense of their experience, and to find new ways of conceptualizing the broad social and economic changes that rock their lives." (Ferguson, 1999: 14)

This effort, Ferguson pointed out, emerged mainly as a tension that led mineworkers and urban dwellers to rethink the relationship between the model of modernity, which, for many, had become an unattainable dream, and native cultures and communities. This describes a broader dynamic aimed at revising their 'global hierarchy of value' (cf. Herzfeld, 2004), and revaluing the abandoned networks and ways of living.

While the key element of Ferguson's work is to study the relationship of individuals with different models of success, and their relationship with traditional and westernised models of life, Stewart explores the relationship between individuals and space in the wake of industrial crisis and collapse. Stewart bases her ethnography on a fieldwork conducted since 1980 in a group of hamlets in West Virginia, USA (Stewart, 1996: 17), which were built as miner's camps in the early decades of the 20th century, and turned into a ruined landscape after the mining crisis in the 1960s and 1970s and the final closure of the pits in the 1980s. Inspired by Bachelard's (1994) reflection on the poetics of places, Stewart examines the emergence and the construction of the "space on the side of the road", a human space peripheral to the glittering narrative of success of the 'American dream', through the words of her informants and the weaving of narratives around objects and places: signs in and of the ruined landscape of the Virginian mountains. In her exploration of a corner of this 'other' America, the words of the interviewees, miners and miners' relatives, and the experience in the field thus become the means by which the landscape is made significant and evocative. In the stories hinged on these signs, the local culture is made manifest: a system of co-presence, where present and past coexists in the phenomenology of narration (Stewart, 1996: 20). The ethnographic practice thus becomes, to Stewart, the attempt:

> "To represent the shifting memories and desires of a haunting absent presence, to capture a 'system' that has the fragmentary contested qualities of the discursive process itself, to trace 'culture' through the tense of confabulation of social and discursive practices in use." (Stewart, 1996: 27)

The description of this system highlights the relevance that the mining industry still had in the community. It was the main, haunting but the meaningful absence on which the idea of place hinged for the (ex-) mining communities. In De Certeau's terms (1984: 117), it made the 'place' a meaningful 'space' of social interaction and memory, although this construction was based only on the ruins and debris (cf. Stoler, 2008) of that economy: abandoned machinery and huts, rusted carcasses of cars, loud silences in the human landscape of the mountain. In her phenomenological description of a community suspended in an eternal present, Stewart demonstrates the importance that an industry, even after its downfall and disappearance, can have for the creation of the sense of place and belonging to a place. She also offers an example of a methodological approach to the study of economy and economic crises that goes beyond the historical and economic reconstruction of causes and effects of the rooting of an industry in a particular locale. Focusing on the narrative woven together by various members of the community talking about signs of the landscape or 'remembering and retelling' their histories, she is able to bring to the foreground the emotional (and not just material) living bond that links individuals to a form of economy. In so doing, she brings to light aspects of social and economic life that are external to the area of investigation of economic theory but that appear crucial to understand the social role played by particular forms of production in a community.

Ferguson's and Stewart's works are not framed as ethnographies of an economic crisis, but they offer important elements of analysis and methodology to go beyond the limits imposed by economic theory in framing what an economic crisis is, and its impact on a community. Both of these works explored communities that endured or were enduring the effect of an economic downturn of the principal industry, in both cases the mining industry, on which the entire local economy depended. In acknowledging the economic relevance of the industry and the economic effects of the crisis they noticed, first of all, the material and symbolic role played by that form of economy for the community. The industry was the economic and symbolic instrument through which individuals founded their participation to an ideal of success, be it the 'American dream' or 'Western modernity', and placed themselves in high positions in their 'global hierarchies of value'[10] (cf. Herzfeld, 2004). This cultural role showed, in the first place, that production activities and goods and capital exchanges are not simply 'embedded' in society as proposed by Granovetter (1985). They represent a foundational element of the sense of belonging (Lovell, 1998) that gives meaning to a local community. Consequently, an economic crisis, that is, the interruption of those practices which are substantive in the sense of belonging, becomes a paradigmatic moment for the entire community: a moment that leads to the reconsideration of the self, the remodelling of society, and the shift in meaning of the very idea of the locale.

This reconfiguration was explored through different and, in my view, complementary methodologies by the two scholars. On the one hand,

---

[10] The emic worldview in which overlapping patterns of life generate hierarchies that span from apical models of social life, considered successful and central to the social body, to inferior ones, singled out as examples of failure and social marginalisation

Ferguson offers an analysis of the despair of miners sacked after the mining industry crisis, through a socio-historical approach, framing individuals' expectations as the very foundation of the constitution of the local. On the other, Stewart investigates the way in which miners experienced their landscape and expressed their sense of history and their relationship with a (disappeared) form of industry.

These studies and the more recent literature offer an alternative and complementary response to the one given by economic theory to our question about the meaning of an economic crisis. They show that a crisis not merely a slowdown or an interruption in the exchange of goods and capital, and to answer the question it is necessary to reintegrate economic activities into their original bedrock, that is the social and cultural life of a community (Bourdieu, 2005: 1-2). Thus, we must embrace a broader perspective that also encompasses an enquiry into the social, symbolic and emotional bonds that link individuals to a form of economy, the relationship between a community, the form of economy and the space of the community, and the way in which these connections change after the transformation in flows of goods and capital[11].

Fieldwork

Drawing on this scholarship, I have built my arguments on the materials collected in over two years of research (December 2008-January 2011), including 13 months of fieldwork in the city. Although the district of Valenza extends outside the city, encompassing a territory of approximately 300 km^2 and 11 other municipalities between two provinces and two regions – the province of Alessandria in Piedmont and the province of Pavia in Lombardy –, the research was conducted mainly in Valenza itself, the centre of the ID and the area with the greatest concentration of companies and people working in the trade[12].

---

[11] While anthropology of IDs has shown the potentialities of a methodological approach that combines ethnography and historic analysis, recent anthropological studies on rhetoric (e.g. Carrithers, 2005, 2009; Gudeman, 2009; Campbell, 2010; Emery, 2010) have provided fertile ground for understanding the way in which economic events and objects are perceived and enacted (see Chapter 1). Thus, the study of rhetoric appears as a further method to investigate local industry and its cultural meaning; a method I am going to employ in this research.

[12] Although, occasionally, following goldsmiths and jewellery merchants, I extended the area of my enquiring to other cities neighbouring Valenza, such as Alessandria, Casale Monferrato and Pavia, or more distant ones, such as Milan, Rome and Birmingham.

The fieldwork was carried out by combining archival research, conducted in the archives and libraries of Valenza, and Alessandria, with ethnographic methods.

The archival research was aimed at reconstructing the economic history of the city and the trade, in particular in the last forty years. Scholars such as Gaggio (2007) and Lenti (1994) had largely investigated the first century and a half of the industry's history offering a documented account of the origins of the business in the early 19th century, until its boom in the 1970s[13]. The archival research was aimed at filling gaps the information already available and providing a more complex account of the socio-political transformations of the city and its jewellery industry. From an examination of local and national newspapers and periodicals, the investigation involved the study of the deliberations of the Valenza City Council, Valenza goldsmiths' job associations and the Alessandria Chamber of Commerce.

The research included participation in the life of families of goldsmiths and non-goldsmiths, following the family members, where it was possible, in the different activities and moments of their daily lives. It involves, moreover, the visit and observation of workshops, mostly of small or medium size, where I was allowed to conduct observations of the daily production activities for prolonged periods. Unfortunately, none of them were any of the large establishments of the city. In the course of the research I conducted in-depth interviews with goldsmiths and non-goldsmiths of different ages, backgrounds and employment status. The information gathered enrich a more broad corpus of interviews, conducted either with goldsmiths or non-goldsmiths and focused on specific issues of working and social life in the city. I can also count the numerous meetings and casual conversations, which notes constellate my field-notes.

Finally, this research also draws from my experience as a journalist in Valenza. The most relevant experience took place between March and May 2009. I collaborated with the local radio news station, *Radiogold*, as one of the columnists for their programme "*Valenza: le persone, l'oro, la Crisi*" [Valenza: gold, people and the crisis]. This broadcast aimed to describe the effects of the downturn on the entire city of Valenza, as a holistic event that was changing not just the jewellery industry, but the way in which Valenzani – that is people of Valenza – were perceiving the business and their city. For this programme I was asked to write 9

[13] A local historian, Maggiora (2010), has recently produced a compendium about the history of the 20th century in Valenza. Although it represents a resource for economic and political data concerning the city, his account is often superficial and missing of a proper apparatus of historical sources and references.

editorials, freely available online, for the episodes of the series. I informed those articles with elements and data drawn from my early months of fieldwork, openly working against the precept of Kuper who suggested that "ethnographers should write for [other] anthropologists." (1994: 551)

My work as a journalist proved to be a further means of participation in the community I was studying. To be a journalist was to be a voice and a participant, not just an observer, in the public debate of Valenza. Here, I am not claiming to have changed the course of the city's history or that my contribution to this debate was particularly original, but the experience itself and the feedback I received further enriched my understanding of Valenza and its change.

Outline of the book

This book is divided into two parts. In the first part (Chapters 1-4), the connections between Valenza and its jewellery industry appear through the widespread identity rhetoric (Chapter 1), the deep penetration of jewellery production into the urban fabric (Chapter 2), as well as in the goldsmiths' way of understanding the production, *'artigianalità'* and entrepreneurship (Chapters 3 and 4). In the second part (Chapters 5-8), I have analysed the downturn (Chapter 5), and its effect on the participation of the community in the jewellery industry. On the one hand, the loss of their jobs obliged (ex-) goldsmiths to re-think and re-shape their world, by abandoning the practices, spaces and social networks associated with their previous work (Chapter 6). On the other hand, the worsening economic conditions led to a ruination of the industry that led goldsmiths to question their economic model (Chapter 7). More broadly, the downturn led Valenzani to challenge the identity rhetoric and start discussing the futures of a city without gold (Chapter 8).

In Chapter 1, I consider the identity discourse of Valenza that is symbolised by the trope of the '*città orafa*', goldsmith's city, and the wider identification of the city with its jewellery industry. By considering different nuances with which this identification is expressed, I offer an analysis of how this discourse is (re) produced by different actors, such as Valenza's policy makers, the press and the city's population.

In Chapter 2, I focus on the recurring metaphor, employed by my informants, that identifies Valenza with a big jewellery firm. Starting from this comparison I will explore the role that the industry has and has had in determining the rhythms and the landscapes of the city.

In Chapter 3, I will examine the way in which jewellery production is organised in the city. From the example of the production management of a large batch of rings ordered by a multinational corporation, I examine the structure of the jewellery business in the city and its articulation in a social and economic network that situates firms and producers in an integrated web of production. In light of this network and the historical process through which the network came to be I consider the theory of IDs, highlighting the limits that this theory has in describing the actual cosmos of this local industry.

In Chapter 4, I investigate the concept of *'artigianalità',* which goldsmiths commonly use to distinguish local industry. By considering the main meanings that are associated with this category, I point out that *'artigianalità'* represents a particular way of thinking and experiencing jewellery making that is achieved during the various stages of goldsmiths' careers, so that it represents the driving principle that behind the individual's engagement with the industry.

In Chapter 5, the first chapter of the second part of the book, I present the downturn and its effects in the city. In particular, by considering the conceptualisation of the downturn as an object of knowledge, *'la Crisi'*, I highlight how multiple narratives, i.e. multiple causes, are related to this object. In so doing, I outline the different historical trajectories of change that Valenzani use to explain the decline of the local industry. This tangle of trajectories stands *de facto* against a causal simplification of the downturn such as the one imposed by economists, who see in the downturn a mere effect of the Credit Crunch, and outlines a 'non-linear history' (cf. De Landa, 1997) of the downturn.

In Chapter 6, I examine the effects of the downturn on the goldsmiths, focusing on the experiences of those workers who lost their jobs after 2008. Being unable to be (quickly) reintegrated into the industry, they experience unemployment as a moment of profound, personal transformation and radical distancing from jewellery production, so deep as to make this experience be part of a process of un-becoming a goldsmith, that is the abandonment of *'artigianalità'* and individual's disengagement from the industry.

In Chapter 7, I move the focus to the jewellery industry as it has been transformed during the two years of my research. I bring to light a dual transformation: on the one hand, the intensification of power in the hands of outsourcing firms and the overall reduction of the exchange flows among firms; on the other, the desolation of the workplaces after the numerous layoffs. These interconnected transformations, I argue, represents an overall precarisation of work in the city. This is jeopardizing the condition for which even the smallest firms could participate in the network economy and goldsmiths achieve the dream of wealth and success that spurred individuals to engage jewellery production.

Finally, in Chapter 8, I take into account the effects of the downturn in the city. After having shown how the discourse of '*la Crisi*' came to be associated with a decline of the entire city, I will consider the material transformation that the downturn caused in Valenza. I will then analyse how these changes led to the problematisation of the identity paradigm of the goldsmith's city, which is still central to the city discourse and ways of portraying the city, and signifies the population of the city's decreasing confidence in and engagement with the trade.

PART I:

THE "CITTÀ DELL'ORO"

Fig. 1: Workshops in the Coinor area

Fig. 2: The Expo-Piemonte exhibition centre

CHAPTER ONE

JEWELLERY AND THE IDENTITY RHETORIC OF VALENZA

> "Valenza... can one imagine Valenza without its jewellery... its goldsmiths? No, nobody can... and this is because Valenza is its jewellery... Valenza is a '*città orafa*'...."
> —A goldsmith.

Leaving Milan along the SS 494 motorway, after a ninety-minute drive past rice fields and industrial sheds, one eventually reaches the Po River: the border between Lombardy and Piedmont regions. The wide, grey line of fresh water cuts across the landscape and creates a visible interruption between the Lombard tableland and the Piedmontese hills, whose elevations rise just beyond the border. Looking out towards the hills, Valenza is the first settlement in view: small, ochre houses and numerous bell towers characterise the skyline. The city lies on the top of a knoll less than one kilometre away from the river and bridge. From this position, Valenza dominates the course of the river and the surrounding plain. Since the Medieval period, this position has made Valenza a strategic point for the control of traffic along and across the river. In the 14th century, tall towers and walls were built around the town, turning it into one of the most important fortresses on the regional border (Barghini et al., 1993: 30). In 1805, after the defeat of the Kingdom of Sardinia and the inclusion of Piedmont into Napoleonic France, the fortification was demolished (Barghini et al., 1993: 30). Only a small section of the walls was left: the *Bastione della Colombina*, in the northern sector of the city. Without its walls, during the 19th century, the city experienced a profound redefinition of its economy: a town based on agriculture, in less than a century and a half, turned into an industrial city with a flourishing jewellery trade. The legacy of this transformation can be seen today.

Along the motorway, still 30 kilometres from Valenza, many roadside billboards advertising Valenza jewellery firms dots the landscape. Some of them are new; some have seen better days. Approaching Valenza, the number of advertisements increases, introducing the driver to one of the world's most famous centres for the manufacturing of *'gioielleria'*: high quality jewellery mounted with precious stones[1].

The billboards are just the first landmark that suggests to visitors that today, the economy of the city fundamentally relies on jewellery production. Further clues are clearly visible upon arrival at the train station, which is located on a plateau overlooking the city. There, one encounters the modern part of the city: the Coinor neighbourhood, a belt of industrial plants lying in the small valley that separates the station from the city. Damiani (www.damiani.it), Bulgari (www.bulgari.com), Pasquale Bruni (www.pasqualebruni.com), and many other famous jewellery brand names can be read on the façades of buildings or on road signs. Dozens of firms, from small workshops to larger establishments, are located in the area between the train station and the city. They constitute only 20% of the jewellery firms operating in Valenza. The majority of the more than one thousand firms still lies, almost hidden to unaccustomed visitors' eyes (Chapter 2), within the city centre, where the industry originally developed in the 19th century (Chapters 2 and 3).

Since the 1970s, Valenza has been internationally known as one of the three largest Italian jewellery centres and the principal one for the manufacturing of *'gioielleria'* (Lenti and Pugnetti, 1974, Lenti, 1994, Gaggio, 2007, Garofoli, 2004); indeed, the scholarship highlighted the centrality of this industry for the city. The term '*monocoltura orafa*'[2],

---

[1] Unlike English, Italian distinguishes between two different forms of jewellery making, depending on the cost of the precious stones when compared to the price of the metal alloy used. When the cost of the metal alloy exceeds which of the stones, jewellery is termed '*oreficeria*'. When, instead, the cost of the precious stones is greater than the alloy's, jewellery is called '*gioielleria*'. Moreover, by Italian goldsmiths the word *'oreficeria'* is often used to refer to serialised and automated productions, whereas *'gioielleria'* may denote artisanal creations (Lenti and Bergesio, 2005). Despite this distinction, the work and workers employed in the manufacturing of *'gioielleria'* are regularly referred to by the adjective and the substantive adjective *'orafo'*, while *gioielliere* refers to the owners of a high-quality jewellery shop, a *'gioielleria'*.

[2] This definition comes as a local variant of a more common usage that the word '*monocoltura*' has in Italian. In this language, differently from English where 'monoculture' is still strictly part of the agricultural vocabulary and addresses a specific region's specialisation in one or a very limited number of cultivations, the original agricultural meaning has been expanded per similitude. Thus, this word normally is commonly used to refer to all the specific cases of local economies being completely dedicated to one specific form of economy. For example, the

translatable as jewellery or goldsmith monoculture, has often been used to emphasise the mono-specialisation of this trade in Valenza (e.g. Fondazione Gianfranco Pittatore and The European House Ambrosetti, 2011). The term has primarily an economic connotation and does not imply *per se* the pervasiveness of a trade beyond econometric features, such as the concentration of firms or the high rate of employment in the dominant trade. However, in Valenza, the pervasiveness of jewellery surpasses the boundaries imposed by economic theory and goes far beyond the number of employees and firms, the sales turnover and the prestige of some of the local enterprises. Jewellery in Valenza is the very element for which the city is known and represented by both Valenzani and people outside the city.

I will present this profound link in this chapter. Following the methodological suggestions of Carrithers (2005), I will focus on the identity rhetoric that hinges around a particular trope, that of *'città orafa'* [goldsmith city], and its many variants, such as *'città dell'oro'* [city of gold], or *'città degli orafi'* [city of goldsmiths].

Scholars have highlighted the fundamental role that the bounded urban space of cities or villages has played in the Italian identity discourse where it appears as the key element in the definition of an individual's sense of community belonging (e.g. Stacul, 2003; Tak, 1990; Sorba, 1998; Grimaldi, 1993, 2012; Clemente, 1997). In the following pages, I aim to show how through the trope, the jewellery industry is a fundamental element in the construction of the 'sense of place' (cf. Field and Basso, 1996) of Valenza.

After making some theoretical preliminary remarks, I will discuss how Valenzani and non-Valenzani employ the trope and how, in so doing, they bring to the fore a tangle of meanings and beliefs that substantiate their sense of Valenza and its jewellery industry. Although these may appear to be parallel narratives, in the second part of the chapter, I will show how Valenzani and non-Valenzani's narrations represent interlaced trajectories in a broader discourse: a cultural dynamic that also involves mass-media and Valenza's local government. In order to explore this discourse, I will examine the ways in which these two actors affect the discourse of *'città orafa'* and the dynamic that brings together all these different trajectories.

---

definition *'monocoltura industriale'* [industrial monoculture] is used to describe Northern Italian urban landscape (e.g. Morandi, 2006).

Approaching Rhetoric

> "Yes... Yes... Valenza... Valenza, I think, is a city of gold. But I don't mean that all the streets are paved with gold[3]. No... Not at all... It is a city like all the others...But I think Valenza is a *'città orafa'*...A city of goldsmiths. We [goldsmiths] are the motor of the city, the ones who make it unique. We are Valenza."

It was October 2010. My informant, a goldsmith entrepreneur in his late fifties, was comfortably sitting in an armchair at his stand at the annual *Valenza Gioielli* jewellery fair (www.valenzagioielli.it). It was the first time I met him – the only time in my fieldwork – but it was the umpteenth time I came across this peculiar rhetoric hinging on the trope of the *'città orafa'*. Together with its variants, the trope is employed in everyday conversations and public speeches that associate the urban space of Valenza and its population with jewellery production. Thus, this rhetoric sheds light on a peculiar aspect of this locale, namely, how the very idea of Valenza is interwoven with and narrated on the basis of the jewellery trade. Thus, following the example of Carrithers (2005), an exploration of the rhetoric of *'città orafa'* may offer us valuable elements to understand how this community is defined and what role is played by the jewellery industry in this process.

When, in 2005 Carrithers brought the study of rhetoric back to the attention of the discipline, he noted that:

> "Rhetoric adds to [...] previous depiction[s] of human sociality a more vivid sense of (1) the moving force in interaction, (2) the cultural and distinctly human character of that force, and (3) the creation of new cultural forms in social life." (Carrithers, 2005: 579)

---

[3] In Italian, as well as in English, there is a common saying of "a city/country [whose streets are] paved with gold". Drawing from the imagery of El Dorado, this saying aims to portray an opulent place through the use of hyperbole. In this case, the informant's use of this saying appears ambiguous in its rhetoric substance. A possible meaning would be "I don't think Valenza is an opulent city". However, we may also use this example to testify the interchangeability of the tropes. Apparently, the locution 'city of gold' is a metaphor that associates a city with a metal and its vast symbology (i.e. Ferber, 2007: 87). However, the specification that follows indicates the substantial and pragmatic synonym between the first locution and the second, which is a synecdoche distinguishing and making the city recognizable by just a part of its body, the goldsmiths, we can re-read 'city of gold' as a further synecdoche if we consider 'gold' as the emblem of a trade, the jewellery production, rather than just a metal.

The rhetoric dimension, according to Carrithers, is not only an ambit "reducible to speech alone" (Carrithers, 2005: 582), but a complex occurrence of speech and gestures moved by a communicative intent.

Almost a decade before Carrithers, Herzfeld (1997: 139-45) had formulated a similar line of inquiry, framed as 'social poetics'. In this perspective, Herzfeld proposed to consider public and private rhetoric as an ethnographic field of research in order to illuminate new aspects of a society and re-think anthropological interpretative schemata. Rhetoric emerged as a key to better penetrate a culture and society. Similarly, according to Carrithers (2009: ix-x) the study of rhetoric becomes the tool to recuperate the unpredictability of culture-making. Carrithers' theory represents a new step in the engagement of anthropology with rhetoric. With this move, unlike Herzfeld, Carrithers underlines the methodological necessity of including categories and concepts developed in rhetorical studies, such as the attention to the ways in which people address other people, objects and events (Carrithers, 2009: 6-9), and the rich terminology developed to classify figures of speech and their employment (Carrithers, 2008), among the tools for ethnographic analysis, in order to better penetrate the meanings and implications that public and private rhetoric brings with it (for an application of this methodology, see Carrithers, 2007).

In Carrithers' works, culture emerges as a social, collective phenomenon that manifests and is created through rhetoric. In this perspective, he echoes the ideas of the French philosopher Foucault. In Foucault's post-structuralist imagining social life and culture coincide with 'discourse', a dimension that encompasses and characterises human life. The discourse is a whole (1994 [1969]: 29-42) characterised by a multiplicity of actors, who are considered as variables and complex functions of the whole (Foucault, 1991: 118). The discourse propagates through narrations, ideas and imageries created when actors interact (Foucault, 1994 [1969]: 55-67). Narrations follow independent trajectories that interweave, creating the discourse; a space where:

> "Things relate but don't add up, if events occur but not within the processes of linear time, and if phenomena share a space but cannot be mapped in terms of a single set of three-dimensional coordinates. This discursive space is, however, still." (Law and Mol, 2002: 1)

To tackle this complexity, a concept to which this definition refers, is a heuristically obligatory step. While discourse is framed as a system of variants and interconnections (Foucault, 1994 [1969]), Foucault undertook this challenge by mainly focusing on the becoming of some objects, such as the definition of 'normality' and 'pathology', and their implementation in social context, such as the clinical environment (Foucault, 1973). He resolved complexity by describing the apparition, affirmation and implementation of these particular practices and ideas. In his theorisation and in particular in his early works (Foucault, 2001 [1966]; 1994 [1969]), he marginalised the role played by individuals' agency, by describing discourse, as a logo-bounded dimension of human life shaped by an immanent, impersonal and omni-comprehensive force that is 'power' (Foucault, 1978 [1976]: 92-93). Against this marginalisation, an anthropological study of rhetoric draws the attention to individuals' agentive moves and intentions (Carrithers, 2009). In fact, Carrithers pointed out that culture is a relational system of individuals and institutions that is animated by their intentions (Carrithers, 2005).

In the light of Carrithers arguments, thus, exploring a discourse is not just limited to investigating the history and social life of particular objects of the discourse, as Foucault proposed (Foucault, 1994 [1969]), but a social analysis of the actors involved in the discourse. It is a reading of the objects of the discourse that combines rhetoric analysis and a study of the social relations that are conveyed, built and affected through the employment of the objects.

By following this model, previously employed in the study of mass media (Carrithers, 2008) as well as everyday speech (Carrithers, 2009; Emery, 2010), I am approaching the analysis of the *'città orafa'* trope as it was used during my fieldwork, first of all by Valenzani.

"This is the city of gold, isn't it?"

From the billboards along the streets to the tourist materials obtainable in the city's tourist office, the trope is employed to (re) present the city. Above all, it is a pervasive presence in the descriptions that Valenzani, regardless of their actual occupation, give of their city when interviewed or even when chatting in a café.

This usage was explained to me as based on 'ineluctable' geographical and demographic evidence. In the words of Sebastiano, a gem-setter in his fifties who arrived in Valenza in the 1970s to attend one of the local professional schools' courses:

> "Valenza is the *'città orafa'*! Look at the city. Everything is linked to the jewellery industry. Just think about Coinor or the new exhibition centre... Everywhere there are goldsmith firms and signs of jewellery producers, manufacturers, and sellers. Gold, the jewellery trade, is everywhere. Go to the supermarket and ask the customers what their job is and ninety percent

will tell you they are employed in the jewellery trade. One will be a goldsmith, another a gem setter, another will be just a clerk but in a jewellery firm: they will all work in the trade. In this respect, Valenza is the *'città orafa'*."

Like Sebastiano, many other informants, in fact, noted that Valenza is a *'città orafa'* because the jewellery trade pervades the urban landscape. This visceral interconnection is expressed by the presence of certain particular landmarks, such as the Coinor industrial neighbourhood and the Expo-Piemonte exhibition centre, and the widespread presence of firms amid the general urban context. Due to this, in the eyes of my informants, it was almost impossible to discern the difference between Valenza and the jewellery industry: as Fabio Bosco[4] noted during an interview broadcasted by *Radiogold* in March 2009 (Fontefrancesco, 2009d), Valenza appears to its dweller as:

"A *'grande fabbrica'* [a big factory] from which one cannot actually escape."

The trope becomes, thus, an emotional tool to express this sense of being immersed in the jewellery industry when living in the city, even if not directly involved in the trade.

For example, Maria was a forty-three-year-old elementary school teacher. She was born in Valenza to a family of shopkeepers. She has been teaching in Valenza since she was in her twenties. In the 1990s, she married a man from Alessandria, who worked as a clerk for a company near Milan. They were living in Valenza, in a flat in the historic city centre. Describing her daily life in Valenza in January 2009, she commented:

[4] Fabio is a theatrical actor and a writer who, in the past, has worked as a journalist for *la Repubblica* (www.repubblica.it), the most-sold Italian daily, and as a jewellery merchant in his family's firm. In 2004 he published a book of short stories about Valenza, *Oroscuro* [Dark-gold]. It collected eight short stories, which Fabio wrote during the 1990s, describing the Valenza goldsmith community in the years of Valenza's economic boom, between the 1960s and 1990s, through the everyday vicissitudes of ordinary characters of the jewellery milieu (e.g. a polisher, a couple of apprentices, an artisan-entrepreneur owner of a small workshop). Thanks to *Oroscuro*, Fabio had been invited to participate in the radio broadcast and was asked to attempt to narrate or, at least, outline a literary portrait of the city in the 2000s.

> "You see, I am surely not a goldsmith, however... However... This is the 'city of gold', isn't it? *'Mondo Orafo'*[5] is a reality that is waiting for you just outside your door. You open it and, on the same floor, you find the first *'fabbrica'*[6] of your day. You go downstairs and, near your garage there are another two or three firms. You go to the coffee shop, and there are always some goldsmiths there. You go to school and you have to teach the goldsmiths' sons and daughters. You go to the supermarket and you see goldsmiths and their wives or husbands. Must I go on? This is why Valenza is a 'city of gold'...This is the pervasiveness of the jewellery trade, how I experience everyday life in the goldsmiths' city... How the jewellery industry touches my life... And I am just a teacher at an elementary school..."

Thus, the trope becomes the sign of the very penetration Bosco highlighted, and of life in a world so pervaded by jewellery production that it makes even individuals who are not part of the jewellery business feel that they are a part of in the *'Mondo Orafo'*.

From the interview with Maria, another important feature of the trope also emerges. It is not just an inert, neutral locution. It is an emotional tool that is the vehicle of emotions, ways of understanding and feeling the city and its industry. A tangle of emotions pervades this expression; a tangle made with narrations that portray personal feelings, experiences, and psychologies. These narrations describe an expanse of emotional shades that extends from pride and richness to frustration and desolation. In attempting a systematisation of a similar multitude, Bovero (1992), in his work on the perception of the city among its population in the early 1990s, proposed a method based on the profession of the informants, by dividing them in 'goldsmiths' and 'non-goldsmiths' and, thus, making a synthesis of the data collected. This solution may be practical; however, it ends up not accounting for the very blurred dimension that divides goldsmiths from non-goldsmiths.

In a city where almost no family is completely unconnected to the jewellery trade (Gaggio, 2007: 33), to not be a goldsmith may not necessarily mean to be practically and emotionally divorced from that social world. This is well explained by Carolina. She is the thirty-year-old

---

[5] The locution literally means 'Goldsmith World'. It is a recurrent locution used by Valenzani to address the economic and human milieu that constitutes the local jewellery industry.

[6] The most common translation for *'fabbrica'* is 'factory'. However *'fabbrica'* is used as emic terminology to refer to any jewellery enterprise, even the smallest workshop. Thus, when the term occurred in the interviews with this meaning, I maintain the original in the text.

daughter of a gem-setter. Despite being an only child, her parents wanted her to continue her studies and cultivate her passion for writing; a passion she has had since she was an adoloescent. She attended the Turin University, and after obtaining a degree in Journalism she began working for various local news agencies. In 2005 she was hired as a journalist for an Alessandria newspaper where she is still working. Thus, she never developed a direct experience of life in a workshop or of goldsmiths' work; however, to her, jewellery production is far from being an alien field.

> "It may be true that I'm not a goldsmith... However, when I hear people talk about this *'città orafa'*, its success and, more frequently in these days, its crises, or when I see the tools of that trade – a bench, files, drills, *et cetera*, I cannot think that that world [the jewellery industry] is not mine. It is not just because Valenza's economy is based on the jewellery industry or because most of my schoolmates worked in this business. No... It is something about me, my history... My past... What I feel to be home. I don't know how many times I have visited my dad in his *'fabbrica'*. When I was a schoolchild, I spent my afternoons in his workshop. He bought a little desk where I did my homework while he and the others worked. How many times I have seen them working... I have never been a goldsmith... But if I have to talk about me, my youth, my family, I would start from the *'fabbrica'* of my father, from the jewellery making... I think that it is because of that that I feel that the *'Mondo Orafo'* is at the same time distant and close to me... Mine, even though I am not part of it."

The case of Carolina is emblematic of many other people I met who, although not employed and having never been employed in the jewellery business, are linked to it through an emotional bond of feeling and memory. To those 'non-goldsmiths', the jewellery trade, its spaces and signs, the very speech of the *'città orafa'* are 'evocative objects' that, according to Turkle:

> "Exert their holding power because of the particular moment and circumstance in which they come into the [individual]'s life. Some, however, seem intrinsically evocative – for example, those with a quality we might call 'uncanny' [...]. Other objects are naturally evocative because they remind us of the blurry childhood line between self and other [...] or because they are associated with times of transition." (Turkle, 2007: 8)

They are objects able to evoke images and sensations linked to the past and/or the everyday experience of the individual – that is what Carolina explained. In their view, these intangible and tangible objects are able to evoke moments of their childhood and lived experience. They generate a sense of 'at-homeness', a sense of security and comfort that arises from dwelling and interacting with familiar places and objects (Baldursson, 2002, Buckley, 1971). Thus, although people never experienced jewellery production directly, as manufacturers, the jewellery business is described as the pillar of their past, their childhood, and family history.

By acknowledging this fact, in the analysis I prefer to avoid a Manichean division between goldsmith and non-goldsmith. I also intend to avoid a heuristic position, such as Bovero's, that ends up presenting a city, a living cosmos of interacting people and things as a complexity made up through a juxtaposition of different, isolated social worlds. In so doing, I am not arguing that there are no differences between the point of view of someone who works in the jewellery trade and someone external to it, such as the cases of Sebastiano and Maria. Rather, I suggest, these different voices are constituent parts of a discourse – the discourse of *'città orafa'* – where narrations overlap, cross, and interweave.

However, in this speckled fabric some recurring patterns emerge, which distinguish a general way for goldsmiths to perceive Valenza's jewellery trade. During my interviews and more casual encounters with Valenza artisans, the trope occurred hundreds of times in their words. Generally, however, this way of describing the city was mingled with a sense of pride toward the city and the role held by their professional category. In their words, this centrality leads to a further conclusion: Valenza was 'their' city, the *'città orafa'*. To quote Gioacchino, the fifty-year-old goldsmith whose words open this chapter:

> "When I think of this city, I, as a goldsmith, cannot but feel at home. This is a *'città orafa'*; I think... This is our city... Our special, unique place."

Thus, the rhetoric of *'città orafa'* faded into a representation of the 'nest': a precarious, lyrical thing that despite its transitory nature is able to infuse the speaker with a profound sense of confidence towards the world, as Bachelard (1994: 102-4) explains. Hence, the employment of the trope appears as rhetoric pervaded by a sense of 'at-homeness'.

In the words of many people not involved directly in the trade, however, this comfortable sensation is often substituted by a sense of the 'uncanny'. This awkward feeling derived, in this instance, not from "a sense of impropriety, haunting, or an act of violation", as in the case of Cypriot confiscated houses described by Navaro-Yashin (2002: 11), or the resurgence of repressed experience, as theorised by Freud (1919), but from being faced every day by a familiar reality, such as the jewellery industry, not being part of it and, to some extent, feeling one's own job and role in society delegitimised by this productive reality. While talking about the city, non-goldsmith informants often referred to their situation as being almost obliterated by the other Valenza citizens, 'the' Valenzani: the goldsmiths. Thus, the rhetoric of *'città orafa'* becomes their way of externalizing and systematizing this sense of abandonment into the representation of their city. This is shown well in the words used by a public officer of the local health service in an informal meeting we had in summer 2009. She was in her fifties, born and raised in Valenza, the daughter of a goldsmith couple, who worked until the late 1980s in their own little workshop in the historic centre of the city. She decided to not tread the family path but to continue her studies, get a university degree and undertake a career in the civil service. Despite her 'goldsmith' origins, however, she pointed out:

> "This is the 'city of gold' and everybody knows it. Its [economic] fulcrum is the jewellery industry, and everybody knows this. However, if I think about this *'città orafa'* I can only feel a certain sense... Of... Dejection... We [people not employed in the jewellery trade] do not exist, in the eye of the goldsmiths. Valenza is 'their' city. Full stop. All other people seem not to exist. We live in the shadows of 'their' gold... The gold of this city..."

Hence, it appears that the very conceptual foundation of the trope of *'città orafa'*, the centrality of the jewellery trade in Valenza, was not rejected by my informants, and they employed it to describe Valenza in the same way as goldsmiths. However, *'città orafa'* becomes, in their narration, the expression of the marginalisation they feel; it highlights a sense of estrangement that they feel in regard to the city: a very sense of '*Unheimlich'*, 'un-homeyness'.

Diverse, often contrasting emotions are, thus, linked to this trope. They describe a city whose nature is contested between a sense of belonging, it being 'my city', and a sense of marginalisation, it being 'their city': The boundary between these two experiences is less neat that what Bovero (1992), and myself (Fontefrancesco, 2011), described. Within this swinging dimension, the *'città orafa"* expresses the sense of Valenza: a place and a community dominated by the gold.

Knowing without seeing

While Valenzani have described their city as '*città orafa*', I found this rhetoric to be known and recurrent also outside Valenza. People from the neighbouring cities, such as Alessandria, and from more distant ones, such as Milan, and even foreigners, such as Germans, French, British and

Americans, remembered Valenza as a city of gold and jewellery. Many of those informants had never actually visited the city.

The actual use of the trope by non-Valenzani shows, first of all, a dimension of this discourse that surpasses the boundaries of the original bounded community, to encompass the wider world. However, following Carrier's argument about 'Occidentalism' (Carrier, 1992b; 1995), this occurrence raises questions about the actual meaning of this 'ethno-' category (cf. Carrier, 1992b) and the actual origins of this category. Although my fieldwork shows an extension of the discourse that encompasses two continents, I would like to propose an answer to these questions by considering an 'arbitrary location' (Candea, 2007, 2010), Alessandria.

Alessandria is the third largest city of Piedmont (Comuni-Italiani.it, 2009a) with almost 100,000 inhabitants. It is situated 14 km south of Valenza. It is the capital of the Province of Alessandria, the administrative region of Piedmont in which Valenza is situated. While hundreds of people commute every day between the two cities to work or study, the most-read local newspapers, *la Stampa* and *il Piccolo*, and the most-listened-to local news radio, *Radiogold*, have their offices in Alessandria. Despite this strong interconnectivity, the increasing integration of services offered by the two municipalities, and the improvement of infrastructures linking the cities (Fontefrancesco, 2009d, 2009e), Valenza and Alessandria continue to vividly identify themselves as divided, parallel entities: a phenomenon that manifests a strong '*campanilismo*'[7] in these two local communities and what we can consider a distinction of Alessandria as an 'other' of Valenza. This is, however, a very proximal 'other'. One who lives in Valenza, nowadays, cannot avoid visiting Alessandria, at least once in a while, since the province's main hospital, most of the governmental offices, high schools, the local university, and the main train station are located there. Thus, to a person from Alessandria it is normal to count some Valenza among their acquaintances, as was the case of dozens of people I met during the years of fieldwork. Despite the proximity of the two cities and these acquaintances, in Alessandria it is not rare to find people who have never visited Valenza, though they may have seen the city for a few minutes through their car or train window, or from afar. This non-visiting is generally justified by the lack of any particular attraction in

[7] It is generally translated as 'parochialism'. However, due to the negative meaning that taints this word and make it sound like 'narrowed-mindness' –a meaning that is absent in the Italian word– I would suggest, following Clemente (1997), to translate '*campanilismo*' as 'local pride' that better mirrors the actual identity tension that distinguishes this word.

Valenza that would raise the interest of an inhabitant of Alessandria, such as particular shops, cultural facilities (e.g. museums), or amenities (e.g. nightclubs). The lack of experience of the city, however, does not make Valenza an unknown location. It is a place half hour away from home, "just around the corner," using an expression heard so many times. Informants from Alessandria always have an 'idea' of this place:

> "Valenza... Isn't that the city where everybody is a goldsmith?"

This quote is from an interview with Alessio, an engineer in his forties, employed in a study in Turin, who had never visited Valenza. Like Alessio, when they had to explain what they associated with Valenza, and give a brief description of what they knew about the city, all the other Alessandria people linked Valenza to jewellery production. The reference to *'città orafa'* explicitly or implicitly occurred in all my interviews, since all my informants shared the belief that Valenza was a city wholly dedicated to the jewellery trade. However, the link between the city and the trade differed from one informant to the other. For example, a shop cashier, still in her teens, thought the *'città orafa'* was a place crowded with jewellery shops, while a clerk in his thirties described Valenza as an industrial city. Both these fantasies, however, strongly differ from the actual appearance of the city, as I illustrate in the beginning of the chapter and further explain in the following chapters.

The people in Alessandria thus knew without having seen. They had clearly-defined ideas that led them to equate Valenza with the jewellery trade. Even without a direct experience or familiarity with the features of the jewellery trade my informants, like *'bricoleurs'*, modulated this information according to their taste and imagination. The result of this shaping varied due to personal inclination, education, age, etc., but was generally underpinned by a subtle jealousy and a sense of wonder for a city, a community that is imagined to be rich because of its connection with the production of jewellery.

The words of Alessio and the other people from Alessandria, thus, attest the knowledge and use of *'città orafa'* trope outside Valenza. At the same time, they show the crucial role that the trope has to express the 'sense of place' (cf. Field and Basso, 1996) of Valenza outside the city. Similarly to Valenzani, this is an overall understanding dominated by the superimposition of jewellery industry to Valenza. However, in this case, jewellery is not the element capable of creating a sense of belonging or estrangement, as in the case of Valenzani, but turns into a fantasy, "a psychic symptom that survives analysis, critique, or deconstruction", and as Navaro-Yashin suggests "generates unconscious psychic attachments to the very object [...] that has been deconstructed in the domains of consciousness." (Navaro-Yashin, 2002: 4). Through this fantasy, a 'sense of place' (cf. Field and Basso, 1996) is generated. Thus, a place is known, often without having seen it.

A broad discourse

This ethnographic excursus, encompassing experiences of people in Valenza and Alessandria, demonstrates the centrality of the trope in the expression of the 'sense of place' (cf. Field and Basso, 1996) of Valenza that relies on the conflation of the city and its jewellery industry. The diffusion of this trope in and outside Valenza shows, moreover, the existence of a wide discourse that hinges on the trope and in which Valenzani and non-Valenzani alike participate. In this discourse, my informants pointed out, they are not the only actors.

Matteo, a film student in his mid-twenties, who was born and raised in Valenza (and whose entire family was employed in the jewellery trade), but currently lives in Turin, offered a concise description of the extension of this discourse:

> "You head out from Valenza, and people, even without having visited the city, will tell you that Valenza is the *'città orafa'*. You look at the newspaper and Valenza is always associated with gold. You speak with Valenzani and they will talk about the jewellery trade. You listen to local politics and, again, it seems that the only problem in Valenza is jewellery production. What do I have to think about my city?"

In the words of this informant, the individual's awareness that Valenza is the *'città orafa'* does not arise from an imposition of this rhetoric from 'above', a culturally hegemonic act perpetrated by a particular elite, such as the goldsmiths, but rather from their exposure to a tangle of multiple experiences that do not exclusively involve Valenzani and non-Valenzani. Alongside actual face-to-face interactions with other Valenzani, this discourse also encompasses encounters with outsiders, the reading of newspapers, and the actions of Valenza politicians. From exposure to these media, permeated by the rhetoric of the 'goldsmith city', people in Alessandria as well as in Valenza came to know and seize this rhetoric. The trope became part of their vocabulary and their way of understanding when referring to a city that they may not have directly experienced but, through these media, they came to know. Based on this knowledge, they formulated ideas and narrations of Valenza: tales that, in turn, become a vector for the spreading of the rhetoric of the 'city of goldsmiths'. These dynamics express the discourse of *'città orafa'*: a relational system that is described by the agencies and actions of different actors, some of whom I have explored in the previous paragraphs. To complete the analysis of this system, to understand how the jewellery industry becomes a fundamental element in the creation of the 'sense of place' (cf. Field and Basso, 1996) of Valenza, I am going to discuss how the trope is employed and connected with the action of mass-media and Valenza's local government.

Mass-media

Forms of mass-media, mostly radio and newspapers, are important vectors of the rhetoric of *'città orafa'*. As Carrithers explained, in general, the mass-media contributes to changing the public's mind by offering them "a new set of persons, and new sets of feelings" (Carrithers, 2008: 163) and in so doing they move

> "powerfully [public] toward more specificity and more understanding [of the world], even if that understanding is still only speculative." (Carrithers, 2008: 162-63)

In other words, the employment of a particular rhetoric by mass-media is an important element in orientating the knowledge and effectiveness of the public. While Carrithers underlines this point by analysing particular cases in American, British and German media, a similar point has been made by my informants with respect to the employment of *'città orafa'* rhetoric in local mass-media in Alessandria province. In particular, Carolina vividly explained:

> "[Mass-media] bombard us every day with that story so that at the very end you end up to learn that Valenza is a 'city of gold' even if you did not live here."

She, like other Valenzani and non-Valenzani, associate the employment of the rhetoric with a quotidian 'barrage'. This is a metaphor that highlights, in an emphatic manner, a widespread and undifferentiated use of the word to refer to aspects of the city, such as politics, economics, and sport. A simple ethnographic episode from my field notes can explain this extensiveness.

8 am, 9th of January 2009: a typically frosty weekday after days of snow that had transformed the landscape of Alessandria and the other cities of the province into Christmas postcard-like images. The little café in the centre of Alessandria was crowded, and people were packed in front of the counter ordering espressos, cappuccinos, lattes, brioches and other

refreshments. I was waiting there for an informant, while a cracking radio was broadcasting *Radiogold (*www.radiogold.it) – a station broadcasted throughout the Alessandria Province, and in some areas of the surrounding provinces of Vercelli and Pavia. The speaker was reading some fresh news about football minor leagues, offering a brief analysis of the next match for the *'orafi di Valenza'* [Valenza goldsmiths], the nickname of *the Valenzana Calcio team.*

To kill time I decided to peep at the headlines of a daily left on a nearby table. It was the current issue of *il Piccolo (*www.ilpiccolo.net). *Il Piccolo* is a local newspaper published in Alessandria and distributed throughout the province, in which two to four pages in every issue are dedicated to news from Valenza. That day, a long article reported the effects of the snowstorm that had struck the *'città orafa'* in the past few days. On another table, someone had left a copy of *La Stampa (*www.lastampa.it), a national newspaper published in Turin that, in Piedmont, includes a special section dedicated to local news. This section is published on a provincial level, so that the issue I was glancing at was the same that was distributed around the Alessandria Province, including Valenza. In my reading, I checked the page dedicated to Valenza, and there I read that the mayor of *'città dell'oro'* [city of gold] had made some hasty comments about the works of the City Council.

***

The 9th of January 2009 was a day like all the others. However, for the ordinariness of its subject, this 'tale of the field' (cf. Van Maanen, 1988) well demonstrated the pervasiveness of the *'città orafa'* trope in the media landscape described by the newspapers and the radio. As it emerges from even a superficial examination of the articles about Valenza published in recent years by these media, or from a simple search through the archives of *il Piccolo, la Stampa* and *Radiogold*, the pervasiveness of the rhetoric is a custom dating back decades. Some evidence gives us elements to draw a possible archaeology of this imagery.

A first datum is the very name of the station *Radiogold.* Although in 2008 this radio station was set up in Alessandria, it was originally established in Valenza in the late 1970s and was conceived as "the radio of Valenza," as one of its founders, a fifty-year-old disc jockey explained to me.

> "We wanted to create the first, and only, radio of Valenza. For this reason we decided to call it a fancy name that was clearly rooted into and able to

> mirror the 'city of gold'. We found '*Radiogold*'; a name that definitely fitted with our aims. So we adopted it and so named our baby"

The case of *Radiogold* is evidence of the actual occurrence of the trope in the late 1970s, and led to research further back in time. From a foray into the historical collections of the newspapers, it appears that the trope has been widely attested since the 1960s. Headlines and articles in the dailies and in flyers conserved in Valenza's city library show the use of the trope as a fundamental part of public rhetoric since the later years of that decade. The first occurrence I found of the trope in mass media appeared not in newspapers, but in cinema. In the year 1964, AOV started a widespread advertising campaign for jewellery made in Valenza. A 10-minute-long documentary was produced to be broadcasted in the cinemas before film showings. In this film (Orengo et al., 1964), Valenza was repeatedly referred to as *la capitale degli orafi* [the capital of the goldsmiths].

***

Considering this dating, the diffusion of the trope appears to coincide with the success of the jewellery industry in Valenza and its becoming the city's first and only industry (Maggiora, 2010: 137-60); this transformation started in the 1960s with the crisis of the shoe-making industry (Maggiora, 2010: 220), the principal economy of the city in the early years after WWII (Maggiora, 2010: 149-52, Penna Ivaldi, 2008). The transformation of Valenza into a jewellery monoculture ended in the 1970s (RP-Ricerche e Progetti, 1979). At that time the press was already accustomed to associating Valenza exclusively with gold and jewellery, an association also shared by, we can argue, its public, both within and outside the city.

Despite this history, none of the journalists I met knew the origins of the trope. Its use is mostly contextualised in the present and justifies its rhetorical power. As explained by the chief editor of *Radiogold*, a man in his mid-thirties with a degree in Law who has worked for the radio since the 1990s:

> "Why do we use such an expression? Well, it's catchy. It is evocative. Think about a '*città orafa*' and you'll wonder about magic castles and fairies. You see. It is a good rhetorical image! Besides, everybody in the Province, no matter whether they have ever visited Valenza or not, knows that Valenza is a '*città orafa*'!"

The journalist, as well as his colleagues, highlighted the functionality of the locution: on the one hand, the imagery that the expression '*città orafa'* conveys is evocative; on the other hand, all the readers/listeners are accustomed to associating it with Valenza, despite never having visited the city. In other words, there seem to be two recurrent points: 1) the expression makes Valenza memorable; 2) it suggests wealth, magic, and opportunity. Journalists were aware that the rhetoric did not portray the complexity of the city, but employed it for the rhetoric power that it is endowed with, and due to their connection with the public and city's population. Journalists justified their use of the image as a reflection of popular usage in Valenza, and as a response to their readers' expectations. Using the words of a *Radiogold* journalist:

> "[The trope] portrays the way they conceptualise their city; the relationship between advertising and public bodies and private companies in Valenza – they use the image of *'città orafa'* in their campaigns. So, when I write about their campaigns, I have to describe Valenza as *'città orafa'* because it is part of their message, their relationship with the public – the article must be entertaining and understandable to the entire my audience. My audience knows Valenza as *'città orafa'*. I use this locution because they know it and it makes the article more understandable to them."

From the archival research and the daily experience of reading and listening to news from the local media, the wide extent of the trope of *'città orafa'* clearly appears. Because of this widespread usage, we can conclude that the media is among the principal actors that were able to extend and shape the discourse of Valenza by pervading it with the imagery of gold. Since Anderson (1991), newspapers and mass-media in general have been shown to be crucial actors in the creation and spreading of collective ideas of community. While the collective rite of reading the daily newspaper is pointed out as a foundation of the sense of belonging to a community, the public substantiates a particular view of the world – the imagery of a shared community and foreign ones – through the access to the same news presented by the media (Anderson, 1991: 30-36).

These media are without doubt main actors in the weaving of the discourse; however, we should not underestimate the importance of interaction between the public and the media. Although scholars such as Chomsky and Herman (1994) or Sartori (1999) have tended to depict the public as a passive and cheatable subject in the hands of the media, Boyer has, more recently (2005), pointed out the interaction and mutual affection that distinguishes the creation of news. While Boyer examines only the dialectic between media and intelligentia, and the higher strata of German society, in the building the idea of German-ness across almost two centuries, in our case the journalists themselves are the ones who point out the importance of the Valenza and non-Valenza public's response in reinforcing and employing rhetoric, thus spreading the idea of '*città orafa*'. In light of the experience and testimonies of local journalists, we should revise the idea of media as hegemonic entities (cf. Cospito, 2004) that impose imaginaries over the population. We should think of media as participants rather than masters of the discourse. In the discourse, they play an important role in making ideas and rhetoric circulating. Rhetoric, as well as news, can be manufactured by the media but *'città orafa'* rhetoric is an example of an object that exists independently of the media's actions. The media play a fundamental role in making the rhetoric circulate. In so doing, they expand its discourse, and reinforce, rather than impose, the rhetoric. From the interviews with journalists, the employment of a particular rhetoric appears fundamentally subordinated to the needs of their public, that is to say, the actual recognisability, comprehensibility and appeal of a rhetoric and its employment by the narrated subjects. Thus, the employment of the rhetoric appears as a spiral dynamic where Valenzani, non-Valenzani and media are involved, together with local politicians.

Valenza policy makers

My informants saw the media as crucial actors in propagating and affirming *'città orafa'* rhetoric. However, they pointed out another actor that was seen as responsible for the propagation of the rhetoric and the progressive development of Valenza into a city that pivoted only around the jewellery industry: the local government of Valenza, a group of people my informants often referred to as '*Loro*', 'Them'. 'They' are the people "in the control room", the elected politicians in the local bodies. 'They' are perceived as detached from and not influenced by the rest of Valenza's social milieu. In this perspective, 'They' would decide, more or less autonomously from the rest of the city's population, the city's economic and political agenda and carry out the policy-making process. The "normal Valenza person", using an expression encountered many times, depicting the un-elected ones and generally passive participants in the local political debate, would not have any weight in 'Their' decisions. "Normal" Valenzaniwould simply become acquainted with 'Their' choices through the news or by chatting with other Valenzani. However, 'Their' decisions were considered to be crucial for the development and factual transformation of the city. As noted, for example, by a retired goldsmith in his seventies who worked for fifty years in Valenza as the owner of a small firm:

> "If Valenza is the *'città orafa'*, it is also thanks to 'Them', who are in the control room. With Their decisions, They made Valenza what it is and killed any other alternative."

To support this interpretation, despite attempts by the City Council to convince the population of the wider scope of its involvement (e.g. Comune di Valenza, 2009b, Quaroni and Zeppa, 2005), informants cited examples of large public investments made in past decades in support of the jewellery trade, such as the creation of Expo-Piemonte, in the 2000s, Coinor, during the 1980s and 90s, and the tourist advertising mainly based on the promotion of the city with the trade as its fundamental attraction.

To understand the role that 'They' have in weaving the *'città orafa'*, it is crucial to analyse the particular interpretation of politics that the definition entails. It indicates a dichotomic interpretation of the city's politics. On a local level, this vision follows a bipartition known, and in the past, often endorsed, in scholarship (Mitchell, 1991: 76-89): the one that distinguishes between State (politicians and civil servants) and Society. While Mitchell mainly cites examples from political sciences, this paradigm has been also adopted by anthropologists, such as Anderson, who actually founded his hypothesis on a clear distinction between State and Society. By analysing the birth and spreading of nationalism, in fact, he conceptualises civil servants and politicians as forming a group of people differentiated and rather detached from the rest of the population (Anderson, 1991: 163-185). However, as Gupta (1995) demonstrated in his study of corruption in a village of Northern India, the distinction between Society and State relies on a (Western) ideological premise that fails on the grounds of everyday practices, where the State proves to be a skein of multiple agencies and actors (Gupta, 1995: 392).

The State being far from a solid entity, the researcher should investigate the specific modalities and motivations and explain why such a multiplicity is imagined as a unitary reality (Gupta, 1995: 393) and singled out from society. In this interpretative effort, it is necessary to take the category of state divorced from society, and consequently the political divorced from the non-political, seriously and, on the level of the ethnographic analysis, consider them in their aspect of emic realities (Mitchell, 1991: 95; Candea, 2011: 313-14).

With this perspective in mind, the definition of 'Them' appears to be generated by Valenzani to explain to themselves how their city works on the basis of their (often publicly admitted) incomplete knowledge of the policy-making process. The 'cut' (cf. Strathern, 1996) this classification operates in the social milieu is far from sharp: the identity of those who make up 'Them' is quite unclear and imprecise and it changes from informant to informant. Following Gupta (1997), it appears that different imaginations intertwine around "the ones that pull the levers [of power]," using another common vernacular expression. Most commonly, my informants only placed the most prominent elected administrators in this group: the city mayor and the other members of the city '*giunta*', the city's board of governors, the members of which in Italy are called '*assessori*' [singular: '*assessore*']. However, my informants ignored other people employed in the city bureaucracy altogether, for example, the city managers, despite their pivotal role in policy making.[8]

While this distinction tends to separate 'Them' from the rest of the social body of Valenza, elected politicians are still part of, and remember their part in, the social body of Valenza. Thus, the public administrators are not detached from the rest of society; they are part of it, and in their actions they are influenced by the opinions of other Valenzani. Thus, the role ultimately played by these administrators in the creation of a fertile ground in which the idea of '*città orafa*' can take root and prosper must be considered in the light of these dialectics.

My Valenza informants pointed at the voluntariness of the intervention of 'Them' towards shaping the city into the '*città orafa*'. However, this perception of administrative work does not imply that the administrators actually consider their work to be willingly aimed at transforming the city into that model. This clearly emerged from the several interviews I conducted. None of the public administrators considered to privilege the problems of jewellery trade over those of other sectors.

While the social planning of the City Council may not be based only on the needs of the people employed in jewellery production (e.g. Fontefrancesco, 2006b), and the public administrators may not have intended their actions to be directed only at the goldsmiths, in the last ten

[8] An important part is played by the city managers that actually write the policies and protocols. After Law 81/1993 came into force, the mayor and the '*assessori*' have lost their legislative centrality in policy-making. The city managers, appointed officers hired by the city administration, have assumed greater importance because they have become the officials legally responsible for all the legal acts produced by the City Council. A possible explanation for this omission can be found in the sources used by my interviewees to keep them up-to-date about current local political and administrative issues: discussion with other Valenzani and the press. In particular, the local press still presents all the actions and plans launched by the City Council as being the results of the work of the elected politicians alone, silencing the role played by the city managers and other bureaucrats, despite the change in the law increasing the administrative role of such officers.

years the local government has publicly embraced the idea of *'città orafa'* in its public rhetoric, in particular in the case of tourism. Throughout the 2000s, the City Council invested resources in promoting the city nationally and internationally as a place of tourism and culture (Comune di Valenza, 2009b, Quaroni and Zeppa, 2005). As part of this effort, the administration, together with the local goldsmiths' associations, advertised Valenza as *'città orafa'*. Public signs were installed around the city and advertisements were published in many local and national newspapers and online journals, using slogans such that celebrate the primate of the local manufacture of gold and precious gems. In this way, the idea of *'città orafa'* became an immaterial, distinguishing landmark of Valenza. In September 2010, I met the '*assessore*' deputed to tourism and public events and I asked for the reasons for such a strategy. He answered:

> "Yes, when we try to sell Valenza as a possible destination for tourism we speak a lot about gold and the jewellery trade. It is not because I think Valenza is only the jewellery trade, but it is because the image of *'città orafa'* is effective – ask our jewellery sellers! – and people outside of Valenza already know Valenza as the *'città orafa'*!"

The words used by the '*assessore*' stress a link between this rhetorical action and an on-going practice spread in Valenza. In fact, the use of the rhetorical *'città orafa'* object as a tool to make Valenza a 'sticky' (cf. Gladwell, 2000: 89-132) image in the mind of outsiders: an evocative and easy to remember image. Thus, as pointed out by many informants, it is a way commonly used to increase the value of Valenza production, by associating it to an image of opulence. Thus, we can consider the administrative action, rather than as an authoritarian action that shapes the collective imaginary, to be an example of the interconnection between 'common Valenzani' practices and the administrative actions taken.

Going back to the examination of the work of the administration in the 2000s, the use of the rhetoric of *'città orafa'* can be considered to be linked to a different, important role in another of the City Council's large-scale plans aimed to spur on both tourism and the city's economy. The City Council, along with the Provincial and Regional Governments, launched the Expo-Piemonte program in 2002. This program aimed to create, in Valenza, Piedmont's second largest trade fair centre, and involved the building of an exhibition centre, Expo-Piemonte, on the outskirts of the city (Zemide, 2002, 2005; Il Piccolo, 2010). The new building, moreover, would answer the growing need expressed by the goldsmith community for a large exhibition centre in which to host *Valenza Gioielli*, the annual international jewellery exposition that started running in the 1970s[9]. This fair continued to grow over the years, and in the 1990s the need for a new exhibition centre had become acute. The new building was inaugurated in 2009 and became *Valenza Gioielli*'s official location. No other events are organised in the large building, apart from this four-day event, *V+*, a three-day national technology exposition event and services for the jewellery trade,. However, some of the rooms are, instead, used as the seat of AOV.

Despite the good intentions of the public administrators, the Expo has been perceived by Valenzani as a facility for the jewellery trade, rather than something opened for development of new businesses, services and tourism; it is a new landmark that manifests the centrality of the jewellery trade in the city. This perception was explained by my informants as being based on the characteristics of the few events held in the structure, which only concern the jewellery trade, and by the physical presence of AOV. In the eyes of the local politicians, Expo-Piemonte was still an open project aimed at creating a new business opportunity for the city that was also – but not exclusively – able to answer the needs of the goldsmith community. In their view, it still provides a possibility for development and economic diversification to the entire city and cannot be considered a project "only for goldsmiths". However, a dominant interpretation, shared by goldsmiths and non-goldsmiths alike, sees it as an extremely expensive project that answered only the need of the goldsmithing community to have a large and modern venue for their fair. It appears that the interpretation of the policy-makers emerges as a contested place: while politicians considered it as oriented towards offering a possibility of diversification through tourism to the city, goldsmiths and non-goldsmiths in the public saw it as a further step in actively shaping Valenza into the *'città orafa'*, the city thoroughly and utterly dedicated to the goldsmiths. This analysis shows the gap between the interpretation given by the public administrators and other Valenzani. The Expo-Piemonte is an example of how the action of bureaucracy and administration does not only play a direct role in reinforcing and spreading a particular idea of community – in the case of Valenza, the rhetoric of the *'città orafa'* – they also have a highly

---

[9] The event, organised by AOV, has run since the 1970s. To hold *Valenza Gioielli*, AOV built Valenza's first exhibition centre, Palazzo Mostre, in 1983. Due to the constant growth of the event, the large building, located in the west sector of the city, rapidly became too small to effectively house the exposition. In the 1990s, AOV began works to expand the building, but they were stopped in 2000 when discussion about the Expo-Piemonte project started. In the eyes of the AOV members, once it opened, the Expo-Piemonte building was to become the new location for the jewellery exposition (AOV, 2006).

significant indirect role. The local community may perceive administrative projects and actions from a different angle than the administrators, and may consider only the factual entity of these actions, as in the case of Expo-Piemonte. These differences may bring members of the local community to an interpretation and comprehension of administrative actions that diverges from the one of the public administrators. Because of this gap – a gap that can be traced back to a lack of communication by the politicians towards the city and the low level of interest and participation that Valenzani show towards the city's policymaking – even those actions that were not meant to reinforce a particular idea of the city and community are experienced as just such reinforcement.

Narrating and Imagining

Previous paragraphs show different trajectories and discursive practices in which the trope is employed and that are underpinned by the rhetoric. These intersect in the description, in the imagination of a city. Calvino (1993) pointed out that the act of narrating a city, imaginary or real, visible or invisible, is far from just describing the anthropomorphised landscape.

> "A city is an ensemble of many things: memories, desires, and signs of a language. Cities are places of exchanges [...], but these exchanges are not only of goods; they are exchanges of words, desires, memories." (Calvino, 1993: ix-x)

To narrate a city is to describe a society, a complex cosmos of objects and people and their interactions. However, as Reed (2002) showed in the case of London walking tours, this ensemble and the affective cosmos that individuals link to it are mobilised in order to recount and explain their universe of men and objects. It is the very word '*città*' that introduces the listener to this complexity. In any Italian-English dictionary one can find that the translation of this word is 'city'. In its simplicity, however, this straightforward definition hides an important difference that differentiates the meaning of the Italian word from the English one. *'City'*, although it stems from the Latin *'civitas'*, currently refers to a large and/or important town, or an urban area. However,

> "'*Civitas*' was not 'city' in the modern sense [...]. '*Civitas*' was the general noun derived from '*civis*' [Lat. citizen], which is nearer our modern sense of a '*national*'. '*Civitas*' was then the body of citizens rather than a particular settlement of type of settlement." (Williams, 1983: 56)

Like '*city*', the contemporary Italian '*città*' also stems from '*civitas*', and like the English word it also denotes an urban space and large settlements. However, unlike 'city', it also maintains the original Latin meaning. Thus, '*città*', more than its English counterpart, is able to represent the image of a community dwelling in a physical, urban landscape.

To talk about a '*città*' is to mobilise a living cosmos of men and objects. As Portelli et al. (2006) demonstrated in their study of Rome's Centocelle neighbourhood, it is to make an idea of community, its place, and its activities explicit in a broad narration that defines not only a city or a neighbourhood, but also yields much information about how persons consider themselves part of this cosmos (Portelli et al., 2006: 3-7). In the case of Valenza, this idea of the city is emblemised by a trope, that of '*città orafa*': a particular object that is able, from its very rhetorical structure, to portray a tension between the vital cosmos of a '*città*' and one of its elements, the jewellery industry.

In a rhetorical perspective, '*città orafa*' can be classified as an epithet (Mortara Garavelli, 2003: 219-21), often employed as an *antonomasia* (Mortara Garavelli, 2003: 173-75), when it substitutes the use of the noun 'Valenza' completely in referring to the city and its people. From the previous paragraphs, it emerges that the use of this trope has been a consolidated discursive practice occurring since the 1960s, as we have seen in the case of the press. Besides this historicity, it is relevant to note the rhetorical strategy that is associated with this trope creates a revealing bond between the city and its jewellery industry, which constitutes only one aspect of it. Analysing the structure of this epithet, it appears that '*città orafa*' is a synecdoche, a construction through which a whole is identified through one of its details (Mortara Garavelli, 2003: 152). A synecdoche has a duple descriptive effect: on the one hand, it brings the detail into the foreground and manifests its importance; on the other hand, however, it silences the rest of the whole, almost negating its existence. This trope can evoke a particularly vivid image of the subject: a 'poetic' image that, as explained by Bachelard (Bachelard, 1994: xxii-xxix), is able to trigger 'poetry', an emotional understanding of the world that goes beyond the rational, and causalistic comprehension. Due to this strong evocative power, a synecdoche can result in a moving and 'sticky' image (cf. Gladwell, 2000: 89-132), and a powerful and convincing tool. As we have seen, the case of '*città orafa*' follows this general trend, being strategically used by the local government, Valenza jewellery merchants, and the press for its persuasive and suggestive efficacy, as demonstrated by the earlier examples of people from Alessandria and Valenza.

Moreover, our case shows this image is the very centre of 'fantasies' of Valenza and its industry.

Navaro-Yashin (2002), in her ethnographic study of politics in Istanbul, used the category of 'fantasy' to address and explain the role that the State has in the everyday life of the city's people. In our case, what escapes deconstruction is the jewellery industry and its crucial role in the city. This is the centre of narrations, of ways of sensing Valenza and a subject capable of releasing and disclosing poetry (Bachelard, 1994) and emotiveness that tells us how jewellery production is experienced and understood by people. The jewellery industry is the subject of dreams of affluence for people in Alessandria, the badge of pride and honour for goldsmiths, the mark of marginalisation for non-goldsmiths: different narrations wrapped around the jewellery industry that make the industry meaningful and constitute its evocative, symbolic power. While the rhetoric of the *'città orafa'* shows that the jewellery industry is a fundamental part of the definition of the sense of Valenza, the analysis of this rhetoric showed that this sense is not universal and univocal. From this multiplicity emerges the affinity between *'città orafa'* and a 'boundary object' as theorised by Star and Griesemer (1989; see also: Bowker and Star, 1999).

> "This is an analytic concept of those scientific objects that both inhabit several intersecting social worlds [...] and satisfies the informational requirements of each of them. Boundary objects are objects which are both plastic enough to adapt to local needs and the constraints of the several parties employing them, yet robust enough to maintain a common identity across sites. They are weakly structured in common use, and become strongly structured in individual-site use [...]. They have different meanings in different social worlds but their structure is common enough to more than one world to make them recognizable, a means of translation." (Star and Griesemer, 1989: 393).

The definition fits well with our case and describes the actual dimension of the value that the epithet has in the different 'social worlds' I explored. It helps us to clarify a situation of complexity, where multiple actors co-act and mutually modify their work in response to the others' positions and actions. However, whereas in Star and Griesemer (1989) the 'boundary objects' are seen as the fundamental ideas that allow social words to interact in the completion of a common goal, such as the preparation of Barkley's Museum of Vertebrate History, in our case there is no such common goal. Actors seem to move on different, almost parallel trajectories. However, it is by observing the occurrence of the epithet in the different discourses, in the different social worlds they describe, that is possible to see a pattern of interaction and mutual influence. In other words, we come to see a web of 'ordinary affects' (cf. Stewart, 2007: 2) that binds people together into an impalpable network that we may call society, "a world of affinities and impacts that take place in the moves of intensity across things that seem solid and dead." (Stewart, 2007: 127)

It is in acknowledging this network and its sociality that the very role played by the jewellery industry emerges. It is not just a production experience. It is the very discursive element through which the discourse of this society is interwoven.

By disclosing this fundamental role, we can make a final remark. *'città orafa'* testifies well to how the boundaries of an industry extend farther the mere concatenations of action-connected goods' production, to encompass the individuals' ways of understanding and affecting. From the words of the informants, it appears that the jewellery industry is embedded deeper than the level of social relations and personal interactions examined by Granovetter (1985), to be engraved in the very 'soul' (cf. Bachelard, 1994) of the actors of our discourse. However, by taking this element seriously, in order to understand and explain what an industry means for a locale, we are forced to abandon a heuristic attitude that brought scholars, who based their analyses and centred their definitions of industry on the physicality of places and means of production, to objectify industries into definable and defined entities. We have to employ a new understanding of production that, potentially, will answer the appeal that Hart et al. (2010) recently made for a new understanding of the economy. The one they hope would be founded on, what I would term, an economic Copernican Revolution that places humanity at the centre of the system and would shift the focus away from the economy by considering it to be "made and remade by people" (Hart et al., 2010: 5). Such a move, however, implies that we should start considering the economy on the basis of people, hence through their ways of understanding and sensing it, bringing the analysis to re-consider the economy as 'complexity' (cf. Law and Mol, 2002: 1), rather than as a linear process.

Moving to a conclusion of this chapter, it appears that the interrogation of the discourse of the *'città orafa'* has led to the shedding of light on a variegated cosmos of people and objects. I started this chapter intending to introduce Valenza and its jewellery industry. In so doing I decided to present the very discourse that brings together a city and its industry in the formulation of a narration of an urban society. This is a discourse that goes beyond the settlement's actual material borders, to involve people who live outside Valenza. This discourse is marked by the occurrence of a particular trope, that of *'città orafa'*. Through this trope, Valenza is imagined and narrated by different subjects, but in so doing it is evocative of feelings and fantasies. Producing a list of narrations where the trope is employed and explained, I attempted to show how this discourse is propelled by different actors and to display a vast human cosmos of sentiments, ways of understanding, seeing and imagining a city. While each narration traces an independent trajectory, I showed the interconnections among those and the way in which these different trajectories and actors affect each other, creating a complex plot of the discourse. Individual agencies, often without realizing it, mutually interact in shaping the image of '*città orafa*' and reinforce personal fantasies about the '*città*' and its jewellery industry. In this way, the discourse is continuously generated and regenerated, consumed and propagated. In the previous pages I meant to offer an account, although ineluctably limited, of this grand cultural dynamic. Thus, by analysing the narrations and considering the role played by the jewellery industry in contributing to and creating an image of a city, I have ultimately commenced a broader critique of the very idea of industry, by showing the necessity of re-thinking even the very borders of what an industry is and acknowledging in it a role and a dimension that go beyond a mere account of production places and means.

In this chapter, the jewellery industry has been explored as a fundamental element in the creation of the 'sense of place' (cf. Field and Basso, 1996) of Valenza. However, it remains an object concealed in the shadows of a trope. Dissipating these shadows, in the next chapter I will further the analysis, by focusing on the ways in which the jewellery industry shaped the space and time of Valenza community, so as to become its metre and metronome.

Fig. 3: The North-Western corner of Piazza Gramsci

Fig. 4: An invisible 'fabbrica' in Piazza Gramsci

CHAPTER TWO

JEWELLERY: SPACE AND TIME OF A CITY

At the beginning of May 2009, I was with Fabio Bosco (Chapter 1) and one of *Radiogold*'s journalists in one of the station's studios during the broadcasting of an instalment of their series, *Valenza: le persone, l'oro, la Crisi*. On that occasion, I had been invited, along with Fabio, to talk about Valenza and its recent transformations through the lens of a subject other than economics; the lens of literature and poetry. Our discussion continued along after the 20 minute instalment. During this conversation, Fabio pointed out:

> "Valenza... If I think of Valenza, as it was and how I learned to love and hate it, I picture it like a '*grande fabbrica*'. It is hundreds of invisible workshops scattered all over the urban fabric. It is a living place from 8 [am] to 8 [pm], when cars and people whizz past you in a frenetic dance. Then, the desert during the night when the workshops close: No cafés, no cinemas are open. Nothing and nobody is in the street. Nothing but the light of street lamps or neon lamps filtrates through the curtains of house windows or the shutters of some firm that is carrying out some overtime. Nobody because firms may be closed but people continue their work in their homes, their domestic *'fabbriche'*, until they go to sleep. And they sleep until the new day and another day of crafting. Valenza... Valenza is a city that every day pulses with the beat of her jewellery industry... It is *a 'grande fabbrica'* from which none can actually escape."

During the interview, Fabio employed a particular rhetoric to describe Valenza. He equated the city to a '*grande fabbrica*'. In Italian, *'fabbrica'* usually refers to an industrial establishment in which mechanised manufacturing is carried out. Thus, a '*grande fabbrica*' could be translated as *a big factory*. However, in Valenza, *'fabbrica'* assumes a particular meaning. It is commonly used to refer to any jewellery firm, even the smallest workshops. Thus, the image of '*grande fabbrica*' could be considered just another variant of the rhetoric of the *'città orafa'* that expresses the 'sense of place' (cf. Field and Basso, 1996) of Valenza as explained in the previous chapter. However, if we take this similitude[1] seriously, *'grande fabbrica'* leads us to investigate the basis on which Valenza can be perceived as a gigantic jewellery firm, that is to analyse the linkage between the time and space of the city and its jewellery production.

As Applebaum (1986a, 1986b) and Burawoy (1979) pointed out, the industry is not a form of production organisation that affects only the work within the perimeters of a firm; it strongly impacts on the space and time of the community outside the production site as well. The word 'impact', however, describes a physical clash between two, or more, solid objects that does not imply any degree of merging between these entities. After the collision, in fact, they remain extraneous to each other even in the eventuality that they get stuck to one another. In the light of this semantic note, referring to Valenza, I prefer to employ the word 'permeation' that in implying the contact between objects also provides a sense of their merging and becoming one.

In this chapter, taking as a starting point the words of Fabio, I am going to present the permeation that affects the space and time of Valenza. I will consider the actual permeation of production within the urban fabric, highlighting the actual presences of firms all across the area of the city. In so doing and in order to explain this presence, I offer an account of the history of Valenza jewellery production; an industry that challenges an idea of industrial landscape based on large shelters and the division between residential and production areas. In the second part of the chapter, I will consider the permeation of jewellery production into the domestic spaces of goldsmith families; this makes houses into a further space of production. Finally, I will consider the permeation of jewellery production into the time of the city, by describing how this industry and with its rhythms end up marking the time of the city as the distinctive foundation of the articulation of the public calendar of a community.

Invisible 'fabbriche''

"Valenza is an industrial city with more than one thousand *'fabbriche'*." My informants repeated this sentence innumerable times. It was reiterated along with the rhetoric of the *'città orafa'* in official speeches and publications, as well as in the pages of national and local newspapers, among friends chatting in an informal situation, and by

[1] A similitude is a rhetorical strategy of describing an object through the characteristics of another one (Mortara Garavelli, 2003: 249-51).

professionals and scholars during formal meetings. In these different contexts, by affirming the manufacturing vocation of the local milieu, Valenza was described as '*industriale*' [industrial] and its workshops were called '*fabbriche*' [factories].

'*Industria*' [industry] and '*fabbrica*', in Italian as well as in English, bring to mind images of large plants, smoking chimneys and production lines: a human landscape that anthropology has studied since the early 1920s (for a retrospective see: Baba, 1998, 2006). In the case of Italy and Piedmont, this imagery may fit production realities such as Turin with its large establishments linked to the car industry (e.g. Morandi, 2006; Petsimeris, 1998; Oliva, 1988; Governa et al., 2009), but it does not fit with the majority of Italian industrial experiences. Since Bagnasco's studies (1977), scholars have repeatedly indicated that Italian industry is mainly based on small and middle size enterprises, generally localised within geographically bounded areas[2], such as Brianza (e.g. Ghezzi, 2007; Yanagisako, 2002) or the Marche region (e.g. Blim, 1990). The landscape of these areas is characterised by the massive presence of small and medium firms, nested in industrial concrete sheds that form uninterrupted expanses of grey buildings and grey streets that ring the residential city centre: a landscape that, although lacking large industrial plants, is characterised by the easy distinguishability between residential and production neighbourhoods. Relying on this model, a visitor, a '*furesté*' in the local dialect of Valenza, may expect to see a similar city structure in Valenza, but risks being surprised. The jewellery industry is barely visible to the eyes of a '*furesté*', as well as to the eyes of Valenzani, since in the industrial Valenza no chimney stands out against the sky in the city.

In 2008, Valenza industrial milieu was made up of about a thousand registered firms (Bellini, 2009).Only about fifty of those were located in the Coinor area, the small industrial area that lies between the train station and the city in the western periphery of Valenza; the majority, instead, was in the city centre. However, their presence is almost invisible, since no chimneys and no concrete shelters mark their location, and only very few have large premises. Thus, the invisibility of these '*fabbriche*' arises from their indistinguishability within an urban fabric of modernist condominiums built from the 1960s onwards, and short brick buildings, mainly built after the second half of the 19th century. You may be in front of dozens of them

[2] A vast bibliography explores the history and the development of Italian industrialism. Recent exaples are: (Malanima and Zamagni, 2010; Colli, 2010; Rabellotti et al., 2009; Sforzi, 2009). For further details concerning the actual economic and entrepreneurial characteristics of Valenza's industrialism, see next chapter.

and not acknowledge their presence, as happened to me during an afternoon in the beginning of August 2009, looking around Piazza Gramsci[3].

***

Roberto and I were sitting on a bench, chatting. He was the owner of a jewellery business and an activist in one of the jewellery firms' associations. He was in his forties. Black hair and black beard, he was a goldsmith born and raised in Valenza who had inherited his profession and firm from his father. He started working as a goldsmith when he was a highschool student at ISA Cellini school (see Chapter 4 for further details), in his father's workshop. After he finished his studies, he joined his parent and, when the father retired in the late 1990s, he and his siblings continued the family business.

I met him at the beginning of my fieldwork and, from then on, I regularly visited him. This time, when I rang at his door, he invited me to go out for a coffee. After the coffee we sat for a while on a park bench along Viale Oliva, a short boulevard in the centre of Valenza, in the hot summer afternoon. He was scanning Piazza Gramsci, the square at the end of the boulevard. Its expanse was almost free from cars, as is generally the case in August. Still watching the square, he was talking about the profound penetration of the industry within the city. To prove his point, and in reaction to my puzzled expression, he proposed we play a 'game'.

> "You don't believe it? Well, tell me, how many firms do you see over there?"

He pointed at the square and the buildings around it. I decided to try, and I spotted three *'fabbriche'*, thanks to the neon signs that communicated the firms' presence with their bright light and bold fonts. When I said the number, he laughed.

---

[3] Located on the edge of the historic centre, Piazza Gramsci is the one of the largest squares in the city. The square is ringed by short condominiums. These were mostly built in the 1960s, although there are still a few early 20th century small houses. The square itself is a public car park with about one hundred spaces. From September to July, from 8am to 8pm, it is hard to find a space free, but, after the patronal feast of St. James, on the 25th July, most firms close for the holidays and people leave the city almost deserted. Further information about the rhythms of Valenza is provided later in the chapter.

> "You see. You don't see them. But they are there. As far as I know, there are twenty *'fabbriche'* there, but most of them are almost invisible: you get their presence from small clues you should know."

While saying this, he pointed at some apartments on the first and second floors of the buildings in front of us. To my eyes they appeared to be 'normal' flats: venues indistinguishable from all the others used for residential purposes with nearly empty balconies.

> "You need a skilled eye, and even with a lot of practice it is difficult to know whether or not there is a workshop in a building or in one nearby... The best way to detect their presence is just to know they are there...At the end of the day, however, I think it is not really important to know where they are, because you know that in any case, the jewellery industry is around you, it surrounds you wherever you go."

I never directly verified the accuracy of Roberto's assessment. Although in the phone guide only a dozen firms involved in the jewellery trade were listed, it is not rare for small studios to not have a phone. Regardless of the accuracy of the numerical datum, Piazza Gramsci and this episode revealed an urban landscape where production and residential spaces are juxtaposed and almost indistinguishable from one another. On the front of a condominium or a detached house, as Roberto pointed out, few signs allow to detect the presence of a jewellery firm within those walls. A plate with the name of the firm on the condominium's entry phone panel or on the door, solid bars installed on the windows, the presence of CCTV cameras on the main and secondary doors of the building, and metal cages, easily confusable with normal metal lockers but used to store and protect the acetylene cylinders needed for welding, installed on the balconies, or outside a door or window if the firm is set up on the ground floor. Despite these signs, which even goldsmiths who have lived and worked in Valenza for decades find indicative but not exhaustive to identify workshops, the jewellery industry remains invisible, indistinguishable in the urban fabric of Valenza.

In this respect, Valenza's industry echoes the productive geography of a Mediterranean city, such as Naples, where it is not clear the separation between production and residential spaces (Troin, 1997: 38-41). As described by Pardo (1996) and Goddard (1996), in this Mediterranean metropolis, industrial production is mostly carried out in small production sites that are nested inside small venues, within houses and condominiums across the entire city. These establishments, which fall into a category between industrial plants and artisan studios, create a distributed network of 'invisible' workshops that encompasses the entirety of Naples. In

Valenza, as in Naples, industry involves the entire urban fabric. This emerges quite clearly from the maps, which localises all the firms listed in the 2010 Valenza phone guide – about 400, roughly half of the estimated existing firms. The entire urban fabric is covered with dots, showing the extent of the production network and a high density of workshops in the historic centre. By considering this map, we can see a permeation of the jewellery industry in Valenza that makes the city into a distributed production plant, since the entire city is in fact the space of this industry.

This characteristic spatial configuration is an inheritance and a continuation of the history of the trade in Valenza. Lenti (1994) described it in detail, from the birth of the first studio, which was opened in 1824 by Francesco Camora near Santa Maria Maggiore, Valenza's main church that is often called *the Duomo* [the cathedral] by Valenzani. Throughout the history of the trade, despite the success of those single firms that were able to expand to over one hundred workers, such as Vincenzo Morosetti's (Lenti, 1994: 120-6) or Vincenzo Melchiorre's (Lenti, 1994: 139-46; 1998), the majority of local enterprises has remained small-scale (for precise statistics concerning the growth of the trade, see: Gaggio, 2007: 88).

The oldest among my informants, people around or over 80 years of age, still remembered the appearance of those workshops established in the last decades of the 19th century or in the early 20th century. The firms crowded the courtyards of the historic centre[4].

---

[4] These old Valenzani offered vivid descriptions of those "unhealthy but beloved" studios. An example is the depiction offered to me by Vittorio, a retired goldsmith who turned 80 in October 2010, a few days before I interviewed him: "Most of those studios were just a damp room, scarcely ventilated and illuminated. In that room of a few square metres, two or three artisans worked cheek to cheek from dawn to dusk. They were often old stables, become empty after the massive prevalence of bikes and scooters. The landlords rented them to the artisans for their work for a handful of 'Lire' per month. Sometimes, the goldsmiths bought them. They became their 'fabbriche', but they were so damp! After a few months working there you started getting arthritis. I remember where my father worked. It was near Via Po, a few metres from Duomo. His studio was so damp. All the walls were stained by the humidity and, in some places, were covered in moss. However, my father worked there, alone, twelve, fourteen hours a day. And he loved that place. It was his 'fabbrica'; the centre of his life."

Map 1. The map gives the location of all the firms, about 400, that had a land line listed in the telephone book in 2010. Each dot corresponds to an address. Thus, where multiple firms share the same address, due to being located in the same building, on the map they are represented as one only spot. This is the case of the firms located in the Coinor area, which despite their number appear here as three spots (the ones just under the uppermost blue box SS 494). This map offers a clear picture of the spread of the enterprises but not of their density.

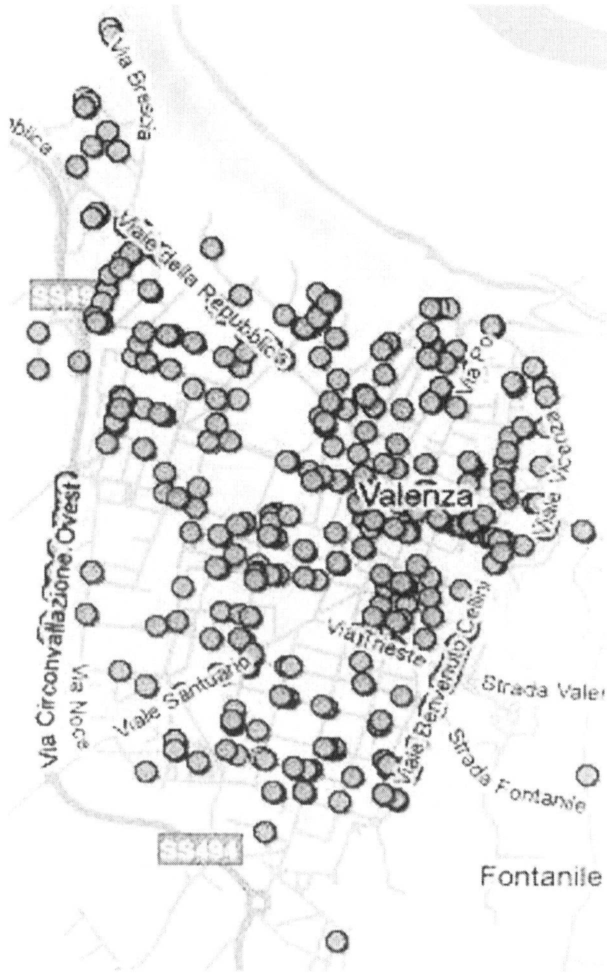

Map 2. In this re-elaboration of Map 1, in grey is highlighted the historic centre, whose perimeter corresponds with the boundary of the city in the 1920s.

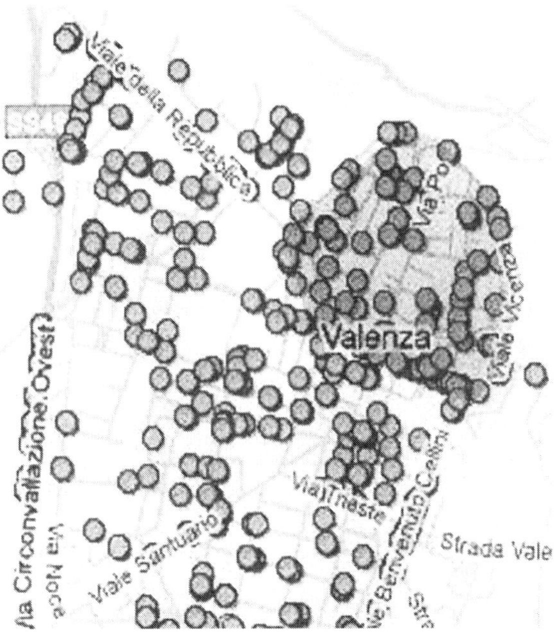

In the second half of the 1950s (Maggiora, 2010: 141), the city's demographic boom brought with it a rapid expansion of the city outside its historical borders. New neighbourhoods were built and, over two decades, the urban area of Valenza quadrupled (Maggiora, 2010: 112). The jewellery industry expanded quickly over this period. It clearly emerges from the three industrial censuses completed from 1951 to 1971: in 1951 there were 335 firms with 1,972 workers; in 1961 the number increased and reached 575 firms and 4,068 employees; in 1971, 1,031 were active with 5,562 employees (Maggiora, 2010: 234). New firms were opened in the new neighbourhoods created after the demographic boom while old enterprises aiming at expanding their scale moved into these areas, where they were able to find larger venues for their production workshops.

Because of the precarious conditions of the city centre workshops, in the 1970s, the City Council launched campaigns aimed at encouraging producers to improve the conditions of their workplaces, mainly by relocating their activities to the new areas. With this goal in mind, in the second half of the decade, the local government planned the construction of a new industrial area entirely dedicated to jewellery production facilities, located close to the train station in the western periphery of the city. As intended by the Council, this area, called Coinor, was to be an alternative for goldsmiths still working in the city centre to allow them to relocate their firms to new and healthier structures placed in an area logistically better connected to major infrastructures: the rail station and the SS 494 motorway. The new buildings were inaugurated in 1984 and offered new spaces, mostly designed for firms that employed at least ten employees: large venues, over 200 m2 each, and composed of multiple rooms. Clearly, they were profoundly different venues from the old studios and ill-fitting with the necessities of the previous entrepreneurial model. Retrospectively, it is no surprise that only a very few firms bought these workshops, and decided to relocate there: mostly large jewellery firms, such as Corova-Bulgari or Pasquale Bruni, which found in this the opportunity to further expand their facilities. However, the majority of firms is still located in the centre of Valenza.

From the 1980s onward, due to the coming into force of new national laws concerning health and safety requirements for workplaces (for an overall history of this legislation see: e.g. Brolis, 1991, Soprani, 2006), every firm had to meet new and progressively more restrictive standards of ventilation, heating and illumination. Firms had to renovate those frugal and gloomy spaces, which represented the artisan world described by Vittorio, to meet the new standards. Some of them undertook this work, so that, even in the days of my fieldwork, in the courtyards of the houses around the Duomo, it was possible to admire the last of these studios. However, the majority of those enterprises just closed, leaving behind them memories and some empty venues that thanks to their barred windows and heavy armoured shutters still betray a past as a goldsmith's studio.

In the 1970s, while old studios ceased their activities or were renovated, new workshops were opened across the entire city, occupying old and new spaces in the fabric of the city. Besides the firms that created their workshops in the Coinor area, most firms were opened in condominiums or in smaller houses built after the 1960s. Small firms were generally located in flats converted into production workshops, while large firms were usually located on ground floors or basements, adapting spaces intended as garages or warehouses. Thus, buildings originally designed just as residential spaces have become hybrid realities, 'between and betwixt' residential and production functions: ambiguous elements of the urban landscape, the actual functions of which remain a quality that barely leaks out from their ordinary façades.

An example of these hidden presences is given by Gustavo's workshop. The gem setting studio owned by Gustavo is a significant example of this hidden presence. This *'fabbrica'* is a small studio that thrives thanks to the manual ability of its few employees. The studio was opened in the mid-1970s by Gustavo and a partner.

Their workshop is set up in a two-room flat, about fifty square metres in size, located a few hundred metres away from Piazza Gramsci, on the third floor of a five storey building. From the main street, looking at the facade, nothing betrays its presence, since it looks like the other flats in the building. Inside the flat, the organisation of the rooms has been left as originally intended, even though they have been repurposed. The kitchen-dining room has become the shop floor; the bedroom, the office. The space is well illuminated and clean, although only basically furnished. The only pieces of furniture on the shop floor are four workbenches with their stools placed in the centre of the room and four metal closets placed against the wall. In the office, the furniture consists of a large desk and some metal cabinets placed along the walls of the room. The only touch of colour to the premises is provided with the photos hung in the entrance and the office, which portray Gustavo and his colleagues from the time they opened the firm onwards.

This *'fabbrica'*, when I met its owner, employed five people (it had started as a two-person firm; over the course of the following decades, it expanded by employing another two gem-setters and a part-time accountant[5]), and is a representative example of the socioeconomic composition of a good percentage of local enterprises (Chapter 3).

Gustavo's is an example of the invisible *'fabbriche'* of Valenza and the entrepreneurship that they embody. It is one of the hundreds of workshops of Valenza that turn the city's urban fabric into a space where jewellery

---

[5] The expansion was, however, to some extent limited: "Our work is in a difficult equilibrium. It is not possible to continue expanding. First of all because new artisans need space and, if you do not intend to buy or rent larger premises, a *fabbrica* like mine cannot contain more than four or five people. Besides that, our trade is based on continuous booms and busts, and if you don't want to hire just to fire people when the situation worsens, you limit your size and, instead, try to specialise yourself in more profitable manufacturing. We did it and in doing so we were able to thrive and maintain the same premises where we started this firm."

production is widespread and every building can host dozens of invisible workshops. In this geographical context, the permeation of the jewellery industry substantiates the sense of intimacy, of constant and reciprocal interaction (Kahan, 2005: 416), that pervades the words of Roberto, and that ends up in creating the grounds for the metaphorical transfiguration of the entire city into a *'fabbrica'*.

A bench at home

In his description, Fabio hints at a further direction of the permeation of jewellery production into the living fabric of Valenza: a pervasion into the domestic space of goldsmiths and their families that makes these spaces into work places; small *'fabbriche'*. Often goldsmiths refer to their home as their second, small workshops, and overt expressions like "my home; my small *'fabbrica'!*" were not unusual. These sentences, in their hyperbolic (Mortara Garavelli, 2003: 178-81) nature, describe the actual coincidence of production with residential spaces: a substantial overlapping of functions that stands against a theoretical tradition based on Marx's works that has seen a distinction between production and domestic spaces as a characteristic of industrialised societies.

In the first volume of his *The Capital,* Marx (2010 [1867]: 257-83) described the advent of industrialism as a progressive process of externalisation of any production function of a house, which in non-industrialised societies and localities represents not only a residence but the most important production place, as remarked by anthropologists such as Gudeman (2005; 2008; 2010), Bourdieu (1977: 89-91) and others (Sanjek, 2010). With the mechanisation of manufacture came the creation of a new place of centralised production: the factory.

After one hundred and fifty years, Marx's theories are still echoed in recent works (e.g. Mollona, 2009: 12; Parry, 2005; Yanagisako, 2002), in which factory and home are theorised as separate, though interconnected[6],

[6] Since Engels' studies on the interconnections between reproduction and production functions (Engels, 1972 [1884]), scholars have noted the interdependence between these two realms of individual and collective lives. Examples of this interconnection were given recently by Mollona (2009: 12) in his account of Sheffield's (UK) metal industry. He highlighted production and non-production spaces are principally connected in two ways. First of all, the possible low and insufficient wages gained from the factory would oblige workers to externalise the production function from the factory to other social worlds, ending up (re) internalizing production into the home. Secondly, the industrial work itself, as already pointed out by Carrier (1992), would be the source of workers' perceived

social spaces. The distinction between the two, however, lies on a twofold simplification of the understanding of the complexity of industrial work. First of all, this assumption seems to limit the production activities that make up industrial production to the activation and use of machinery, not considering all the other possible practical and intellectual activities (e.g. planning, designing, and accounting) that are constituent parts of this form of production. Secondly, the assumption implicitly reduces industrialism to a univocal and universal reality associable to automated and serial commodity making, where the human factor, the manual and creative skills of individual workers, holds a subordinate role. However, this idea clashes against the fact that industrialisation emerged as a multi-faceted phenomenon that, even in the same country, presented automated productions based on cumbersome machinery side by side with productions that require a more significant employment of human factors and smaller tools.

The different production contexts that are facets of contemporary industrialism bring with them different ways of being and, consequentially, ways of understanding and participating in the production in and outside the perimeter of a factory. Thus, this theoretical generalisation seems to exclude a wide range of possibilities that opens up in circumstances where the distinctive boundaries of the domestic space as a non - production place crumble. The home can have an economic and production function within and for an industrialised economy, indeed making the home a small factory. Industries, such as the shoe industry in the Italian Marche (Blim, 1990), in Naples (Goddard, 1978; 1996) and in the Spanish Valencian territory (Benton, 1989; Narotzky and Smith, 2006), are characterised by a limited mechanisation and the co-presence, along with factories, of a widespread, often informal, cottage industry. Valenza's jewellery production is a further example of this form of industrialism.

Since its origins in the 19th century, Valenza firms have been distinguished for their specialisation in medium and high-quality productions and a minimal employment of machinery in manufacturing, as is well described in the research and collection completed by Mollina and Manenti (1994). Centres such as Arezzo and Vicenza, the other two main poles of Italian jewellery production, made their fortune on the basis of the ability of their workers in creating and modifying machinery in order to develop mass productions of pieces (Gaggio, 2007: 128-203). Instead, Valenza developed productions based on minimally-mechanised productions predominantly based on the creative and manual skills of goldsmiths

distinction between home and factory, and their continuous exposure to this form of work furthers this perception.

(Lenti, 2010). Moreover, being mostly a milieu of small firms, in most of the local *'fabbriche'* Marx's categorisation between capitalist factory - owner and proletarian workers is not applicable, since in the past as well as in the present the owners directly work in jewellery making, as goldsmiths, gem-setters or polishers (Paradiso, 2008a; Benzi, 2004a).

In this industrial context, the distinction between domestic and production spaces is weak. Often, goldsmiths remarked that the jewellery industry leaks into their homes and makes them part of the production network. This permeation passes through objects and, above all, people. Through carrying out some management or manufacturing activities connected to production, or simply by talking and thinking about work, goldsmiths described how jewellery production follows them into their domestic space. In so doing, they have highlighted a sense of continuity between their work and domestic life that stands against the sense of industrial alienation that, in Marx's terms would derive from the commoditisation of individuals' work and creativity into the commodity of labour (Marx, 2010 [1867]: 117-23); a process that according with Carrier (1992a) would be the basis of the sense of utter division between the social spaces of factory and home that characterises modern industrial societies.

In this respect, the experience of Gustavo is relevant. Talking about the role that jewellery production has in his life, he noted that:

> "It is funny to think that my work, making jewellery, could remain outside the door of my home... It leaks into the house because I *am* a goldsmith. Being a goldsmith is what I am, not just what I do for a living. When I go home I leave my *'fabbrica'*, but it does not mean I quit thinking about my work. I don't know how many times, after dinner, I've spent time calculating the cost of labour for particular orders, I've called clients and suppliers, and I've finished some piece sat in front of the bench I have at home. Then I speak with my family and friends and we often talk about work, and I come back to think about my work. You cannot really stop. [...] Home is the place where you live, where the people you love live with you, but it is far from being a space free from jewellery production."

His words show us how an industry, such as jewellery production, represents a cosmos of experiences from which individuals are not completely able to divorce themselves once they leave their workplace. In this respect, Gustavo's testimony echoes a major strand of anthropological research on artisanship and work (Bourdieu, 1984; Lave, 1993; Lave and Wenger, 1991; Keller and Keller, 1996; Herzfeld, 2004; Marchand, 2001; 2009, 2010b) that has shown the impossibility of the individual to divorce work from their private life, mainly as an effect of the embodiment of the particular mindset that distinguishes a particular trade. Moreover, it also shows a continuity of economic activities outside the workplace, in the personal space of the home. For example, the activities of Gustavo are not restricted to his *'fabbrica'*, but are often continued outside that space, at home. Thus, it may be a calculation scribbled on a piece of paper, a phone call or the manual work of gem setting, but, overall, these activities make the factory leak into the home, and, in so doing, make the home into a second, small *'fabbrica'*.

From Gustavo's words, it emerges that some objects are particularly able to further this overlapping and give physicality to the ontological statement that opens this paragraph: if home is a *'fabbrica'*, it is also due to the presence, and use, of particular tools that allow the continuation of the activity: the most significant of those is the workbench.

A goldsmith's workbench is a special desk, about 90 - 100 cm tall and 50 cm wide, featuring a work surface, about 80 cm high, which is designed to be at the same height as the artisan's chin once they are sitting in front of the desk. On the outer edge of the surface there is generally a 50 cm long, 25 cm wide semi-circular indentation. At its centre is mounted the bench pin, a wooden wedge that leans out from the space[7]. Under the indentation, it is installed a removable metal box or piece of cloth in which the filings fall to be collected. The entire structure of the bench was designed to provide a wide space to support work, allowing a person to be free in their movements and providing ample space for the storage of tools. Despite the presence of the large indentation, the work surface is still ample and allows one to lay down tools such as drills, files, pencils, and wax. Over the work surface, there is generally another shelf upon which it is possible to install equipment such as a table lamp, mills, or a welder. In the lower section, moreover, a desk can be furnished with drawers.

The workbenches are the principal landmark of jewellery shop floors. Set up in rows and lines, they describe the inside of small as well as large firms, creating a spatial and human geography of production. However their presence is not restricted to the *'fabbrica'*. In the heart of goldsmiths' domestic spaces it is common to find these pieces of furniture. They are a recurring presence in the houses of goldsmiths and gem setters, such as Gustavo. They are placed in well-lit spaces, in the very centre of the

[7]The bench pin is the focal point of the workbench because it is there that majority of the manufacture of a piece of jewellery is carried out. The pin is a flat rectangular surface, one of the short sides of which is affixed to the work top with an adjustable metal clamp. The other side is cut into a truncated swallow-tail shape. This allows the artisan to file or saw a piece and have room to move the file or the saw around and still hold onto the metal.

domestic space, in living rooms, or in dedicated rooms, in the case of large houses. Through these objects, the very spaces that goldsmiths define as 'domestic' and 'private' become an integral part of the jewellery industry in their eyes. Thus, the home becomes an informal place of production often hidden from the State's observation; another invisible *'fabbrica'* where they live and act, as my informants expressed overtly. An example is given by Oreste, a goldsmith in his fifties:

> "You know, this house is a sort of second *'fabbrica'* to me. I don't know how many hours I've spent in front of this bench, working, experimenting, sweating and cursing..."

When he said this, it was about 9.00 pm, in early April 2010, and he was in front of his bench, at home, working. That day, from 8.00am to 6.00pm at work, he had worked on the production of a stock of rings ordered from their firm by a multinational corporation. After work and a walk around Valenza he returned home where he had dinner with his wife. Later, after she left for a book presentation at the City Library, Oreste started his overtime work. He went to his room, the smallest room in the five-room flat.

It was 10 m^2 illuminated by a window that opened onto the balcony, and a ceiling lamp with a couple of 60w bulbs. Originally, it had probably been designed as a storeroom, but it was being used in a different way. Beside the large wardrobe, there was a goldsmith's bench, with the same equipment as can be seen in an official workshop: a small welder, an extendable lamp equipped with a magnifier, an electric drill like the one used by dentists, a complete set of files, nippers and pliers.

He sat in front of the bench and took a cigarette packet from his pocket. From this, he extracted three small envelopes, which contained the three constituent pieces of the rings he had worked on all day, and started working.

Oreste's is just one example of a widespread phenomenon. Goldsmith benches are a common piece of furniture in the houses of many artisans in the city. Their location in the house may vary for reasons that appear to be functional (better illumination, more free space, etc.) rather than ideological, as is clear from another passage of the interview with Oreste. When talking about the bench, he explained that:

> "In the old house [a two-room flat located in the city centre], I had my bench in the dining room: it was the only place where I could keep it. The good part of having the bench there was that my wife and I could chat while I was working. It was nice. It was not a great problem [to have the bench in the living room] when Marco [their son] was a child, and it was

> rare that his friends came home to play. When he grew up and the number of kids that ran around the room increased, however, I found it too risky to have all this equipment in the same place where children play. I mean, you don't want your son to play near a welder... I wanted a separated space so that Marco did not risk hurting himself. When we changed home in the early 1990s, I chose this room as my workshop. It is a bit secluded and I preferred the old way, but you cannot have everything from life. When my wife is at home, however, it is enough that I leave the door open and the TV not at the highest volume and we are able to chat anyway."

The spreading of goldsmith benches through Valenza houses and, more broadly, the custom of having a domestic workshop may be facilitated by several factors: a national health and safety regulation that allows the domestic use of a welder for private use, i.e. a hobby, so long as the gas tank is kept outside the habitation, for example on a balcony; the small number of tools required for the manufacture of jewellery; the low cost of the bench and the tools – during my fieldwork, a second hand bench with all the basic tools for goldsmithing could be bought for a few hundreds Euros, and could be found quite easily for sale. However, the principal reason that goldsmiths gave was the presence of a market, that is, a demand for jewellery pieces or repairs that are not generally answered by the other, 'formal' firms. In many cases, these very firms outsource this work to their employees, offering extra money, often under-the-counter. This was for example the case of Oreste:

> "It is just an agreement with my boss. We have a strict deadline. We have to finish the stuff in a few days, so he is happy to pay us some extra money if we continue the production on our own. I brought these for this reason. It is just a few Euros, but why shouldn't I get them? I have the bench for this. I bought it in the 1980s, a few months after we had our son. To have all these things at home is useful. You know, to get some extra money and to keep you practicing. We had to pay the mortgage for this home and my son's rent, and... Well, it has always been like that... We always had something to pay and some extra money is definitely useful."

Hence, the presence and use of the equipment make these habitations constituent parts of the production geography of the local industry, since it transforms a home into an invisible and informal workshop where the artisan can experiment with new techniques and ideas or bring forward extra production. In this respect, hence, we see that home can be, and is, a second *'fabbrica'*: the most extreme limb of the production that stems from a firm and branches off by including this invisible, informal workshop.

Reconsidering all these points, it appears that this permeation in the lives of people and in their 'stuff' (cf. Miller, 2010) is strictly linked to the spreading of economic activities that we should refer to as 'informal' due to being, after the original definition of the term given by Hart (1973), unregulated and unregulatable by law and invisible to bureaucracy (Hart, 2010: 145). Thus, in order to understand the reasons of the overlapping of home and factory it is necessary to clarify what motivates this informal system of production. In past years Gaggio (2007) had offered a possible explanation to it by describing jewellery production as an industrialism that, *de facto*, developed and prospered from the constant employment of informal housework as a source of qualified cheap labour (pp. 67-68, 122-123). In so doing, Gaggio's thesis echoes the analysis by Blim in the case of San Lorenzo's shoe industry (1990: 145-77), and, more generally, Porter's structural theory of informal economies (1990). For Porter, the informal sector is a direct result of modern industry; it is made by subordinated economic units employed by firms to reduce input and labour costs and increase the firms' competitiveness. If we consider this interpretation in the light of the dyadic distinction between factory and home, it presents the complex relationship between formal and informal economy as subordination of the domestic space under the one of the factory, and the leaking of production into this space as a form of exploitation. This heuristic approach was developed to study large industries, however; when applied in the context of 'alternative' industrialism such as Valenza, it appears excessively rigid in identifying a power relation that, in the description of the radical distinction between workers and firm-owners and the subordination of the former over the latter hides the actual dialectical dynamics between artisans and outsourcers that emerge from the words of Gustavo and Oreste. In fact, although Porter's theory might prove to be a possible key to interpreting Oreste's experience, it cannot be used to explain the reasons why Gustavo, like dozens of firm owners I met, has and uses benches and tools at home to continue their productions. In this respect, it may be more useful to abandon a perspective that characterises a structural approach to an informal economy. Instead, we could recognise this form of production as a consequence of an entrepreneurial choice on the part of workers aimed at improving their conditions of life and, more broadly, expanding their economic possibilities. This does not mean we should ignore the fact that this choice can be forced by particular vicissitudes that a worker experiences, or that outsources and not manufacturers may be the price-makers for the commodities produced at home, but we should simply reconsider the victimisation of (home-) workers as a particular temporally-

and spatially-framed event, rather than an inevitable and universal structural dynamic of modern industrialism. By abandoning that angle, thus, we are able to acknowledge the actual tension of goldsmiths towards their work. In so doing, we end up seeing the leaking of the jewellery industry into their domestic space as the result of goldsmiths' action and their seeking fortune. Thus, we can see in that leaking the artisans' allowing of the industry to leak into their homes, and not just the effects of an oppressive structural process implied in a universal industrialism.

The beat of the city

The previous paragraphs introduced a spatial dimension pervaded by jewellery production. This industry has penetrated the urban fabric and has become its widespread landmark. In the quote that opens the chapter, however, Fabio pointed out a further direction of permeation of the industry that completes our portrait of the characteristic relationship between the city and the industry: time. This direction is highlighted through a poetic image: the beating of a city to the sound of the jewellery industry. Through a metaphor (Mortara Garavelli, 2003: 159-66), a subject is narrated through the characteristics of another object. This trope is thus able to offer solid, almost tactile, descriptions of intangible entities, such as time. This is actually what Fabio did: intertwining a narration in order to give a sense of relationship. However, this rhetorical move is achieved through a particular strategy that passes through the essentialisation of two abstract and complex entities (a city and an industry), and by making the relationship between these two objects explicit in the description of the reverberation of the movements of the latter with the former. This alluded kinetic univocity gives form to a profound, almost visceral union between the two entities by portraying the jewellery industry as the metronome of the Valenza.

If the jewellery industry, hence, the occurrence of social action that substantiates the production economy, marks the time, the days and seasons of Valenza, then to describe the manifestation of these movements allows us to better understand how the industry permeates into this dimension of the city's life. In other words, we can discuss the temporal dimension by considering activities such as the coming and going to and from the factories of hundreds of workers, or the opening and closing of firms during the year, that end up articulating a lay, production and civic calendar of Valenza. These events mark the daily public schedule of Valenza and its '*piazza*' [the square], the physical space of the main square of a community and consequentially its social public space, according to Isnenghi (1997). In so doing, these activities, hence the jewellery industry itself, become a system of temporal and spatial reference, a social calendar, for the city that makes non-goldsmiths participate in the rhythms of jewellery production as well. In fact, to the lay eyes of a non-goldsmith, this calendar unwinds over the course of the days and seasons, first of all, through modifications of the public spaces of the city. It appears through the periodical alternation of the filling and emptying of spaces; of traffic jams and fast flowing traffic; days when finding a place to park a car is a Herculean task and those when only a handful of cars circulates, since most people have left for their holidays. It is in this respect that to recount this alternation is to describe this calendar and this permeation of time by the jewellery industry.

Calendars rely on the definition of particular temporal units, which segment the flow of the world into defined objects. Some of the most significant and fundamental units are days, weeks, and seasons (Halford-Strevens, 2005: 1-17, 64-85). Considering Piedmontese history and culture, these units were the fundamental constituent parts of the traditional calendar (Grimaldi, 1993: 30-34, 50-69), and are useful temporal dimensions to describe our calendar.

To explore the penetration of a trade is to see the everyday dimension of life and interpret its signs that, though they may appear banal and un-meaningful, can disclose the information we seek. To speak about the temporal penetration of the jewellery industry and how it marks the course of days and weeks, is to address one of these banalities: road traffic.

About 17.000 cars circulate in Valenza area every year (Morselli, 2012: 33). This traffic is generally concentrated on particular days and times of the day: from Monday to Friday, from 7.30 to 9 am and from 6 to 7 pm. These are the peak hours in Valenza. During these times hundreds of cars noisily queue to move through the city and to drive the few hundred metres between Piazza Gramsci and the SS 494 motorway, which can take half an hour. The long queues of cars and fuming drivers mark the beginning and end of a normal working day in Valenza.

From Monday to Friday, between 8 and 8.30 am, most of the jewellery firms open, while shops and offices open later, at 9-9.30 am. However, traffic starts half an hour before 8, when goldsmiths flock to the city, slowly moving to reach their workplaces. Some of these are driving to their firms a little earlier to avoid the worst of the traffic, find a parking space close to their firm, possibly go to a café to have breakfast (cappuccino and brioche is a classic choice), and have time to change into their work overalls before the official beginning of the working day. So the traffic congestion slowly intensifies, to reach its apex around 8 am: the '*Mondo Orafo*' wakes up and with it the entire city.

The awakening is as noisy as it is fast. After its peak, traffic decreases after 9 am. At 9.30 am, when all the offices and shops are open, the flow of traffic is again smooth, although finding a free parking space can require a long search, since most of the spaces have been taken an hour or two earlier. In the streets of the city centre, as well as in the supermarkets and in the shops, one finds mainly retired persons, housewives or goldsmiths busy on some errand. Thus, someone who does not know that several thousand people are working in hundreds of invisible firms may have the impression of wandering through a half-empty city.

Only after 6 pm is the spell broken. After 5.30 pm, the workday ends for all the goldsmiths that are not employed in some overtime at their benches. Traffic, slowly, re-congests. People drive back home, or to one of the large supermarkets, such as Coop and Esselunga, or to the city centre to do some shopping. The city is populated by women and men who, during the rest of the day, have no chance to visit the shops. However, after 7.30 pm, the standard closing time for most of the shops and cafés, the streets come to be empty once again. The work may continue in the workshops or at home, but the streets remain deserted until a new, clamorous awakening.

The cycle of noisy awakenings lasts from Monday to Friday. On Saturday, only a few firms work and, generally, at a reduced pace. If it is not the case of some urgent job or a particularly busy period of the year, production halts. Firm owners might do some paperwork with their accountants, or they might finalise an order with some of their workers, or prepare the work for the following week. However most goldsmiths have a free day, often used to complete those domestic errands that were not done during the rest of the week, by going to some shops in Valenza or in the neighbouring cities, or going to the market, which is held every Saturday along Corso Garibaldi and in Piazza Gramsci. It is on Saturday that Piazza Gramsci comes to be a socially-attended public space for meetings and encounters. The '*Mondo Orafo*' comes out from the firms to populate this space as well.

Sunday, the firms are closed, as well as the shops and offices. The only exceptions are two supermarkets, Esselunga and Coop. It is a day of rest, when the entire city seems to be willing to sleep some extra hours. Cafés and newsagents open at about 8, while the rest of the week they open at 7 am. People go out after 9, some of them to attend Sunday service, other just to take a walk and meet some acquaintances or friends along the city centre's streets or in a café. Sunday is generally a day of domestic life, family lunches or trips to destinations not too far from the city: some village along the Ligurian coast, in the Alps, or the Piedmontese hills.

Contrary to a model of industrial cycles as a linear articulation of social life, repeated uniformly day after day without variation in quality or intensity (as proposed by: Grimaldi, 1993: 34), the cycles of the jewellery industry exhibit accelerations and slowdowns. Seasonal fluctuations in production are, as Miron (1996: 15-56) showed, events common to a wide range of activities including the tobacco, chemical and petroleum industries. The seasonality of consumption of commodities (e.g. Miron, 1986) is central to this fluctuation, being connected with the cycle of seasons and particular annual festivities. Likewise, the jewellery trade in Europe and in North America, the main markets for Valenza products (Gereffi et al., 2010; Paradiso, 2008c; 2009), is notably seasonal (Carcano, 2007b: 136-38). It hinges on particular annual events and periods: Christmas and Easter.

Christmas time represents the busiest period for the trade. Demand can become particularly intense and jewellery sales reach their annual peak. In the case of Valenza, about 60% of the entire year's turnover is generated in the last three months of the year when the production milieu is producing for Christmas orders (for econometric data, see: Servizio Studi e Ricerche, 2010b: 173). Christmas is the apex of a longer period of production acceleration that starts in October; a period that is often called '*stagione invernale*' [winter season; also: winter campaign]. During these months activity in the workshops picks up the pace and reaches its apex between November and the early weeks of December.

After Christmas, in January and February, the market normally relaxes, to upturn again in the weeks before Easter, reaching a new, minor peak in the month after the holiday. During this month, in Italy and in a large percentage of Catholic Europe, religious events, such as First Communions and Confirmations, are celebrated; jewellery is among the traditional gifts for these occasions.

After this period, called '*stagione primaverile*' [spring season; also: spring campaign], the demand downturns again, opening the '*stagione estiva*' [summer season; also summer campaign] (June, July and August) of low activity. Due to this slowing of demand, hence of production, goldsmith firms usually close for the holidays at the end of July, traditionally after the feast day of St. James (25th July), one of the protector saints of Valenza.

Thus, the seasonality of the market influences the work in '*fabbriche*', intensifying or attenuating working times and activities. In the '*stagione invernale*', in particular during its apex in December, goldsmiths recalled that it was not rare, in the years before 2008, for firms to work every day, including during the weekend, until late hours to complete orders. Saturday and Sunday, generally relaxed, turned into 'normal' working days. The frenetic activity of jewellery firms ended up characterizing the public space. Again, it is traffic that appears to be the first sign of this situation. In the words of a shop-keeper in her forties:

> "[*'Stagione invernale'*] is a continuous coming and going of cars. Every morning, long queues of cars clog the streets, and even during the weekend it is truly difficult to find a free parking space. Goldsmiths come, goldsmiths go. With them are lots of cars from outside Valenza. They are their customers that come for their orders and to check the goods. Every day is a working day, when *'fabbriche'* are open till late."

Traffic and activity were actually the markers of the end of the years, as a civil servant in her forties whom I met in her office at the City Council in April 2010 commented:

> "It was the coming and going that involved jewellery workshops every day in December, even Sunday mornings at 9 am when the city normally sleeps, that reminded Valenza, reminded all of us, even those who have nothing to do with that business, that Christmas was coming, rather than Christmas lights."

After the Christmas peak, in the *'stagione primaverile'* and *'stagione estiva'* the same firms reduce their working time to 30-40 hours a week. While the *'stagione invernale'* is remembered for its fullness, conversely, the *'stagione estiva'* is remembered for its emptiness. Almost no firms are open from St. James' day to the last week of August. The halt of the industry appears clearly even to the most distracted of *furesté*. The city is emptied and, as in the case of Roberto's episode, there are almost no people or cars in the squares and streets of Valenza. As a Milanese tourist in her thirties commented, while walking in the deserted and silent streets of Valenza one mid-August afternoon in 2010:

> "It is incredible. There is no one. No café is open. Not even a newsagent or a shop. I am walking and walking and I have met just three people and a dog... It is so depressing... Wasn't it a 'city of gold'? It seems to me instead one of Leone's[8] ghost towns..."

---

[8] Italian film director, internationally famous for his western movies, such as *A Fistful of Dollars* (1964), and *The Good, the Bad and the Ugly* (1966).

The frenetic presence or relaxed absence of people and cars publicly characterises and distinguishes jewellery seasons and marks the time of the city. These seasons, however, are announced by particular moments of 'effervescence', "periods [...] when [...] men look for each other and assemble together more than ever," (Durkheim, 1976 [1912]: 241) when the jewellery trade becomes at the centre of public interest and goldsmiths try to forecast the new market trends.[9] These moments correspond to the international fairs of Basel (*Baselworld*, annual fair – March –, see: www.baselworld.com), Vicenza (*Vicenza Oro*, quarterly – January, March, June, September –, see: www.vicenzaoro.it), and Valenza (*Valenza Gioielli*, annual fair – October –, see: www.valenzagioielli.it).

These events open the production seasons and are occasions at which firms can show their products to potential clients (final clients, retailers or other producers) before the actual beginning of the production campaigns. Moreover, during the events, small and large international *maisons* [jewellery houses] present their new collections. Furthermore, the fairs allow producers to meet new potential production partners and open business relations. While participation in these fairs represents a non-trivial investment[10], it is considered by most of my informants to be a potentially useful experience to test the trends of the market and fashion and develop one's business network. On the days during the fair and following it, goldsmiths who attended the event are always asked by colleagues and friends about what they saw, and predictions are made about the future of the market, whether the trend in the following months was to be a *'molla'* [downturn] or *'bonna'* [upturn]. Some signs are particularly important in this game of forecasting: the estimated number of visitors and expositors, the volume of orders that firms have collected – or that they are known to have collected –, the conspicuousness and novelty of collections displayed. These signs are interpreted by people and discussed for hours after work. In this process of forerunning, figures and statistics are not essential; in many cases, the sensations of old or reputedly wise artisans are better trusted. Their opinions, the small and

---

[9] As lay counterparts of holidays, such as Easter or Candlemas, that in traditional Piedmontese agricultural calendar (e.g. Grimaldi, 1993: 250-68) mark the change of season and correspond to sacred (cf. Eliade, 1987 [1957]: 11-13) moments when the peasant community finds ritual signs to forecast the results of the upcoming harvests.

[10] To hire the smallest stand at the Basel fair costs about €30.000; in addition a firm must consider the travel and accommodation costs for its personnel, and an indemnity and theft insurance for its goods. Thus, to attend the event as an expositor can cost at least € 50.000 for a firm.

ephemeral signs collected during the visit to the fair or just the rumours heard in a café become the foundations on which goldsmiths picture the future, the destiny of the market is foretold[11]. These verdicts in turn become the basis on which goldsmiths normally approach the opening of a new season and decide whether to expand or reduce manufacturing, to invest on new collections, or adjust their previous products '*prendendo spunto'*, 'by taking some hints' – often a euphemism to mean 'copy' – from the new collections displayed during the fairs by competitors.

The centrality that these fairs have in the planning of goldsmiths' productions can explain the particular interest that these events provoke in Valenza and the relevance they have in public and private discussions. In cafés, as well as in the firms and in the street, goldsmiths exchange rumours about what is happening at the fair. The newspapers publish long articles with opinions of experts, mainly politicians and firm owners, about the fairs and the situation of the market (e.g. Zemide, 2011). Posters about these events are even put up in the streets. Thus, in this respect, we can conclude that the city is literally permeated by information about the event.

This is particularly true in the case of *Valenza Gioielli*, Valenza's jewellery fair. This is organised once every year in Expo Piemonte, the exposition centre located outside the city, in the eastern periphery of Valenza's territory. Despite this segregation, it affects the life of the city and its space. Car parks, normally used by locals, are reserved for the visitors of the fairs; posters are placed all around the city advertising the event; side events, such as art expositions or concerts, are organised in the city museums and theatre. Although access to the exposition is limited to official jewellery producers or retailers, over the days of the event, hundreds of cars coming from all around Italy and foreign countries flock

[11] In light of the parallels between traditional agricultural and jewellery calendars, a further structural parallelism can be drawn between the forecasting practices that peasant communities associated with particular feasts, such as Candlemas (Grimaldi, 1993: 186-89) or Saint Martin's day (Romano, 2009), and the actions of Valenza goldsmiths. Although peasant practices were read as production strategies rooted in and characterised by a particular anti-scientific ontology defining rural communities and their knowledge (Grimaldi, 1993, 2012; De Martino, 2003 [1948]), if we consider these practices in a perspective less interested in classifying actions according to the antinomian couples of 'magic/science' and 'sacred/profane', in goldsmiths' actions we would see an application of the same deductive cognitive practice that, on the basis of a few, standardised elements (clues), generates an idea of the world on the basis of which they planned their economic activities.

to the city, increasing the normal traffic. *Valenza Gioielli* is thus another visible element of the city calendar that marks, as a un-official opening, the beginning of the '*stagione invernale*'.

Coming to a conclusion of this section, the words of Fabio still resound and reveal their meaning beyond their poetic imagery. Ordinary events, such as road traffic, turn out to be ways in which jewellery production affects the public space of the city. In so doing, jewellery production becomes the metronome of Valenza; the 'beat' that marks the rhythms of the city. Thus, rises and falls in production become the basis of a complex calendar through which daily and seasonal time manifests and become a narratable and an experienceable dimension of life in the *'città orafa'*.

Conclusion

In the previous chapter, we saw that Valenza is narrated as a *'città orafa'*, and that this discourse is rooted into the life of this city. This chapter has provided further elements to understand the link between the city and its jewellery industry. In so doing it completes the ethnographic description of this city of goldsmiths.

As a permeating and characterizing element of the space and time of the city, the trade represents a fundamental key to understanding the city and its being. In this respect, it can be seen as the metre and metronome of the city.

In the light of the jewellery industry's fundamental role, we can re-read Fabio's metaphor, which opened the chapter, and understand its existential substance. I have attempted to make this dimension of experiencing the city emerge, following three directions of permeation of the jewellery industry in the life of Valenza. Thus, while the tempo of the city is marked by the rhythms of jewellery production, and *'fabbriche'* create a diffuse production net that expands over the entire city, jewellery production becomes part of the everyday life of Valenzani, and in the case of goldsmiths and their families, a connecting line that binds together the domestic space with that of the factory. In this respect, Valenza is a *'fabbrica'*, an absolute dimension of living for its population that lives every day to some extent in contact with jewellery production and reverberates with it.

Together with the previous one, this chapter concludes a preliminary ethnographic portrait that aims at introducing and explaining the centrality of the jewellery industry in this city. In so doing, some elements of the actual operation of this industry have been presented to explain other aspects of the life of the city. In the following chapter, these elements will be completed and treated more systematically to better explain how this industry, this diffuse productive network works and is experienced by goldsmiths.

Fig.5: A goldsmith's workbench

Fig. 6: Working in a small 'fabbrica'

CHAPTER THREE

MAKING THE NETWORK

In the previous chapter, I began the analysis of Valenza's jewellery industry and its role in the city. In so doing, and by making sense of two widespread rhetorics that associate Valenza to jewellery making, I have shown that this business is a fundamental element in the definition of the 'sense of place' (cf. Field and Basso, 1996) and a fundamental marker of the space and time of the city. In the analysis I described the jewellery industry as roughly homogeneous and did not discuss in detail the organisation of the business in the city, which is the main topic of this chapter.

In this chapter, I will investigate the structure of the network, by showing the different models of enterprise that coexist in Valenza, the ways in which they collaborate, and the history of this network. Valenza has been presented as an example of an ID (Gaibisso, 1995; Garofoli, 2004; Bassano, 2008). This approach appears valuable in many respects; however, it tends to overlook the dynamism and agency of the actors in favour of a substantial structural determinism in the analysis of a district. To recover this fundamental aspect of the economy, I will examine a case of a network economy in action. In so doing, I will also show how this economy is explained through a language of affects that sheds light on the form of knowledge and interpersonal relationships that underpins the network. Furthermore, this chapter opens out to a broad reflection on the experience of jewellery making that will be completed in the next chapter.

Models of firms

Let us return to Map 1. Looking at the map, we see dozens of dots that cover the surface: they that mark buildings in the urban fabric; dots that mark the presence of dozens of *'fabbriche'* scattered all across the city. These are signs of a diffuse entrepreneurship, the actual consistency of which goes beyond the numerical entity of those spots to encompass about 1200 firms in 2008 (FDI, 2011).

The Valenza's landscape is dominated by small firms, like Gustavo's workshop presented in the previous chapter. These generally employ up to five or six workers (FDI, 2011), and, as pointed out by Benzi and Fugagnoli (2004b) and Paradiso (2008a), commonly work for other Valenza firms, completing only part of the production cycle, such as gem-setting, like in the case of Gustavo.

Firms with more than 15 employees are referred to as '*grandi*' [large] '*fabbriche*' by Valenza goldsmiths. These are about 30% of local firms, and almost all of them have less than 50 employees. These firms may be specialised in the processing of particular phases of production (e.g. gem-setting, polishing, casting) but more commonly they process the entire cycle of production although they may outsource part of their production to local suppliers, and combine their activity as suppliers of other firms with direct sales of their collections to buyers, such as jewellery shops or private customers.

The '*fabbrica*' of Roberto, a jeweller we met in the previous chapter, is an explicative case of these '*grandi frabbriche*'. His firm employs about thirty employees, about five times the average number of workers of an average firm. The business was started by Roberto's father, Renato, in the late 1960s. Renato was a goldsmith who worked for almost ten years for a large firm in the city. After that experience, he decided to work as an independent artisan and opened a small studio. In the 1980s, he decided to expand the activity and bought the premises where Roberto's workshop currently is. The firm is set up in the basement of a condominium, in a roughly 450 m^2 premises, a few hundred metres away from Piazza Gramsci. However, from the main street, the '*fabbrica*' is almost unnoticeable, since none of the windows open out from the façade, and no other obvious signs, such as a plate with the name of the firm on the condominium's entry phone panel (one has to ring the entry bearing the name of Roberto's father), betray the presence of this firm.

Roberto's firm started out as a supplier for other firms. However, since the 1990s, he has created and expanded his own commercial network, mainly thanks to the involvement of Roberto's siblings in the business, to cover key positions in the management. They complete the entire cycle of production of a piece of jewellery; however, for some particular tasks or in case of large orders they may outsource part or all of the production to other '*fabbriche*'. While the firm occasionally works as a supplier for other firms, it mainly markets its own branded collections, with customers in Italy, Spain, Germany, and in the United Arab Emirates.

While firms like Gustavo's and Roberto's constitute almost the totality of Valenza's industrial milieu, there are a few other firms that complete the panorama. These are firms with more than fifty employees, some of which employ more than 250 people (e.g. Bulgari, www.bulgari.com; Damiani, www.damiani.com; Pasquale Bruni, www.pasqualebruni.com; Vendorafa, www.vendorafa.it). They are generally internationally-known firms that, as in the case of Damiani and Bulgari, may be part of international corporate groups, like Damiani.spa (www.investorrelations.damiani.com) or LVHM (www.LVHM.com), listed on international stock-exchanges. Moreover, they are also set up in large, dedicated production buildings that lie mainly in the western periphery of Valenza, in or near the Coinor area.

The establishments are usually multi-storey buildings, covering thousands of square metres, where administrative as well as creative and manufacturing activities are carried out. Although some of the firms, such as Damiani or Bulgari, may have their HQs and part of their creative studios set up in other cities – in Milan and Rome respectively – the management concerning production is carried out in Valenza, side by side with the actual jewellery manufacturing. Offices are generally located near the main entrance of the premises, while the inner rooms are used for production. Jewellery-making is carried out in large areas, long, wide rooms whose open space is marked by rows and lines of workbenches supplied with the equipment necessary for particular phases of production, such as drills, welders, microscopes: the same tools that are employed in all the other, smaller, firms of the city. Looking at these spaces, these buildings appear to be modern industrial 'works', production spaces organised in a way that recalls 19th century manufacturing plants where production was clearly segmented and employees are organised on the basis of the needs of production (Hunter Bradley, 1999). However, unlike the space of a metal factory such as the one described by Mollona (2009), no large machines are employed, and manual work and workmanship still occupy a central role. In these firms, the entire cycle of jewellery production is completed, from melting to polishing and gem-mounting. Similarly to medium firms, as scholars have pointed out (e.g. Gereffi, 2007; Benzi, 2004b; Paradiso, 2008a). These firms often outsource part of their production to smaller, local firms, temporarily augmenting the firm's production capacity for unexpected increases in demand or seasonally during the *'stagione invernale'* (Chapter 2).

From this summary, it emerges that, beyond the constellation of dots and an indistinct industrial presence of Map 1, lays a production cosmos in which entrepreneurship is inflected in different, and complementary forms. While jewellery manufacturing is conducted largely through technologies and techniques shared by both macro- and micro-enterprises, the widespread nature of the outsourcing and supplying practices mentioned in this paragraph creates in a production network that covers the entire city; one that has been studied in the light of ID theory since the 1970s.

A network, an ID

In the introduction I discussed the concept of ID as it has been developed in the scholarship since Marshall's (1920) theories. In brief, an ID is an economic local system characterised by the prominence of a particular industry, a widespread entrepreneurship that creates a milieu in which firms are related through 'horizontal' (competitive), 'vertical' (input-output), and 'diagonal' (related services and instruments) activities (Becattini et al., 2009: XVIII). The role played by the local community – defined as an ensemble of practitioners who share a common work ethos and skills – is particularly important for the strong social and work mobility, which scholars have found to be a common characteristic of IDs. It propels the industry, sustains creativity and spreads ideas within the milieu (Markusen, 1996; Becattini et al., 2009).

As shown in earlier studies (Lenti and Pugnetti, 1974; AOV, 1972; Barozzi, 1976), already in the 1970s Valenza's industry appeared as a fabric of hundreds of small workshops and few large enterprises. The work of the RP research team (1979) highlighted the integrated nature of this entrepreneurial network with other industries and services present in the territory, such as banks and insurance companies. In this respect, this study is a first attempt at making sense of this industrial reality by foregrounding the interconnection between different economic activities through the definition of Valenza as an '*area attrezzata*' [equipped area]: a geographic area that pivots around the jewellery industry and that provides all services required to sustain this industry.

Following RP's research, scholars investigated the economic interconnection between economic activities and the nature of this interconnection (e.g. Magni, 1999, Garofoli, 2004; Gaggio, 2007; Gereffi, 2007) producing models of the network's structure. While all of the research has read Valenza as an example of an ID due to the interconnection of the firms' economies and the coherent business vocation of the region, it has also highlighted a hierarchical structure in the city's industry. Recently Gaggio (2007) and Gereffi (2007) have offered articulated studies of this structure. Gaggio read it as:

> "A three-tier pyramid made up of a restricted number of commercially oriented agents on the top level, a larger group of official subcontracting firms on the middle level, and on the third level an even larger number of

individual – and often undocumented – cottage workers who were generally active only a few months a year." (Gaggio, 2006: 31) [1]

A slightly different description of this structure has been provided by Gereffi who has noted the existence of a further level, between the second and the third, made up of small firms, such as Gustavo's, that work exclusively as suppliers of other firms. Moreover, according to Gereffi, the hierarchy and power within this structure are based on a firm's access to the market – the ability of a firm to market its products to final customers rather than to other production firms.

In their view, thus, outsourcing represents an economic glue for the entire industry and, at the same time, a means of domination, since small firms, such as Gustavo's, being unable to produce pieces by themselves, would be strictly dependent on orders from the all-round enterprises. Consequentially, the latter would emerge as the only factual motor of the local economy, while the former would be merely subordinated.

Comparing this organisation with the information provided by historical sources and accounts, a profound similarity emerges between the present network structure and the organisation of the district that emerged during the 19th century and became established after WWI. Moreover, from a historical analysis, it becomes possible to trace the genealogy of this organisational model, as I will do in the next paragraph.

At the roots of an ID

Jewellery production dates back to the 1820s, when the first documented goldsmithing studio was opened in Valenza[2] (Lenti, 1994: 118-19). The workshops that were opened in the first half of the century embraced a model of entrepreneurship that is reminiscent of a medieval goldsmith's workshop, as described by Sennett (Sennett, 2008: 53-81) and others (e.g. Lucie-Smith, 1981: 130-34; James, 2007; Franchi, 2009). Production was not segmented between different workers, and jewellers completed the entire cycle of jewellery production mainly by hand. Moreover, jewellery was generally sold locally, and was thought to satisfy

[1] See also: Benzi and Fugagnoli, 2004b; Gereffi, 2007; Paradiso, 2008a.

[2] In 1824, a new law was promulgated in the Kingdom of Sardinia (the pre-unitary state of Italy in which Valenza was located). It obliged all the silversmiths and goldsmiths to register their firms and hallmarks at the provincial trademarks office (Abrate, 1966 pp. 177-192; Lenti, 1994 p. 94). Thus, Valenzani had to register their marks in Alessandria: thanks to the documents generated because of this law, we have information concerning the origins of the trade in the city.

the demand from Valenza and the neighbouring cities, such as Alessandria, Casale Monferrato and Pavia.

In the 1850s, a new form of entrepreneurship had started to spread in the city. New firms opened; unlike the previous studios, these were large establishments that employed dozens of workers. The first example of such firms is the one opened in 1858 by Carlo Bigatti, a goldsmith and engraver from Alessandria. Established as a studio employing six people, this enterprise rapidly expanded. By 1861, it employed twenty-four goldsmiths and became one of the largest firms in the city. Besides the number of employees, Bigatti's is an interesting example because it is the first *'fabbrica'* cited in historic sources as employing a segmented manufacturing process (Lenti, 1994: 124). The artisan specialisation we see recognised by Bigatti in his employees foregrounds a fragmentation of production that would become a common phenomenon in the following decades and that is still applied in contemporary production (e.g. Benzi and Fugagnoli, 2004a; 2004b). Although jewellery production remained hand-made, the segmentation of the process represented the departure of Valenza goldsmithing from a medieval model of craftsmanship *à la* Sennett (2008: 53-81). A growing number of artisans became specialised in particular phases of production. In the last decades of the century, thanks to the parcelling of production and a growing market, the scale of jewellery plants, as well as the number of firms, increased, prefiguring a process of industrialisation of production and creation of larger, Fordist plants (Lenti and Pugnetti, 1974: 17-19), as occurred in other jewellery production centres, such as Vicenza and Arezzo (Gaggio, 2007: 128-203). WWI, however, prevented this scenario.

While the international, and in particular European, demand for jewellery had already dropped in August 1914, Italian participation in the war also caused a plunge in domestic demand and a surge in the price of the raw materials necessary for manufacture (gold, silver, coal, gas, diamonds, etc.). Furthermore, general conscription forced large numbers of Valenza's goldsmiths to abandon their studios. These circumstances brought Valenza's jewellery industry to a structural crisis. At the end of the conflict, only 14 of the 51 firms open before the conflict survived, and no new enterprises had been established during the years of the war. However, although WWI almost obliterated the entrepreneurial landscape of the city, the community of practitioners survived and expanded. In fact, only a few goldsmiths were among Valenza's fallen[3], and during the

[3] During the war, 139 Valenzani died and 39 remained mutilated or in any case unable to go back to work (Maggiora, 2010: 35).

conflict, the manufacturing had massively relied on the work of elderly craftsmen, as well as women freshly trained for the job. In addition to the mass of veterans these women became a new skilled workforce available on the labour market after the war.

In the years after the conflict the demand for jewellery suddenly increased. Due to the contraction of the production milieu, the load of orders became concentrated in the hands of the few surviving firms. In order to cover the demand, these establishments hired new personnel. However, even with the increase in the workforce they were not able to directly complete all the orders. Thus, they started outsourcing to other, unemployed artisans. These artisans were asked to process part of the production in the form of lots of jewellery, or just through the completion of particular phases of production. In this perspective, unemployed artisans were reintegrated into the production cycle. Instead of being employed as workers, however, they were encouraged to open their own studios. Thus, outsourcing drove the recovery of the production milieu and offered concrete opportunities for (re-)starting activities to the artisans who were expulsed from the trade during the previous decade. At the same time, jewellery production became a collective effort that involved different firms in the production network. In this respect, the jewellery industry can be read as a production network that started rapidly expanding in the years after WWI involving informal work and turning it into a particular form of formal entrepreneurship.

Nine years after the war, in 1927, there were 152 firms and 796 people working in the jewellery trade. These data demonstrate the growth of the jewellery industry (Gaggio, 2007: 59), but above all highlight a radical change in the entrepreneurial structure of this industry. In 1911, nearly as many people were employed by only 47 firms, less than a third of the 1927 number. The size of the average firm shrank: in 1911, firms with less than 10 employees made up about 58% of Valenza's firms; in 1927 they represented more than 84% (Gaggio, 2007: 59). This narrowing can be explained by the conditions that outsourcing and the presence of an intense national and international demand created after WWI. In fact, they guaranteed security for minor entrepreneurs, since, by supplying other firms, they minimised their entrepreneurial risk, being fundamentally guaranteed to sell their entire production. Moreover, the suppliers were almost certain to reduce or nearly eliminate idle stock time. Furthermore, these firms barely needed to invest any resources into the creation of commercial networks, since they could base their trade entirely within the city. Alongside these contingent economic factors, the production specialisation in high-quality jewellery itself sustained this trend. In fact, unlike other productions, such as the manufacturing of medals or chains, it did not require the use of any particularly sophisticated machinery (Cappellieri, 2008; Lenti and Bergesio, 2005), but relied on the artisan's manual skills and a few, cheap tools (Molina and Manenti, 1994). Thus, the centrality of the individual workmanship and their production self-sufficiency, the low entrepreneurial risk and the inexpensiveness of the means of production did not force artisans to associate together in large plants in order to start a new business. On the contrary, these factors permitted small enterprises, such as workshops with less than ten employees, to succeed. These firms tended not to develop their capacity to interface directly with the national and international markets; instead, they looked for Valenza firms to find orders. As many firm owners explained to me, the workshops became a cheap and available resource for those market-oriented firms to cope with large orders without having to expand their production facilities: outsourcing became a viable and cheap solution to cope with the volatile jewellery market and reduce entrepreneurial risk without being obliged to engage in recurrent, thus uneconomical, processes of expansion (that is, to hire new personnel and buy machinery) and contraction (that is, to lay off workers and sell machinery). At the same time, for the workshops, their small scale and the lack of a need for developing a marketing network combined with the low cost of the required means of production allowed sunk costs to be limited and made it easy for an individual enterprise to enter and exit from the (local) market.[4]

On these economic premises, from the ashes of WWI, it emerged a model of network industry that developed without major structural transformations throughout the entire 20th century (Gereffi, 2007). On the basis of historical and econometric data, there appears to be a strong continuity between this model and the structure that characterised Valenza over the course of the last century, as pointed out by Gereffi (2007) and other scholars (e.g. Gaggio, 2006; 2007; Lenti, 1994; 2010; Maggiora, 2010). This continuity was often also indicated by my informants, who

---

[4] While anthropologists who worked in Italy had pointed out the fundamental role that kinship plays in articulating economic networks, in Northern (Yanagisako, 2002; Ghezzi, 2007), as well as Southern (Schneider and Schneider, 1976; Schneider, 1998; Pipyrou, 2011; Goddard, 1996) Italy, in the case of Valenza kinship plays a secondary role in the choice of the business partners (Gaggio, 2006; 2007). Other forms of relatedness come to play. In particular, it is valued the direct knowledge between the partners, as explained later in the chapter. A language of kinship, however, is used to define the relationship between firms. This is the case of workshop *figliolanza*, explained in the next chapter.

provided me with detailed explanations of the overall dynamic of the district. An example is the explanation by Armando:

> "The structure of Valenza's industry is quite easy and straightforward. Over the fifty years I have worked in this city there have been always some large firms or traders that made the economy turn. These people have contacts outside the city. They go to jewellery shops, and most recently, look at the case of Damiani, they open their 'boutiques'. They collect orders from the market. Large amounts of work – if we are lucky. Part of these orders they [the large firms] produce by themselves and, if the order is large enough or the time for delivery is too short, the rest they just outsource to other firms. They pump the jobs in the city and make everybody happy. [...]When there is not much work, well they pump less or don't pump into the system. The network is like a big body. We are the heart of the system: if it stops pumping the rest dies... We [small firms] die. We close. It is painful, but economically it is not as bad as you can imagine. You lose a bit of money. A few hundred '*Lire*'? Something like that... We closed, however, generally, during WWII – colleagues or mine told me – or during the other difficult times, for example in the 1970s after the Yom Kippur war, when the market plunged. Those firms survived – maybe they fired part of their personnel but they survived. And this was good for us, the heart was safe and once the market was restored, after a few months we were able to revitalise the local economy. New and old studios opened and filled the void left by the fallen... To start up a workshop is not so expensive... The only important element is to maintain the contacts with other, bigger, firms... New workshops open and the jobs begin to flow again within the body... And history continues."

Armando was a born and bred Valenza bench-jeweller in his mid-seventies. He left school when he was 14, after having completed a course at a local professional high school. From the early 1950s had worked in a large firm for nearly twenty years, and went on to open his own small workshop that closed in the mid-2000s. Despite the lack of a formal education, Armando was able to offer a vivid portrait of local industry through the metaphor of a (radial) body. Within this picture, Armando identified two main categories and profiles of Valenza firms: a hard core of large firms that gather orders from the market and distribute jobs to a second group of smaller firms, which base their economy just on this outsourcing.

The overall status of Valenza's economy is based on the dynamic equilibrium created in this two-step articulation of the flow of jobs: while the market grows, jobs flow to the small firms making this constellation of enterprises flourish; however, in case of a recession, the flow stops, causing the 'death' of small firms: this demise, however, is only temporary, since, once the demand increases again, the flow restarts and new small firms take the place left by the old ones. Although this scheme may rely on a simplification of the actual characteristics of the milieu, the path so described corresponds overall to the historical trends that the industry experienced in the last century and resembles the model proposed by the scholarship (Gaggio, 2007; Gereffi, 2007).

Scholarship and emic idealisations seem to identify Valenza's industry with a dynamic and adaptable structure that closely resembles a model of flexible, post-Taylorist industry originally theorised by Piore and Sabel (Piore and Sabel, 1984) and discussed in the introduction. While in its structure Valenza resembles this model, neither the development path proposed by Piore and Sabel nor the time scale of Italian ID formation indicated by the anthropological literature (Blim, 1990; Cento Bull and Corner; 1993, Ghezzi, 2007) fit in this case. In fact, the structuring of this network occurred in the same year in which Taylor was formulating his thesis about industrial scientific management (Taylor, 2004 [1911]). Thus, Valenza's industry represents an alternative to, rather than a consequence of the decline of Taylorist industry, and followed a path that actually also anticipated other Italian industrial agglomerations, such as the jewellery industries of Arezzo and Vicenza (Gaggio, 2007), the textile and furniture industry in Brianza (Cento Bull and Corner, 1993; Ghezzi, 2007), and the shoe industry in Marche (Blim, 1990).

Moreover, while Piore and Sabel (1984) have seen in outsourcing a positive economic practice that was potentially capable of reducing production costs and creating a production system adapted to the volatility of the market, Valenza's model shows the critical aspects that outsourcing implies. While the downturn that began in 2008 had proved to be the context to study ethnographically, the 'dark side' of outsourcing, Gereffi (2007) had already pointed out that, in a local production system such as Valenza, where the level of reliance on outsourcing from other firms is often inversely correlated to the level of direct access to the market, network production can become a system of domination ruled by outsourcing firms which also possess a direct access to the market. While for these firms, outsourcing is just a useful resource for reducing the fixed and variable costs of production, to supplier firms the flow of jobs that originates from the outsourcing firms may well be their core business: a fundamental economic pillar of their activity, the disappearance of which would constitute a fatal blow for the firm (Chapter 7). In order to guarantee this resource, these firms will tend to subordinate their decisions and economic strategies to the outsourcers' plans to the point of simply accepting without any negotiation the prices and deadlines imposed on them from the outsourcing firms and, regardless of their formal independence, becoming to a great extent their business 'prisoners' (cf. Gereffi, 2007: 31).

This interpretation, while highlighting an imbalance of power that I also noticed during my fieldwork (see next paragraph for an example), also conveys a profound subordination of supplier firms to outsourcers that contrasts against the social and economic dynamism that I experienced during my time in Valenza. Failing to address this dynamism, Gereffi's account proposes a conceptualisation of the network as a structure in which the owners of supplying firms appear to be individuals frozen in subordinate positions, rather than the active actors I met. Present scholarship, although profoundly engaging with the problem of the industry structure, does not challenge this static conceptualisation.

I agree with Gereffi in seeing an imbalance of economic power among firms in Valenza. However, I intend to recover the missing dynamism and show how economic power comes to be exercised, that is to show how networking is organised and how the jewellery industry is experienced and perceived by goldsmiths. In order to do so, I want to present an ethnographic case of network-building that occurred between a large multinational corporation, Rossi, a '*grande fabbrica* – Gianmario's –, and a network of gem-setting studios employed by Gianmario's firm to carry out the Rossi order, so as to show the active role that subsidiary firms can have in weaving the network. I will do so by focusing on a particularly revealing moment of this process which occurred in Spring 2009.

Rossi rings

During my pilot, in December 2008, I met Gianmario for the first time: he was a distinguished person in his sixties. A friend and client of one of my informants, who occasionally worked for him as a designer and modeller, introduced me to him. Thanks to this mutual friend, in April 2009, Gianmario allowed me to carry out an observation, over a few days, of the activities of his workshop, to understand the dynamics and operations within his firm. I started in the early days of May.

With his twenty employees, his firm might have been considered a '*grande fabbrica*' by many Valenza goldsmiths. It employed ten goldsmiths, five gem setters, a modeller – who was also one of the firm's designers, together with Gianmario, and often supervised the other goldsmiths in their work – three polishers and a secretary-accountant, Clara, who was Gianmario's wife. Most of them were over thirty-five and had worked for Gianmario for more than five years.

The firm was located not far from the Coinor area, in the western periphery of Valenza: a one storey modernist building, originally intended for a shoe-making firm, when it was built in the late 1950s, but since the 1970s had been subsequently used by a string of jewellery firms – at least until the 1990s when Gianmario's was established.

Five days a week, from Monday to Friday, the firm opened at 7.45 am. At that time Gianmario arrived and opened the workshop. At 7.50 AM the early workers arrived and changed their clothes, making them ready for the work day that officially started at 8 am and lasted until 6 pm – with a lunch break from 12.30 to 2.30 pm. On Saturday the workshop was generally closed, unless some special order needed to be quickly processed.

That day, the activity followed this general scheme. I had full access to the shop floor. However, my presence was completely ignored by the goldsmiths. Nobody tried to explain their work to me and I received only very hasty answers to my questions. They were completing an order for five complete sets with diamonds and emeralds ordered by a Roman jewellery shop. People mainly worked silently, and only the noise of the drills and grinders filled the air. At 10.00 am the modeller and his colleagues kindly invited me to "do something useful" and bring the workers some coffee from a coffee shop a few hundred metres from Gianmario's firm. I agreed, and about ten minutes later I was back with fifteen cups of espresso and a handful of bags of sugar. However, something must have happened in the meantime.

There was a vibrant atmosphere on the shop floor. Gianmario, who generally works in his office, was in the middle of the room. He was surrounded by all his workers, all dressed in blue overalls: the only one missing was Clara, who, I was told, was in her office.

He was speaking aloud, gesticulating wildly, when he saw me.

> "Come! There is big news, I was just telling them. We got a big order from Rossi."

He was exulting, and it was the first time I had seen him so excited in the almost six months we had known each other; the reason for this excitement was the economic opportunity that had just arisen for the firm: a large company had just confirmed a large order from them.

It was an unexpected event in those times. Gianmario started the firm in the 1990s: it was a small workshop that mainly worked as a supplier for large firms. In the mid-1990s, Gianmario diversified his business, starting to produce his own collections that were sold in jewellery shops in large Italian cities, such as Milan, Turin, Genoa, Florence and Rome. This diversification gave Gianmario an opportunity to expand the firm and reach its current scale in 2005. Despite the good results from the sale of his collection, however, Gianmario never abandoned his role as a supplier of other firms: this trade continued to represent the firm's core business. However, the economic crisis that began in 2008 corresponded with an overall reduction in orders for his products and the almost complete disappearance of orders from large firms. Gianmario had commented angrily, during an interview we had two days before that morning in his office:

> "They have stopped outsourcing. They prefer to keep all the work for themselves. They are still fat, but we starve now..."

While he was answering my question, he was assembling a set of jewellery samples that he would be presenting the next day to a prospective client. When I asked whom the client would be, Gianmario did not reveal their identity, and explained his decision in these terms:

> "It is just '*scaramanzia'* [tr. to ward off ill-luck]. Too many times, in the past months I went to visit old clients and possible new clients, showing them my collections and what we are able to produce. But too many times I had to come back empty handed or with very small orders that were more a loss than a gain, because you cannot refuse them – even if they are badly paid – because you don't want to lose a client for the future, but on the other hand, they don't give you enough to sustain twenty people or even only one..."

As a result, he had grown cynical to the possible results of his visits: so cynical that

> "I don't want even to talk about those... Just to not create expectations in me and the people there [on the shop floor] that I know may be frustrated."

That morning, I discovered that the possible client whose identity I was not told was Rossi, and that they had just confirmed the largest order Gianmario had received since summer 2008.

While addressing his employees, Gianmario had a ring in his hand. Its surface was to be covered entirely in stones, mainly diamonds. He passed the ring to his workers who, one by one, started studying its surface, welded joints and style of setting.

> "We are to produce three hundred of them in two weeks..."

One of his gem setters abruptly interrupted the speech. He was in his early forties. He was not the oldest of the gem setters, but appeared to be on familiar terms with Gianmario. His accent betrayed his central-Italian origins:

> "Gianma', we cannot do it. One hundred, maybe. Maybe somewhat more, but three hundred is too much for us."
>
> "I know, I know. I was going to say that our normal suppliers will help us in part of the production. Clara is contacting them. They should come in a few days to take the job. I have a couple of unset rings as models; I need for us to start working on it today."
>
> "We are still working on those necklaces you asked for," said one of the goldsmiths.
>
> "You can work on that until the casting is finished. Then, forget them for a while. That guy does not pay as fast as he should do, so he can wait for a while. Instead, if Rossi is happy with our work, it will be good money and the first breath of fresh air for all of us... Let's go back to work! And Michele, come as well."

I followed Gianmario in his office. The modeller was also there with us. He was in his fifties and had worked for Gianmario since the early 1990s when he opened the workshop. At that time, it had been smaller, with just six workers, five goldsmiths and a polisher – they outsourced all the setting at that time. He was not the youngest of them, but he was the only one that remained: the others either retired, or tried to open their own firms, as he remembered:

> "With little success. One failed in one year and another just closed the firm a few years ago, but that was for health problems."

At the firm, he had become a sort of factotum. Mainly, he was the modeller and the designer of the firm, the one in charge of the production of models and their casting. However, since he was also the most experienced amongst Gianmario's goldsmiths, he supervised the shop-floor, when he was not occupied with preparing the prototypes.

In the office, Gianmario gave the un-mounted ring to him and asked him to prepare the casting trees needed by that evening. Once he had left, Gianmario turned to me:

> "Today is a great day. This is a great opportunity for this firm and also for our suppliers, I would say. This is a good order, but above all I am more interested in becoming one of the suppliers of Rossi. I know just one other firm whom Rossi asked to produce a lot of rings similar to this one. Even though this work is not paid as much as other works we have done in the past, Rossi is a multinational corporation and to work for them means to be sure you are not going to lack work. We are going to produce all three hundred settings and a third of them will be set by us. My wife is contacting five gem-setting workshops right now – they work well, and

generally we were happy with their work – and asking to mount, let's say, forty rings each. They will have no more than one week. If they can do it, I am going to pay them the right price. If they don't, I won't pay them at all. Take it or leave it."

Only four of the five workshops, all small firms of which the largest employed six gem-setters, accepted the binding contract offered by Gianmario. One of them was Gustavo's. The fifth, a workshop that employed four gem-setters and an accountant, declined the offer, explaining that it was impossible for them to complete the order in time. This decision was accepted with coldness by Gianmario who, when Clara told him the motivation behind their choice, said:

"So much the worse for them, because they are not getting any money, but for us it is better this way than to get a surprise at the last minute. At least they were correct."

In two weeks, thanks to that particular allocation of work, the three hundred rings were ready and were delivered to Rossi.

Drawing the network

The case of Gianmario and the Rossi rings is an example of the many similar practices that are undertaken in the city every day. These practices portray the substantial dynamism and a degree of unpredictability that marks the actual articulation of production among firms. This episode is a good demonstration of how a network economy is in constant becoming. It is generated through the active role played by different actors: primarily Gianmario, but also Rossi and Gianmario's suppliers. In displaying this variety of actors at work, this episode also allows us to conduct some analysis on the characteristics of local entrepreneurship.

First of all, however, this episode offers us a map of a network. Considering the final products, those three hundred pieces branded 'Rossi', they are the result of the combined work of at least six firms: Rossi, which designed the ring; Gianmario's that reproduced them; and another four firms that, together with Gianmario's, completed the manufacturing. As we can see, production expands beyond the limits of an individual *'fabbrica'* to involve other actors, who become co-protagonists of the production. Jobs, thus, flow from one *'fabbrica'* to others. In so doing, the structure of the network is described. If we focus our attention on the articulation of flow, we can schematise the entire network as a process divided into three levels: a level zero, where the flow originates, a first level, where the work flows through a first group of supplying firms, and through them reaching new firms that represent the second level of our scheme.

This network involves a large, international firm, Rossi[5], a medium firm, and a series of small studios. In this respect it appears to be an example congruous with the schemes proposed by scholars and presented earlier. In fact, we notice that moving from Rossi to its numerous suppliers, we see a progressive reduction of the scale of the firms involved and the reduction of the range of activities carried out in the individual workshops – from the entire production and commercialisation of the product to only manufacturing, to the processing of just a particular phase. However, as noted by Gereffi, this hierarchisation of scale and work specialisation cannot be taken as a mantra, since in particular cases we can see large firms supported by orders coming from smaller enterprises: this is the case of independent jewellery merchants, often one-person enterprises that do not own any production facilities, who outsource the entire production of their orders to other firms.

In the ethnographic example we observe some elements of economic subordination among the firms. In all the exchanges between Rossi and Gianmario and between Gianmario and his suppliers it appears that the price of work is to some extent imposed on the suppliers. This is starkly clear, in fact, in the case of the outsourcing from Gianmario to his suppliers, where it is actually Gianmario who fixes the price and leaves as the only options to the supplier to either accept the conditions or refuse them. In this perspective, we could re-think the network as an economic hierarchy dominated by Rossi; a network that binds firms together through chains of entrepreneurial subordination. However, while the current literature on Valenza conveys an image of the supplier firms as passive actors of the economic process, the case of Gianmario gives an alternative interpretation of the role played by those enterprises and their owners.

Gianmario played a far from subordinate role, since he is in fact the person who established the network by establishing contacts and collecting

---

[5] Rossi is an international player in the jewellery market and its brand is internationally advertised, including in the magazines, such as Forbes and Vogue. The firm sells its production all around the world through its exclusive shops, which are located in cities such as New York, London and Dubai, and through other independent retailers. Its access to the jewellery market is not mediated by any other enterprise. Its main production is generally completed in its own establishments in Valenza and abroad. However, occasionally it can expand its production through outsourcing to cope with an increase in demand or for particular orders, such as the one described in the ethnographic example. In so doing, the company ends up relying on a number of suppliers.

orders from Rossi, and redistributing jobs among a number of suppliers. Thus, aside from the actual decision of outsourcing part of its production, it is relevant to remember that the network was not created by Rossi. While its externalisation made it possible, Rossi did not determine the structure of the entire network – its externalisation made it possible – because did not select all the firms that actually co-operated in the production. Its part was limited to the selection of a few suppliers: Gianmario's firm and, probably, other partners that in our graph represent the first level of externalisation. The firms of the second level are, instead, chosen by suppliers on the basis of their entrepreneurial strategy. In this respect, the active agency of suppliers is revealed and appears to be the key element in the assembly of the network itself.

Thus, the case of Gianmario encourages us to rethink a certain structural determinism that permeates the scholarship about Valenza's network industry, by showing the crucial contribution that a firm, which lies in a subordinated position within the organisation chart of jewellery production, has in shaping the entire network.

"Like a girl": a matter of knowledge and trust

Moreover, this ethnographic case brings to the fore the space and principles on which the network is built. In an economic perspective, outsourcing appears to be organised on the basis of mediation between maximum instantaneous profit and long-term security. This calculation, however, is not performed in a vacuum. Rather, it is decided on the basis of the social relations that links Gianmario to the other firm-owners. In so doing, Gianmario would:

> "Straddle two supposedly separated spheres of action; the social world and the market world." (Ortiz, 2005: 74)

The division to which Ortiz refers is a heritage of classic economic thought and describes a worldview where social actions, such as the exchange of goods and the calculation that underpins these exchanges, are perceived as divorced from other forms of social interaction and relatedness. In the last half of the century, economic anthropology has tried to re-establish the unity against this division, by demonstrating the inseparability of those actions and thoughts commonly referred to as 'economic' from other forms of social relatedness, such as affectivity, cultural institutions, such as kinship, and practices, such as religious rituality (Hart and Ortiz, 2008; Hart, 2008). In connection with this analytical effort, the case of the Rossi rings and Gianmario's words demonstrate not just the union between social and economic worlds, as suggested by Ortiz, but their fundamental unity, which emerges from the role played by Gianmario's trust in his partners in the organisation of the entire network.

The role of trust in IDs has been a fundamental subject of scholarly enquiry. In anthropology, scholars such as Narotzky (1997; 2004) and others (Ghezzi, 2007; Yanagisako, 2002; Blim, 1990) have considered it to be the fundamental bond that sustains networking. In the case of Valenza, Gaggio (2007) showed the importance of these relationships in shaping an industry that he defined as a 'pyramid of trust' (Gaggio, 2006; 2007). In so doing, Gaggio indicates trust and norms of mutuality as the fundamental principles through which outsourcing is established. Thus, Gaggio clarifies the place of trust in the sustenance of economic systems. However, the scholar does not explore in depth the qualities of this social knowledge (Corsín Jiménez, 2011: 179). While he defined goldsmiths' trust in the context of the debate in social theory (e.g. Fukuyama, 1995; Sztompka, 1999; Seligman, 1997; Misztal, 1996; Cook, 2001), I intend to explain it from an ethnographic perspective, by drawing from the ethnographic case I have presented and the interview that followed that morning.

The same day in May, later in the afternoon, I met Gianmario in his office to ask some questions raised by the events of the morning. He was visibly happy about the order. Maybe driven by this euphoria or just by the fact that he was becoming accustomed to my presence and my questions, when I asked for some more details about how he got the order and the way he was managing the production, he answered in a very friendly, informal and convivial way, instead of the usual sober tone that marked his answers on the previous days. When I came to ask him to tell me more about the process of selecting production partners and the nature of the interrelations between firms, Gianmario explained them in these terms:

> "When I have to manage a job such as these rings, I don't select my suppliers just on the basis of the price they ask. The price is not the real issue.
>
> It's a golden rule that works not only in the economy: you must know a partner before you bring them in. It works with women and *'fabbriche'*. A cheap price is like a girl who, on the first meeting, already wants to sleep with you. Nice, sometimes it is great and a lot of fun... That night, but in few, very few cases might she be the woman of your life. Most of the times, it is just disappointing after desire.
>
> In selecting your partners, you must be steady. You want a bit of security, don't you? [To guarantee you that,] you must approach your possible partner. You start with some small orders just to understand how they work. Then, you can test them with some interesting orders. Finally,

> when you get *'conoscenza'* of them [you know them], you can be sure of them, and can *'aver fiducia'* [trust] them because you know how they work and that they are not going to let you down.
>
> You nurture this relationship in many ways, however. It's not just work, work, and work. With your partner you can go out for a coffee, or play football together, for example. Every Friday, with one of the gem setters we called, we run together. At the end of the day, you are talking about people, and if you don't like a person you are not going to work with them; even if they are the best person in the world, you don't want to share anything with them.
>
> This is how it works in Valenza and how the jewellery market works. You should not rush. In this way you can select good partners and not get a last-minute bad surprise. Then, if you have such a partner you will prefer to work with them, even if they are not the cheapest chap you can find around. In this city it is always like I said. With the four gem-setters we are more or less stable partners, instead, the wooing has just started with Rossi, and, yeah, I would be really merry with them!"

Gianmario's answer stands out for its descriptive vivacity among the many I collected in the months of fieldwork; vivacity rooted in a description of the economy that is visibly gendered. It is underpinned by a masculine description of jewellery production and, in particular, entrepreneurship. The text can be seen as the contextual result of Gianmario's attempt (as an older man involved in jewellery production) at establishing a kind of familiarity and camaraderie with me (a younger man interested in the jewellery industry), by employing an idea of masculine entrepreneurship widely attested in the Italian discourse (e.g. Bellassai, 2004; Huysseune, 2000, Bruni et al., 2004; Yanagisako, 2002). This description hints at a possible gender division of roles within the industry that leads to women being marginalised in entrepreneurship; a form of marginalisation that has been described by other ethnographies of Italy (e.g. Goddard, 1996; Yanagisako, 2002). It may have been suited to describe the past of Valenza's industry, but does not fit with its present. As it emerges from historical accounts of the industry (e.g. Gaggio, 2007; Lenti, 1994), this division is visible before the 1970s, when the national family laws subordinated the role of women to their fathers and, after marriage, their husbands. With the Law Lg. 151/1975 and the recognition of equal duties and rights for both women and men, the number of female owners of firms in the city rose. About half of the firms in Valenza are run or co-owned by women (CCAl, 2011b). In the past thirty years, moreover, Valenza experienced a more general rise in women's employment to reach about 50% of the overall sample size (OPML, 2011), although, as I will point out when presenting the biography of Lucia in the next chapter, some form of gender division of work is still present in the jewellery industry. Thus, this gendered rhetoric, I would argue, must be seen as a fundamental metaphor to highlight the work of *'conoscenza'* and *'fiducia'*, two key-concepts in goldsmiths' description of the articulation of Valenza industry.

'Conoscenza' and *'fiducia'* are interconnected elements of a broader process of information creation and management that involves firms and firm-owners and underpins networking. *'Conoscenza'* literally means 'knowledge'. It is described as the knowledge of firm A of another firm B. *'Fiducia'*, trust, is a bond of mutuality, which binds the two firms. However, to understand the social significance of these categories – that is the quality of knowledge implied by these categories (Corsín Jiménez, 2011) – it is necessary to reconsider an object and a category that, so far, I have used as a fundamental trope of this account: the firm. ID theory, scholarship on Valenza jewellery making, Valenza goldsmiths, and my account so far have emphasised the role of firms in the description of the city's economy. Firms have been described as actors: complete and discrete entities that carry out actions within the space of Valenza. However, the concepts of *'fiducia'* and *'conoscenza'* often invoked by Valenza goldsmiths refer to relationships that animate the city and its economy (Thrift, 2004: 59-64; Amin and Thrift, 2002), and in so doing, cut into the solidity of these actors. In fact, they are not abstract forms of relatedness that bind abstract entities, but bonds revealing the centrality of agency of the individuals that are involved in jewellery making, in particular firm-owners. Thus, to better appreciate the magnitude of the effect of *'fiducia'* and *'conoscenza'* it appears useful to open the 'black box' (cf. Latour, 1987: 15) of the firm by allowing its constituent processes, until now subsumed into the (assumed) consistency of the entire object, to emerge.

A firm is a legally recognised organisation, which is engaged in the trade of goods and/or services. It encompasses its owners – who can be one or many individuals or firms – capital, productive infrastructures, and the employees. In other words, it is an 'assemblage' (cf. De Landa, 2006) of humans and objects that are bound together by formal and informal agreements, self-interest and affections (Swedberg, 2003: 74): a tangle of circumstances, intentionality and affects, which cannot be summarised by the simple goal of making profit. In this network, every person carries out some functions that are necessary to complete the production of artefacts and their exchange: to make a phone call, design and file a ring are examples of these operations. In this network, the firm-owner is the one who actually establishes the extension of this network and ratifies it through the formal tools (such as contracts) that are offered, produced and enforced by the State. In this respect, Gianmario could establish his firm by hiring the personnel and buying machines and a building. After the establishment of these boundaries, the production network can be further expanded and shrunk, affecting the shape of these borders, by buying or selling objects or hiring and firing personnel, or not changing them. This is the case with outsourcing. As the production case of the Rossi rings shows, outsourcing is a practice through which other firms, other production networks are involved in the production of specific artefacts, and in which their work is exchanged for goods or a token of value (i.e. money) offered, produced and enforced by the State. In other words, through outsourcing, a single production network is actually expanded for a limited time through the establishment of temporary bonds, which may be formal, when they are ratified through the tools offered, produced and enforced by the State (e.g. contracts), or informal (Chapter 2), when these connections are established through other tools than those of the State. In fact, while in national law as well as often in scholarship (as explained in: Hart, 2010), production and non-production spaces are seen as separated realities, kept apart by the materiality of a firm's walls, the two spaces permeate each other in a social perspective. The participation of an individual as a worker or an entrepreneur in production does not preclude them being contemporarily involved in other relational networks, such as kinship, friendship, the affiliation to a club or association, etc. Even during working hours, individuals continue to participate in all of these networks and these networks, as Yanagisako (2002) clearly documented, can directly affect the quality of the individual's work and the very structure of a firm.

Thus, while firms appear to be complexities of humans and objects, the firm-owner holds a fundamental role in shaping this network and determines, to some extent, the extension of the firm and production. While *'conoscenza'* and *'fiducia'*, as it emerges in the excerpt, are not abstract bonds between abstract entities, but effects that involve firm-owners and direct them in their action of production, they also appear to be categories through which firm-owners face complexity and tackle it.

'Conoscenza' is a specific knowledge that is interwoven into two main, distinct understandings: the knowledge of the firm-owner A of her partner B, intended both as a person (the firm-owner B), and the quality and speed of production of firm B. Thus, it is a dual knowledge that is fostered through different practices. Interpersonal knowledge among owners is nurtured not just by A and B collaborating in business, but also by building familiarity often through participating in shared extra-production

activities, such as taking part in leisure activities together. Knowledge of firm production, however, also grows when A visits B's production line, and through a constant process of business interaction, which creates the bedrock of experience, as Gianmario explained, to acknowledge the potentialities that B's production network can achieve.

While 'conoscenza' grows by accumulating shared experience, it is described as a long process of nurturing a communal sense of familiarity between the firm-owners (rather than abstractly between firms and a better awareness of the production potentialities of the businesse); in other words, a progressive improvement of the capacity to predict the outcomes of production. This is why *'conoscenza'* is a crucial element in creating *'fiducia'* [trust] among firms: it is a feeling that combines expectations based on knowledge of the quality of the work of the partner, a sense of security in the outcome, and a conviction that "the trustee (firm owner B) will not take advantage of one's vulnerability" (Cook and Gerbasi, 2006: 290; see also Jensen, 1991; Doney and Cannon, 1997) due to the familiarity between the firm owners. While *'fiducia'* is the fundamental bond up on which networking is based, it should not be understood as an alternative logic around which this economy is articulated. When goldsmiths manage their production, they attempt to maximise their gains in the short and long term, but they see in the sense of familiarity that links entrepreneurs a guarantee against unfair competition, and in *'fiducia'* a partial antidote against risk — the risk that the trade involves. In other words, echoing Ingold (2000: 70), it is a system of control over the other that safeguards the individual firm from deception by their partners and a way of mitigating the uneven distribution of power among the network's actors.

Despite *'fiducia'*, however, risk cannot be removed from the business. Often goldsmiths pointed out the risks of their business: suppliers may delay their deliveries, outsourcers may not pay, firm agents may be robbed, the price of metals and stones may suddenly plunge or rise, etc. (Boholm, 2001: 160). Thus, by listing these possible risks drawing from their direct experience, goldsmiths outlined an element of ineluctable uncertainty within which an individual or a firm must operate. These risks, as highlighted by Daniell (2000: 10-12), are negative instances that for jewellery entrepreneurs affect prioritisation, resource allocation and opportunity costs. However, while Beck and Beck-Gernsheim (2001) suggest individualisation as the most common effect of risk-management, we notice that in Valenza, jewellery entrepreneurs tread a different path. Instead of pursuing individualisation of production, that is, to reduce the firm's involvement in the economic network faced with a centralisation of production, entrepreneurs like Gianmario have continued networking with other firms and maintained an entrepreneurial structure developed over the course of previous decades. This trend has been explained through two main premises: the strength of the system of control based on *'fiducia'* and *'conoscenza'*, and the continuous expansion of the market context that characterised the last fifty years of the jewellery trade. These premises proved to be misleading. Gaggio (2007), Bosco (2004), and goldsmiths during interviews have all shown that the bond of *'fiducia'* in Valenza did not prevent the spread of recurrent practices of unfair competition, such as copying and theft. The abrupt downturn, which followed on from 2008, represented the refutation of the constant growth of the market: a situation that made the structural weakness and imbalance of power of Valenza's network become apparent, as I will explain in Chapter 7.

Conclusions

In this chapter, I meant to present the jewellery industry of Valenza as a diversified entrepreneurial milieu based on the networking among small, medium, and large firms. By taking as a heuristic starting point a historical account concerning the development of the trade and the theory of IDs already used in other studies of the city, I took into consideration the present networking among firms.

Current studies, influenced by ID theory, have pointed out a hierarchical organisation of the network, and in light of this structure, have depicted a deterministic articulation of the business and its development. I intended to challenge this structural determinism. I have done so through ethnography of the actual structuring of the network in a case of outsourcing. This case highlights the dynamism that actually characterises local entrepreneurs, including those whose enterprises literature has described as passive or subordinated in the business, and the role that trust plays in the structuring.

Although the focus of this chapter has been on the firms and their relations, Gianmario's vicissitudes together with the other fragments of daily life in the industry show the constellation of people, experiences, expectations and dreams that develops alongside a daily exercising of production skills and knowledge. While this element underpinning the jewellery industry has only been mentioned so far, I will explore it deeper in the next chapter by analysing the meaning of *'artigianalità'*.

Fig. 7 Chiselling a plate

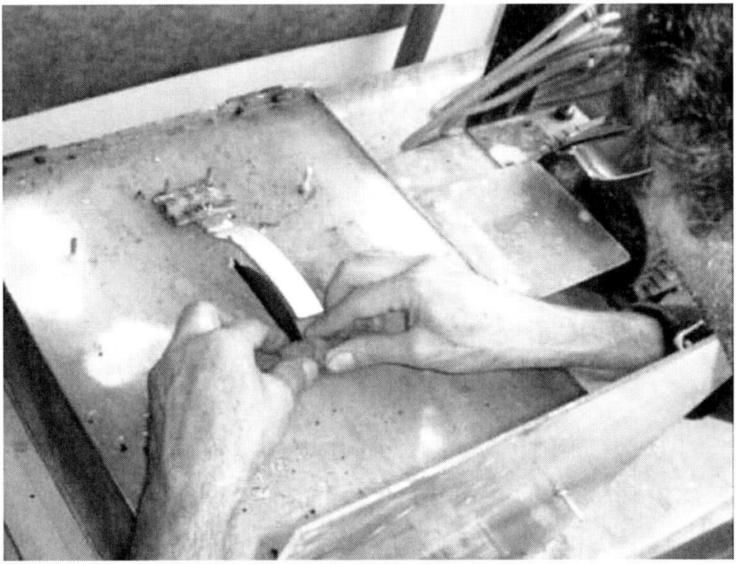

Fig. 8: Stone-cutting

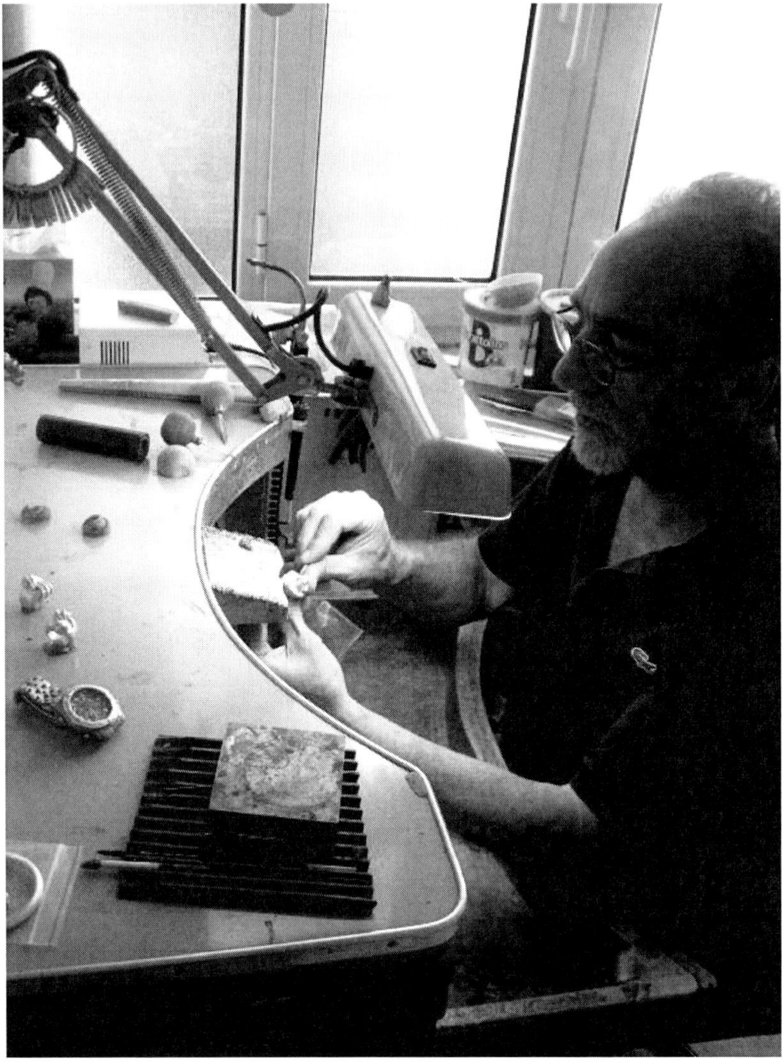

Fig. 9: Goldsmith polishing a lion-shaped ring

CHAPTER FOUR

WORK AND '*ARTIGIANALITÀ*'

Valenza is *a 'grande fabbrica' (*Chapter 2); a city permeated by the jewellery industry in which hundreds of firms create a wide production network. In the previous chapter, I closely explored this network, its articulation, and economic and historical development. While Valenza shares with Arezzo and Vicenza – the other two main centres for jewellery production in Italy – a strong horizontal and vertical interconnection among the firms (Becattini et al., 2009: XVIII) that constitutes the local milieu (Gaibisso, 1995; Bassano, 2008; Gaggio, 2007). However, Valenza is distinguished from them by its form of production. As Gaggio (2007) documented, while in Arezzo and Vicenza, during the 20th century, jewellery production has mostly relied on the work of automated machines and skilful mechanics able to build and modify the equipment, Valenza trod a different path of industrialisation. As shown in the previous chapter, while jewellery production and goldsmiths' activities were divided so as to fit the different phases of the cycle of production, the employment of automated machines was marginalised to carry out the most repetitive phases of production, such as chain making, milling or pressing, and to allow a certain degree of serialisation of production (Lenti, 1994; Molina and Manenti, 1994). Thus, goldsmiths' manual skills retained a central role in manufacturing. Because of these peculiarities, Valenza jewellery is internationally known as 'crafts-based' production (Bassano, 2008; Lenti, 1994; Gaggio, 2007).

While the previous chapter sheds light on the overall organisation of the industry, in this chapter I intend to focus on how production is experienced by jewellery makers and how a goldsmith's career is articulated, offering an account of the practices and skills that are employed and the way they are understood by jewellery makers. Due to the importance of crafts – intended both as an ideal and a practice of production – in establishing the reputation of the city, I will move the focus of my inquiries to the exploration of *'artigianalità'*. This word, literally translatable as 'artisanship', often occurs in public speeches, the press, scientific publications, and informal chats to portray the specificity of Valenza's jewellery productions. Aside from these public occurrences, *'artigianalità'* is part of the everyday vocabulary of jewellery makers who use it to explain the uniqueness of local jewellery and their understanding of the profession. It teases out a tangle of meanings that encompass a tension between crafts- and machine-based production, and the relationship between skills and equipment. *'Artigianalità'* describes the space of an individual's interaction between goldsmith, tools and jewellery, expressed through a participation in production that involves the goldsmith's manual skills and labour together with their creative and mental work. At the same time, *'artigianalità'* is perceived as a fundamental driving principle of Valenza jewellery making: a way of perceiving and practicing the profession that slowly develops through a process that marks a goldsmith's career. Consequentially, *'artigianalità'* expands into a fundamental concept that sheds light on the individual and collective aspects of being a goldsmith.

At dinner with *'artigianalità'*

To explore this concept, I will take as my starting point a conversation I had during a dinner with three goldsmiths (and their partners). This ordinary event, which took place in Valenza in March 2009, clearly shows the penetration of *'artigianalità'* into the lives of goldsmiths, and how, through it, goldsmiths describe Valenza jewellery making in a narration that embraces individuals and the community within an intricate tangle of meaning. By contextualizing these threads within the discourse of the city, I will explain the different understandings and rhetorical patterns that the concept underpins. After having presented this ethnography and having framed *'artigianalità'* as a fundamental 'keyword' (cf. Williams, 1983) of Valenza's discourse, I will explore how *'artigianalità'* plays a fundamental role in a dynamic of definition of the locale through the formulation of its authenticity. I will then move to show how *'artigianalità'* is employed to explain a particular mode of engagement of the individual with production. Finally, by explaining how a goldsmith's career is articulated, and how its different phases are connected to *'artigianalità'*, I will point out that this concept represents a possible key to understand the structure of the career and its goals.

The episode took place in a large flat, in a residential area of the city, in late March 2009. I was invited by Marco to his place for an informal dinner with some of his friends and colleagues.

Marco was a goldsmith in his late fifties. Even though he was born in a village near Venice, he had lived most of his life in the city, in which he arrived in the early 1960s with his family. Since the late 1960s, he had been employed as a goldsmith in many workshops, and now he was working in a large establishment in the Coinor area. I met him in the early 2000s, when I was engaged in previous research about the city and its social services (Fontefrancesco, 2006b). Since then, we have had occasional but friendly contacts. When he knew I was returning to Valenza for Easter that year, he decided to invite me so as to introduce me to some possible informants.

It was an informal dinner: not many people, a dish of pasta and other delicacies prepared by Marco's wife and a few bottles of wine. We were seven at dinner: Marco and his wife; Lucia, a former trainee of Marco's who was working as a freelance modeller, and her husband, a civil servant in Alessandria; Astolfo, a gem-setter in his late fifties and owner of a small '*fabbrica*', and his wife, a housewife; and I. I was introduced to the guests as an English scholar who was doing research on Valenza's jewellery industry. After such a solemn presentation, the other guests were puzzled and uneasy at my presence, but fortunately, after a few glasses of wine and some time, the atmosphere turned friendly and colloquial.

For most of the time there, we talked about our lives. They asked about how England was and I answered, and asked about a bit of 'their' Valenza.

During this conversation, Lucia came to talk about the new training course for CAD/CAM (computer based design and modelling technology) in which she had recently enrolled and her new classmates, mostly twenty years younger than her, more or less the same age as when she was trained by Marco. Telling her story, she concluded, addressing Marco, by adding:

> "Do you remember when I was a teen and you taught me and the other apprentices the basics of this work? We were willing to learn the manual techniques, and master them. At the end of the day, we were coming here [to Valenza] for that; to learn how making jewellery... To become goldsmiths. You repeated to us that, no matter how good a machine is, you cannot hope that it will solve the problems you find while working: a real goldsmith must tackle difficulties and overcome them. Now, I see these new generations... They think that all you need is a PC to make jewellery... They do not get the point, that a computer is not everything... To be clear, I have nothing against computers, I use them in my work, and I enjoy it because they allow me to do stuff I was not able to do before... But I know that the computer is not the whole of jewellery making. Them? No, not at all! It seems they believe one should trust a program, and the program will provide you with the perfect jewellery. They are reducing themselves to being barely appendages of the machine... They barely know how to hold a pencil and a file in their hand, or even think that these manual skills are important, and when they encounter some difficulties they moan that it is

> the computer's fault. What they are doing, however, it is the tomb of *'artigianalità'*. If they do not know how 'to use their hands' [their manual skills], and make the machine part of them, and not vice-versa, how do they imagine achieving any form of *'artigianalità'*?"

To her, born in the neighbouring Alessandria and having moved to Valenza to attend the ISA Cellini goldsmith high school (see later in this chapter), then being trained as an apprentice in the same workshop where Marco worked, it appeared shocking to acknowledge in her fellow students an attitude that appeared to betray what she learned to consider the pillar of her work: *'artigianalità'*, a special relationship between man and machine mediated through a constant exercising of manual skills and knowledge.

The other goldsmiths agreed with her. Astolfo exclaimed, "*Mala temporum corron,*" 'bad times are upon us' in an improvised Latin, while Marco commented:

> "I don't know... It seems that everybody loves these modern gizmos so much... Valenza is Valenza because has been a city of artisans. It is not Arezzo or Vicenza. They made their fortune on machines. We did not do that. Machines are big and noisy, only good to make tons and tons of... Cheap stuff... Machines make anonymous jewellery. It is the only manual work that makes jewellery special. It gives the jewellery a special touch. We handcraft our jewellery. We make it by hand. There lies our *'artigianalità'*... In handwork..."

The others nodded. However, Marco had moved the semantic centre of gravity of *'artigianalità'* to emphasise a contraposition between manual and machine work. The movement was also noted by the other table-companions. So that Astolfo sardonically noted:

> "Ok, ok... I think I have already heard this story too many times in this city... Maybe machines are 'bad' but they make your handwork easier."
>
> "I am not saying you should not use your microscope, dear," responded his friend, alluding to the microscope for gem-setting that Astolfo had recently bought, "I am just saying: have you seen one of the many pieces entirely made by machines? Maybe they are even nice and polished, but when you substitute man with the machine you lose something. And that something is what makes our jewellery special."

Then, Lucia asked:

> "So, do you think that *'artigianalità'* is just a problem of hand vs. machine? Maybe it is just a problem of how you use those machines..."

Marco and Astolfo became silent. Then, the former, with a grave expression, said:

> "Uhmm... I really believe that *'artigianalità'* is that final extra touch that crafts-based jewellery has... Then, maybe you would say that the problem is how to give that extra touch... So how to use your hands... How to use your tools... Fair enough..."

Astolfo sneered. Lucia did not reply. Acknowledging that the tension was mounting, Marco's wife steered the conversation away, starting speaking about the quality of the first course. The Astolfo's wife followed her, and asked the opinion of her husband and Lucia. Thus the discussion took another direction, leaving the argument about *'artigianalità'* unresolved. The conversation headed away, turning into an elaborate treatment of the proper recipe for homemade pasta.

***

Dinner came to its conclusion. I was in the living room, with Astolfo and Marco, sipping a glass of liqueur. While chatting, we resumed talking about my project. Astolfo, considering the research I had done in some workshops, commented:

> "I think your research may be interesting, but to understand this particular city you should look at its *'artigianalità'*. We talked about it earlier, didn't we? Look at how it is created and acquired over the course of our careers... Over the course of our lives. From apprenticeship, to becoming a fully-fledged goldsmith, and then, why not, when you open your small *'fabbrica'*. We build our *'artigianalità'* step by step. During the apprenticeship you get accustomed to it, you make it part of you by learning how you should work properly. Then you nourish it during all the rest of your life. On it, we have built our fortune... We may have had nothing, not even to speak Italian, but we create our fortune…"

With a nasal, inarticulate sound, Astolfo kept the sentence suspended, while Marco was looking at his friend smiling, and slowly nodding. After a few seconds, Astolfo continued,

> "Apprenticeship, employee and employer. Then sometimes back to being an employee, and again an employer...Yes, this sounds more or less like the career that all of us have had... The way in which *'artigianalità'* grows and circulates. The way in which it became our small stairway to success... *'Artigianalità'* has been our stairway to success... Yes... You should write about it."

***

About an hour later I was the only guest remaining with Marco. Thinking back to the conversations of the night and the occurrence of *'artigianalità'* with different meanings, I asked him what, at the end of the day, was *'artigianalità'*.

He looked at me, puzzled. He stayed silent for a while, then suddenly:

> "Bah!? I am afraid there is not one definition... Maybe there are one and many *'artigianalità'*... Maybe you should not just be looking for the right one, but take them all and understand the world they describe...And if you find contradictions, it may be because our reality is made of contradictions... I don't know... I don't know if there is an answer to your question...However, I am sure of one thing: *'artigianalità'* is what makes Valenza, its goldsmiths and jewellery unique."

A keyword

The concept of *'artigianalità'* occurred many times that night and became subject of reflections and confrontations about what is and what should by jewellery making, and jewellery industry (in Valenza).

'Artigianalità' is a common word in Italian that stems from Latin. While in the Italian legal vocabulary this word is used to refer to small scale industries (e.g. *Costituzione della Repubblica italiana*: art. 45), in common parlance *'artigianalità'* relates to crafts-based productions. Thus, it is commonly translated into English as 'artisanship' or 'craftsmanship'. Following this usage, *'artigianalità'* here might have been translated directly as 'craftsmanship', and possibly the entire text would have been rendered more readable. I doubt, however, that it would have been more understandable. To argue that my hosts and fellow guests were talking about 'crafts' would have risked suggesting that they were talking within an academic cultural frame, which is the case of the scholarly debate on 'crafts'. Moreover, it would have risked hiding, under a pleasant linguistic greasepaint, the specificity that this term has in the city, that is how crafts are experienced and conceptualised specifically by Valenza goldsmiths to talk about their industry. Consequentially, in these pages, I will use terms such as 'crafts', 'artisanship', 'craftsmanship' to refer to the categories debated in academia; I keep the Italian originals when I am referring to the emic formulation of these concepts embedded in the local discourse.

Artisanship is a concept still under debate in scholarship. It has been often associated with concepts such as design, manual work, small production, originality, oral lore, and traditions (Adamson, 2013; Nas,

2002, Greenhalgh, 1997, Sennett, 2008). In its current use, craftsmanship is generally opposed to mechanical reproduction on the basis of an ideal contraposition between a non-alienating form of production (crafts-based) and an alienated one (machine-based). With this meaning, the term can be dated back to the 19th century (Adamson, 2013; Greenhalgh, 1997; Spooner, 1986), and the meaning can be considered as an effect of the cultural and economic changes brought about by the Industrial Revolution. These changes triggered a heated cultural debate during which intellectuals rejected the process of mechanisation and commodification of production (Adamson, 2010: 135-38), and celebrated a romanticised ideal of pre-industrial methods of production (Jones and Yarrow, 2012). In particular, scholars, including Marx and Engels, saw in pre-industrial production a way of experiencing production in which creative, physical and mental abilities were exercised together. Instead, the new methods imposed a division between the creative mental work and physical labour of the worker. According to Marx (1959 [1844]), labour was made 'external' to the individual, detached from her, so that the worker "becomes an appendage of the machine, and it is only the most simple, most monotonous, and most easily acquired knack, that is required of him" (Marx and Engels, 2000 [1848]: 8).

As I mentioned, echoes of this debate and theorisation can be found at the present in social sciences. As Jones and Yarrow (2012) noted, in this debate authors, such as Ingold (2000) and Sennet (2008), read craftsmanship as "a special human condition of being engaged" (Sennett, 2008: 20) that "suggests ways of using tools, organizing bodily movements, thinking about materials that remain alternative, viable proposals on how to conduct life with skill" (Sennett, 2008: 11) against a model of life and production based on modern detachment of body and hand (see also Ingold, 2000: 396). Due to this engagement and the radical diversity of understanding materials and creation that the two modes of production (crafts- and machine-based production) impose, crafts have been seen as a way of problematising a (Western) modernity dominated by machine-based production, and finding alternatives to it (Adamson, 2007; 2010: 136).

Moreover, scholars have investigated the practices through which this form of production is transmitted down through generations. These studies have particularly focused on the relationship between master and apprentices, exploring the way of teaching crafts and involving new generations. The work by Lave and Wenger (1991) has been particularly significant in explaining this process as a participatory dynamic that involves apprentices and gradually introduces them to the learning that covers the production practices, social behaviours, and worldviews involving in becoming an artisan. Drawing from these studies, anthropologists have also shown how this process is socially embedded in a broader emancipatory dynamic through which members of marginalised social groups, such as peasants (Herzfeld, 2004), or women (Maher, 2007; Venkatesan, 2009), acquire the knowledge, production skills and economic means to improve directly or indirectly their condition.

This academic debate, besides offering tools to interpret and consider *'artigianalità'*, may have informed the development of this concept in Valenza. However, to understand its meaning, it is necessary to consider the history of *'artigianalità'* in the Italian language, the broad social discourse from which Valenza's is taken.

The etymology and current use of the word, which stems from the Latin '*ars*' [art], refers to special aesthetic and technical (manual) skills learned by workers and used by them in their activity. *'Artigianalità'*, thus, is etymologically close to '*artisticità'*, which is the characteristic of an artist or an artistic work; however, it is generally opposed to it. While *'artisticità'* implies a sense of uniqueness in the production techniques employed and the aesthetic outcome, *'artigianalità'* implies a sense of standardisation in skills employed, a higher implication of communitarian work, and a lower degree of aesthetic uniqueness in comparison to the work of an artist. Moreover, while, in the past two centuries, Italian intellectuals have been engaged in the intellectual debate that I mentioned before, *'artigianalità'* has also been at the centre of an ongoing cultural debate concerning the value of crafts that has led to the proliferation of scholarly definitions (Mazzocchi, 2006). In this ample and intricate national discourse, *'artigianalità'* is currently used to denote limited and generally scarcely mechanised productions (e.g. food, clothes, utensils). Moreover, the recognition of *'artigianalità'* entails an acknowledgment of traditionality, local authenticity and exclusivity of a product. In this respect, in the academic debate this concept occurs in broader discussion concerning the recognition, preservation, and exploitation of local intangible heritage (e.g. Grasseni, 2007; Grimaldi, 2012; Porporato, 2010; Bravo, 2005) in which local crafts are seen as fundamental resources for local development (Micelli, 2011; Benini, 2010; Mazzocchi, 2006; Grasseni, 2003).

In Valenza, the word maintains this broad usage. However, it has assumed a particular meaning in reference to the jewellery industry; a meaning that expresses the peculiarities of local productions and the role played by the industry in the city. In Valenza, as demonstrated at the dinner, *'artigianalità'* is "one and many". "One" in referring to the jewellery production and its output; "many" insofar as it evokes different, disparate aspects and ways of experiencing goldsmithing work: a local authenticity, a tension between crafts- and machine-based production, the relationship between skills and equipment, the process of achieving mastery in crafts, and the very idea of the structuring of the jewellery business. These are the different trajectories of meaning that emerged during the dinner, which show an inchoate expanse of emotions, personal experiences, expectations, and ways of understanding the jewellery industry, and more broadly, the world. Thus, *'artigianalità'* is a polysemic, prominent and controversial word, at the centre of the goldsmiths' debate about the peculiarities of local jewellery production. In this respect, *'artigianalità'* appears to be a 'keyword' (cf. Williams, 1983) of the local industry.

Durant explains: "*keyword* is a figurative expression, evoking privileged ways into something (a small door into a large room, lifting the lid off a casket)." Williams (1983) employed this term to refer to particular, prominent and debated words (such as 'anthropology', 'democracy', 'society') that have been at the centre of intense cultural debate over the centuries. Studying the debates around these words, that is studying the different meanings given to the words, offer us the keys for understanding the development of the society that promoted them.

While Williams urges us to mostly study the way meanings of specific words change through time, thus to address diachronically the polysemy of a 'keyword' (cf. Williams, 1983), I will instead approach the polysemy of *'artigianalità'* in a synchronic perspective. In this way I do not aim at drawing the cultural history of *'artigianalità'* in Valenza. Rather I will untangle the semantic bundle that underpins this word in order to bring to the fore different aspects that distinguish Valenza jewellery making in the eyes of goldsmith community. Exploring these different meanings, I will highlight the everyday experience and the ways of understanding and embodying jewellery making. Thus, I will explain the social and cultural role this industry plays in Valenza's community.

In this investigation, I will start from the sense of local authenticity that is associated with this word.

Crafts, Machine and local Authenticity

While Lucia introduced *'artigianalità'* into our discussion, Marco's comment represented a moment of friction in the conversation. Thinking of Valenza's industry, Marco affirmed his conviction that crafts-based production was superior to machine-made jewellery. To express this conviction, often professed to me by numerous other goldsmiths, Marco pointed out the 'love' of his colleagues for new technologies and techniques that appeared to him to go against a mode of production valuable for its outcome and its apparent local specificity. Due to their inchoate nature (Carrithers, 2007), Marco's words were taken as an accusation by his dinner companions, who felt reproached as partners in the distortion of the 'authentic' production vocation of the locale. I had the impression that Marco's statement was a thought spoken aloud, rather than a comment – let alone an accusation, aimed at his friends. However, in this tension and the reasons that led to it, we find elements to understand a first rhetorical pattern associated with the categories of crafts-based and machine-based production.

In Marco's sentence, even before unpacking and explaining these concepts, appears the fundamental hinges of an identity rhetoric of local authenticity and otherness.

$$\begin{cases} \text{crafts-based} = \text{Valenza} \\ \text{machine-based} = \text{non Valenza} \end{cases}$$

As Astolfo noticed, this identification of Valenza's jewellery industry with crafts-based production framed in a context of radical contraposition between crafts- and machine-based creations is a prominent feature in Valenza's public rhetoric. In the last fifty years, this identification has been found in films (Orengo et al., 1964), art exhibitions (Lenti, 2010; Molina and Manenti, 1994), scientific publications (Lenti and Pugnetti, 1974; Lenti, 2010) and narrative works (Bosco, 2004; Prandi, 2000). Moreover, it has been used by public institutions, such as the City Council, as well as by private enterprises, to promote their services, productions and the Valenza area in general. In these occurrences, the authenticity of local production lies in the human mastery of jewellery making, which is seen in the ability of an individual to carry out all of the phases of jewellery production with the support of simple tools completely under human control (Regione Piemonte et al., 2010: 17). This mastery is contrasted against a de-humanised production carried out by machines.

As mentioned in the introduction, this identification of Valenza with crafts-based production may repose on a historical datum: the failure of Valenza's industry to develop into a mechanised light industry, as it was instead the case for other Italian cities such as Arezzo and Vicenza. However, aside from this historical fact, in this contraposition are visible the seeds of the process of commodification of the local, as explained by Comaroff and Comaroff (2009).

In their comparative analysis of commodification of local heritages, Comaroff and Comaroff (2009: 140) have argued that, when a community engages in a process of commodification of its traditions, it is inevitably involved in a process of definition of the self and the other. This process leads the community to emphasise, and often create, local peculiarities. In other words, local traits are selected, and turned into an 'ethno-commodity': an identity 'black box' (cf. Latour, 1987: 15) in which the local is subsequently enclosed, ready to be sold and advertised, its possible contradictions and discrepancies hidden from the outside. Interpreting Valenza's identity rhetoric, it appears that the city's unusual path of industrial development has been subject to a process similar to that of Zulu dances or American Indian heritage described by Comaroff and Comaroff (2009: 140). I would argue that this trait has become an 'ethno-commodity' (cf. Comaroff and Comaroff, 2009: 20). Valenza is, thus, constructed through this box: the city's production is described as crafts-based, a result of local *'artigianalità'*, while any form of machine-production is ascribed to the outside, called "different", "non-proper", and "non-Valenza". In this context of radical contraposition, a decision such as to employ CAD/CAM in jewellery modelling appears to be incompatible with and betray the local authenticity, thus potentially dangerous to the integrity of the locale, thus to be blamed and avoided.

The words of Marco appear to hint at how the coherent image of the local used to convince the external world has reverberated inwards, towards the community. As Comaroff and Comaroff (2009: 117-38) pointed out, in the process of commodifying the locale, the imagery created for the outside is reflected back inside, ending up being internalised by the members of the community. Comaroff and Comaroff outline the possible final result of this process: the trait of authenticity selected for the world outside the community becomes the 'real' tradition, the silenced discrepancy between actual local practices and those which are promoted is forgotten, and the 'ethno-commodity' becomes the real form of the local traditions (Comaroff and Comaroff, 2009: 20-21). Although the dinner shows that the 'ethno-commodity' of *'artigianalità'* has been internalised by goldsmiths, Lucia and the subsequent comments by Marco also show that the process of determination of the 'ethno-commodity' is still not complete, since goldsmiths are still able to open the 'black box' (cf. Latour, 1987: 15), recognizing the variety of local practices despite the meaning of the rhetoric. This recognition, thus, blurs the neat contraposition of crafts vs. machines. However, it does not resolve the ambiguity.

Machine, Crafts, and Quality

The contraposition between crafts and machine is the subject of another rhetorical pattern, fundamentally interwoven with the previous one: that of quality. Marco's words echoed an intellectual tradition rooted in the works of the "Arts and Crafts" movement and authors, such as Ruskin (1851), and Morris (1888), who placed artisanal manual work above and in opposition to any machine-based production on the basis of an aesthetic and technical judgment of the outcomes of the two modes.

Referring to machine-made jewellery, Marco spoke about its 'anonymous' character: not just the lack of a name, but, more broadly, the lack of any specific characteristic that makes the product particular and unique in the eyes of the beholder. In other words, to goldsmiths, like Marco, machine-based jewellery lacks the "the extra [distinguishing] touch" that craftsmanship would bestow upon it.

Goldsmiths refer to those pieces entirely manufactured by machines as '*gioielli fatti a macchina*' [machine-based jewellery]. To explain this kind of production and the limits of its final outcome, goldsmiths frequently used the example of the chain-making machine[1]. This was the case, for example, of Dario, a fifty-year-old goldsmith, owner of a small workshop in which, in spring 2009, only he and his brother were working. During the visit, Dario often tried to explain the properties of crafts-based versus machine-made jewellery. To do so, he showed me a chain-making machine he had in his '*fabbrica*'.

> "Do you see these bulky, iron machines? They are designed to complete the entire cycle of production of chains: by starting from the metal wire, they cast, cut and bend the metal to create rings that are assembled in chains. These machines automatically complete all these phases, almost without any need for human work. While using this machine, a goldsmith does nothing. He just stands here and oversees the machine, checking the quality of the manufacturing, and preventing eventual breakdowns. He is not an artisan. No. He is an appendage of the machine.

---

[1] Starting from a metal wire, plate or rods, this machine threads and welds rings to make chains of different shapes and length. The shape of the chain and its links is determined on the basis of predetermined models. Any model sets the movements of the machines' presses and welder that operate automatically, without the need for any human assistance. So, to complete the manufacturing, human agency and knowledge are mostly limited to activating and deactivating the machine. Humans can set up new models, but the process requires technical and mechanical knowledge that is not as widespread among the goldsmiths as the use of these machines.

> Now, look at the pieces you obtain with this machine. Every piece is the same as the next. No risks: each ring will be perfectly similar to the others. However, you are limited in the possibilities that the machine gives you. You can make hundreds of metres of chain, it is not a problem...But they will all be the same. Moreover, if you work with this machine you know that you cannot accomplish the complicated designs that handiwork can produce. You can make hundreds of metres of chain but you have to accept that those chains will have not even a pinch of '*artigianalità*'."

As the words of Dario bring to the fore, machine production is qualified, first of all, by a peripheral involvement of the goldsmiths in production: while the machine processes the vast majority of the production, starting from a semi-finished product, such as a gold rod, to the assembly of the finished product, such as a chain, humans act as mere machine operators. In this sense, humans are perceived as appendages of the machine. Besides this operative marginality, the 'anonymous' character arises from the uniformity of the output and the limited number of models that machines, such as chain-makers, can produce.

In contrast with this mode of production, goldsmiths point out that 'special' jewellery is jewellery made through the direct employment of '*tocco artigiano*', the artisan touch in manufacturing. This is not only the handiwork but also the individual's ability to develop new designs and respond with their skills to the manufacturing difficulties as they occur during production. A new hinge for a bracelet or articulation of a chain, a new way of mounting stones or welding parts together, are all considered proofs of goldsmithing mastery, and their result is recognised as the distinctive 'extra-touch' of an object made with '*artigianalità*'. The involvement of these capacities would offer a far greater aesthetic variety and novelty to the products, making them stand out in a crowd of machine-made objects.

As an example of this contraposition, Dario's chain-making machine was able to produce only curb chains in six different sizes; expanding this array required mechanical adjustments that nobody in Dario's firm was able to carry out. Dario and the other workers were able to produce a larger array of chains – he showed me twelve examples – however, while the machine produced several metres of chain in one hour, the goldsmiths were able to make at most five or six metres of those 'special' chains in a day.

On an ideal level, thus, goldsmiths draw a neat contraposition between machine production that provides a large output but constrains manufacture to rigid aesthetic possibilities, and manual production that allows a vast number of aesthetic solutions but requires longer to reach the same quantity of output. Thus, considering the difference between these modes, goldsmiths argued that their products cater to different markets. Machine production is a system designed for standardised mass productions, useful to respond to large demand while minimizing the employment (and cost) of human personnel. Conversely, handwork is a viable way to create unique, or at least limited, productions endowed with an aesthetic complexity precluded by machine production: the kinds of products that may answer the needs of a customer who wants to distinguish themselves through objects different from those available to the masses (Appadurai, 1986: 38; Bourdieu, 2001 [1979]: 283-301; Franchi, 2009; Mosco, 2003).

Crafts, Machine and Engagement

Despite this discussion about quality, in the light of the discourse around authenticity, would suggest Valenza as a milieu completely devoted to handmade products, as the example of Dario suggests, Valenza's jewellery production is a hybrid that combines elements of machine-based and manual productions. Despite this hybridity, goldsmiths individuate Valenza's production through an overall expression of *'artigianalità'* in the quality of work and manufacturing that it conveys. The apparent discrepancy between this claim and the ideal system that backs it, discloses a further dimension of *'artigianalità'* that goes beyond a simple contraposition between crafts- and machine-based productions. In fact, *'artigianalità'* appears to be rooted not in a radical refusal of machine-employment, but a particular ethos in its use. In this respect, the words of Lucia are revealing.

It had been almost thirty years since Lucia had started her experience in jewellery production, when she talked that night. She is one of the over 3000 women employed in the trade. Until the 1970s, goldsmithing had remained a 'male' profession (Chapter 3), although women had been employed as polishers or bench-jewellers since the mid-19th century (Lenti, 1994: 124). However, design, gem-setting and many aspects of jewellery production remained, in the general consideration of goldsmiths, 'male' professions to be transmitted from one generation to the next. The boom of the jewellery industry in the late 1950s-1970s together with the institution of the two professional highschools brought a radical transformation in this conception. Since the 1970s, an increasing number of girls have enrolled in the courses offered by these institutions. There, they learned the design, how to craft pieces of jewellery and set gems in them. Thanks to the schools (see next paragraph), they entered into *'fabbriche'*. Over the span of a decade, the number of women employed in the trade reached 45%, the current ratio (OPML, 2011). Today, women cover all the roles in production, although some task, such as polishing, is still mainly undertaken by women (Benzi and Fugagnoli, 2004b) - As in the case of Lucia, some of these women are firm-owners or self-employed. Lucia attended ISA Cellini high school, where she learned the basics of the goldsmithing art and design. She then worked for almost ten years as a bench-jeweller. Over the same period, she began her activity as a designer and modeller. After those ten years, aged around thirty, she was formally hired as a modeller. In the early 2000s, she left the firm and began her work as a freelancer modeller and designer. Trained in manual design and modelling, in the past fifteen years she has looked with growing interest at the onset of new computer technologies, in particular CAD/CAM packages. After some resistance to engaging in computer work, in 2005 she enrolled in courses in computer use. In 2007, she was working with a computer on a daily basis, supporting her (traditional) manual skills with the possibilities offered by computer-based technology. However, she still attended advanced classes to better understand all the possibilities offered by programs, such as Rinoceros™, and its plug-ins. In the light of these experiences, that evening she was talking about her experience as a student and practitioner, and the precarious ground on which *'artigianalità'* was exercised in combining manual with machine work.

Thinking of her fellow students, she noticed their tendency to abandon themselves to the machine, without complementing this practice with other knowledge, concerning manual skills. In this respect, they were missing the possibility of achieving *'artigianalità'*. Lucia's observation echoes the words of Dario about chain-making machines and their use. Like an assembler machine, a computer is a complex field of interaction between man and machine: a place of hybridisation of those two different forms of work and agency, since individuals are not completely free in what they do and, vice-versa, the machine is not completely alone in its work (Rogers et al., 2011). Thus, manual-work and machine-work appear to be linked, bond together in a broad network in which, as pointed out by Latour (2005), by co-acting and completing each other human and non-human agencies make jewellery production possible.

'Artigianalità' appears as the way through which goldsmiths, like Lucia, make sense of human agency in the network and affirm its centrality and primacy. In so doing, *'artigianalità'* is explained not just as an abstract concept, but as the experiential process through which goldsmiths become aware of the network and expand their agency, so as to

involve the entire network into the artisan extended body and mind (Clark and Chalmers, 1998).

This point that transpires from Lucia's words was clearly formulated by another goldsmith, Mauro. He was a goldsmith in his late fifties and owner of a '*grande fabbrica'*, of twenty employees. One afternoon in July 2009, I met him in his private studio, a former garage located in the same condominium where he was living, while he was working on a ring. He was filing the complex beehive grid that would become the mounting for a diamond *pavé*, using different files that were kept on the work surface of his bench. The work was carried out at a regular pace: filing, stopping and checking his work, filing again. Continuing his activity, he answered my questions, alternating looking at me and at the ring. After a while, he showed me the piece, and explained that he was refining the internal part of the setting to permit an '*a-journ*' setting of the stones, which would give a better brightness to the stones. Showing me the piece, he gently rubbed his thumb on the surface of the jewellery, rotating it at the same time. It was not a nervous motion. Rather, it was the motion of a connoisseur who was studying the surface, checking for imperfections, asperities, and discontinuities. I was intrigued by the careful actions of the man in front of me. Suddenly he stopped. While keeping the jewellery in his fingers, he turned to me and looked directly into my eyes:

> "You may be surprised by what I am doing. Maybe you can call it a small demonstration of *'artigianalità'*. To judge the quality of jewellery, sight is not enough. You must use all your senses and, in particular, touch. Where your eyes do not see, your fingertip may find imperfections and where your fingers cannot reach, you can use one of your tools. A file, for example. To do so, you need to be able to extend your senses through your tools. It is not easy. You must become a master of your hands and your body. You must be gentle to feel, sharp and strong to adjust. It takes years; a whole life. It is a continuous process of learning. However, this knowledge and this constant improvement are *'artigianalità'* and this is the very core of our profession: the very soul of this goldsmith city."

Mauro offered a quite articulate explanation of what *'artigianalità'* may or should be. To him, it is not just a matter of better quality of the final output: *'artigianalità'* is the very way this quality is achieved. It lies in the artisan's talent to use all their senses to explore and acquire an intimate knowledge of a piece of jewellery that they are manufacturing. Moreover, it is also expressed by the capacity to extend one's senses through the tools they are employing. It follows that *'artigianalità'* is neither intuitive nor innate, but a continuous process of learning through which, as Marchand pointed out (2010a), skills become a complex mindset through which an artisan learns to see, and to think about production. Jewellery manufacturing, thus, is made possible through the application of this intimate knowledge that involves the perception of an object through all the senses, and arises from a process of mastering of one's body and gestures, and the different tools and techniques employed in jewellery production.

Human touch and machine are, thus, fundamentally complementary. Tools and machines are seen as possible extensions of a goldsmith's body that enhance an artisan's capacities. They offer them possibilities to surpass of the limits of their body, since they make them able to reach experience and manipulate those parts or features of a piece of jewellery that would normally be inaccessible to them. According to this definition, all tools and machines, from the simplest files that Mauro used as an example to complex devices such as CAD/CAM systems, are necessary aids that allow a goldsmith to imagine, sense and forge an object, so that the body and the mind of a goldsmith are extended to encompass them. This interpretation of the human-machine network, which is shared by many practitioners and expressed mostly through talking about their personal experience of jewellery making, first of all, imposes and identifies the centrality of human agency in the network and interprets the former through the latter. However, it echoes the theory of the 'extended mind', proposed more than a decade ago by Clark and Chalmers (1998: 7-8), by presenting examples of people who externalise cognitive activities through and into their tools – in other words, individuals who think with and through things, extending their mind beyond the human body through a use of tools tempered by crafts. Thus, echoing Ingold (2000: 295, 396), '*artigianalità*' can be seen as a form of engagement between jewellery maker and the forged materials, and the bond between human hand and tools: links that celebrate the complete engagement of the individual in their smithing activity.

While '*artigianalità*' celebrates such a level of engagement, this bond is perceived as hard to achieve because of being built on a continuous process of learning and embodying production skills and knowledge that is developed over years of practice. This understanding is acquired through a slow process of training that starts with working at the bench at school, for those who have attended one of the professional high schools of the city, and in the workshops in the early years of career. Starting from their apprenticeship (see next paragraph), goldsmiths learn the fundamental working techniques (e.g. chiselling, filing and welding), and to apply them while working on progressively more complex and valuable pieces. In this continuous exercise, they master their manual and creative abilities, apply them, and expand their knowledge of tools and materials, turning manual skills into a complex mindset through which an artisan learns to see and to think the production. In this way, individuals are involved in an intense process aimed at turning an inexpert hand into an 'intelligent hand' (cf. Sennett, 2008: 152-55), able to anticipate the reactions of the object that is manipulated and lead the transformation where they intend, and a 'skilful vision' (cf. Grasseni, 2004), an aesthetic understanding of jewellery that is shared by all the other members of the local practitioners. Besides these fundamental skills, the most valued understanding that is seen to distinguish a 'true' goldsmith bearer of *'artigianalità'* is an internal tension towards excellence in production and constant self-improvement of skills. This tension, which echoes Sennett's theorisation of craftsmanship (2008: 23), is perceived as a key in establishing the 'right' relationship between human and machine that substantiates 'artigianalità'. While the goldsmiths' animosity towards machines, such as a chain-maker, can be explained by a marginalisation of human agency in production, the hostility towards those devices, such as computers, whose outputs are more attributable to human agency and creativity lies, as Lucia noted, in the risk of dulling the tension towards self-improvement that their use may involve (rather than a hypothetical goldsmith's '*a priori*' refusal of these machines).

In explaining this understanding, Sennett's reasoning on the risks for the integrity of craftsmanship caused by the employment of machines is illuminated. While Sennett, like Valenza goldsmiths, finds in a tension for self- and production improvement the key to craftsmanship, he points out that any tool, from the simplest pencil to a computer, may be a useful aid through which practitioners express their creative ability fostering constant improvement and repetitive practices. However, he notices that individuals in their work may abandon themselves to the machine, self-marginalizing their agency against pre-made options by ceasing any attempt at self-improvement. This is when:

> "Machinery is misused [... because] it deprives people themselves from learning through repetition. The smart machine can separate human mental understanding from repetitive, instructive, hands-on learning. When this occurs, conceptual human power suffers." (Sennett, 2008: 39)

To explain this abandonment and misuse, Sennett makes the case of CAD software (Sennett, 2008: 39-45) when machines are employed to hide and repress difficulties concerning crafting rather than tackling them. In this respect, human work is over determined by the machine (Sennett,

2008: 43), since the person stops participating in the process of learning, delegating this process to the machine.

In light of this reasoning we can explain the animosity showed by Lucia and the other goldsmiths. In a community where *'artigianalità'* is seen to depend on a process of learning similar to the one described by Sennett, new technologies are not 'bad' in themselves: they offer new possibilities of production, and potentially they could be integrated into the extended body of a goldsmith. The problem that raises hostility lies in the attitude of the user. New possibilities and the ease with which they are achieved are seen as the cause of the abandonment of a process of constant learning and the decision to not tackle the difficulties presented with practice, which is the foundation of *'artigianalità'*. In this sense, technology risks becoming "the tomb of *'artigianalità'*": a complete subordination of human agency and creative capacity to machine setup.

'*Artigianalità*' and goldsmith community

Thus, *'artigianalità'* is revealed as an ideal of production focused on a particular form of an engagement between artisans, their tools and their production; a form of engagement that overcomes the rigid limits of a contraposition between manual and machine-made products. This engagement is defined by opposite temporalities. In fact, *'artigianalità'* lies in a constant process of learning and challenging an individual's skills; at the same time, it is explained in the eternal present of this internal tension and in practice. Cast in this ideal space, *'artigianalità'* appears as a fundamental, solipsistic condition where the practitioner is the fulcrum of a system suspended between doing and becoming. In this engagement, however, this solipsistic dimension opens itself to the world, and stretches out to encompass the social and become a foundation of a model of society. Often goldsmiths pointed out that Valenza's (goldsmith) community hinges on *'artigianalità'*. Marco, Lucia and the other goldsmiths that I have presented up to this point have only hinted at this social dimension of *'artigianalità'*. However, this theme was brought to the fore by Astolfo at the end of the dinner.

In his words, *'artigianalità'* characterised the very foundation of the structure of local industry: a structure that is interpreted as a process oriented towards the achievement of such form of understanding and embodiment of production. In this respect, *'artigianalità'* appears to be the core of a shared progression of individual growth, which passes through the increase in competence in goldsmithing skills. This process is divided into three main phases: becoming an apprentice, becoming a (full-fledged) goldsmith, becoming an entrepreneur. Altogether, these phases, which were listed by Astolfo and also by scholars (e.g. Benzi and Fugagnoli, 2004b; Gaggio, 2007, Lenti and Pugnetti, 1974; Bovero, 1992), are described as a "stairway of success": a process shared by practitioners which leads them towards an ideal of success composed of economic well-being and professional, public recognition.

While *'artigianalità'* and its achievement are linked to these different phases, their exploration becomes a way through which we can understand how *'artigianalità'* becomes a collective experience and phenomenon that unifies Valenza's goldsmithing community, and at the same time creates grounds for its division.

Apprenticeship covers the early years of work, about five to ten years which also encompasses the 3-5 years required to complete a degree in one of the local professional high schools. During my fieldwork, there were two professional goldsmith schools in the city: ISA Cellini and Foral. ISA Cellini was opened in 1950, as the first professional high school for goldsmithing in the city. It has been a state school financed by the local government and supported by private institutions, such as AOV. It offered 5-year curricula aiming at offering a practical and theoretical basis to new goldsmiths. After two years, in which practical skills are taught together with classes of Italian, history, geography, maths, chemistry, English and law, during the following three years the students are engaged in classes of theory of design and history of arts, chemistry, gemmology and mineralogy, which offers the theoretical basis of goldsmith practices.

Apprenticeship also encompasses an array of work experiences that includes formal apprenticeship, internships and informal work experiences in workshops (Benzi and Fugagnoli, 2004a). Formal apprenticeship is regulated by a national law (Dgl 273/2006). It is considered a form of temporary work aimed at the acquisition of professional skills through a combination of training and work experience. All people from 17 to 30 are eligible for this form of contract, which is extendable up to three years. Despite the existence of this regulation, apprenticeship is developed through different forms of formal and informal activities in the workshop. Students of professional highschools in their last years of education are often involved in internships in *'fabbriche'*. Moreover, most talented youths will be accepted for a few months as informal helpers by goldsmiths in order to practice their skills and learn by observing elders at work. These training periods are often preparatory to subsequent forms of occupation. Young people can be hired as apprentices (ex-Dgl 276/2003), or other forms of temporary or permanent employment. Although State regulations limit apprenticeship for a maximum period of three years, to goldsmiths there is no precise limit to this initiatory state. It can take a longer period (during which the 'apprentice' is hired under temporary contracts or paid under-the-counter), until, using the sentence I repeatedly heard:

> "You prove that you are able to stay by yourself without the constant watching of elder goldsmiths."

In the years of apprenticeship, the individual is asked to perform more and more complex tasks, from milling a plate, to chiselling, pressing, cutting, welding, and setting stones. During work hours the youth is often left alone. At the end of the day her work is checked by elder goldsmiths who may accept or refuse it.

In this way, the apprentice exercises and improves her crafts. Herzfeld (2004), explaining the case of artisans in Crete, as well as Maher (2007), considering dressmakers in Turin, showed cases where apprenticeship is an antagonistic relationship between apprentice and master. They describe a form of relationship that passes through the attitude of the master of not explaining techniques countered by the apprentice's attitude of secretive learning and practicing them in a manner that the scholars termed, "to steal with eyes". This situation of silence and furtive observation is something I did not observe in the workshops. Verbal descriptions are indeed often avoided, perhaps due to the fact that most of the crafting experience is a tactile one that has difficulty fitting into words, as argued by Sennett (2008). However, masters (who may be the firm owner or an experienced goldsmith in the firm) generally explain by showing their apprentices how to accomplish the different tasks. Masters are not mysterious in their practices. They let pupils watch and, in the case I observed, required their full attention. Moreover, firm-owners may leave exercises for apprentices after working hours: the apprentices are not paid for this work, but have a chance to actually practice with all the equipment of the workshop. In this way, apprentices engage with jewellery-making, learning the techniques and forms of production in a way that closely resembles Lave and Wenger's (1991) theory.

In their analysis of apprenticeship and learning, the scholars interpreted apprenticeship as a social process of legitimation of the individual within a 'community of practice', a group of practitioners who share common social and production practices (Lave and Wenger, 1991). During the apprenticeship, apprentices:

> "Are seen as developing their expertise in these practices through 'legitimate peripheral participation' in the practice. Legitimate peripheral participation allows a novice to take part in peripheral aspects of the

> practice of the community and to be recognized as legitimately so doing, while gradually being inducted into more central, often more complex aspects of the practice. Thus, the novice practitioner gradually takes on more and more expert and important tasks, until eventually she or he becomes an 'old timer,' a central participant with a role in inducting new members. In this process, learners develop not just their expertise in the practice, but also their understanding of and embeddedness in the culture that surrounds it. Through the acknowledged legitimacy of their participation, they learn how to be full participants in the community of practice, with all the many and varied social behaviours and relations that this implies." (Paetcher, 2003: 542)

Apprenticeship in Valenza moves along this interpretative line, offering an apprentice the chance to learn the skills and embody them, through a process similar to the one described by Marchand (2010a) in the case of English woodworkers, and become known in the social space of the *'fabbrica'* and the local industry. It is this process that makes an apprentice a fully-recognised goldsmith.

While in the medieval guild system the apprentice had to prove their mastery through the completion of a particular piece of work (Sennett, 2008: 58), in Valenza there is no formal test or a special initiatory rite that apprentices have to pass to be qualified as fully-fledged goldsmiths. My informants noted, however, that a crucial turning point in this process of legitimation is the first full-time contract. The first contract represents the moment when the apprenticeship ends, although the goldsmith may still be used mainly for easier tasks and can continue their informal training within the *'fabbrica'*. However, goldsmiths defined it an important recognition of the individual's skills, since it means that a firm-owner trusts their ability and, in their terms, "is ready to bet on this new colt", offering them a better wage and a larger involvement in production. After this point, in fact, goldsmiths are employed full time, officially 40 hours a week, but in some cases up to 70, Saturday and Sunday included. During the working day, goldsmiths stay at their benches, manufacturing the pieces that the firm-owners allocate to them: hour after hour, from 8 am to 6 pm, with generally a two-hour break around 12 pm. Senior goldsmiths can be asked to undertake some errands in the city, but for the majority of the people employed in the firms, their life is spent in the *'fabbrica'*, a micro-cosmos made up of a few rooms and workbenches and tools. In this space, the solipsism of the personal exercise of skills is socialised, by talking with colleagues, by observing them. In this respect, it is not rare to overhear praise or loathing for colleagues' work. There is competition, esteem, envy, love in those judgements of work and skills. These discussions demonstrate well how the work of a goldsmith is taken seriously by their peers. It clearly appears that the individual is legitimated by the others, considered worth of being spoken of, while the work of an apprentice is generally barely considered by goldsmiths and her work, almost never discussed, apart from particular cases in which the apprentice demonstrates particular ability, such as winning design competitions, or made particular 'disasters', such as wasting precious metal or stones.

The passage from apprentice to goldsmith mainly operates on the grounds of the achievement of skills and understanding production that is '*artigianalità*'. However, Astolfo, like many other goldsmiths, noted that the individual's career is not concluded with this achievement, but with that of turning from a worker into an entrepreneur. After WWII, in a context of the expansion of the Italian and international jewellery markets, can be found common examples of artisans who attempted to open their own independent businesses. To have a *'fabbrica'* was at the same time an opportunity for a larger income and a status symbol, as many highlighted. In Astolfo's words:

> "To have a *'fabbrica'*, a firm, was considered to be the apex of one's career. If you had a *'fabbrica'*, you were no longer an employee. You were a boss, an important person... Without people above your head."

This perception portrays entrepreneurship as a means of self-realisation. In doing so, it makes Valenza echo a similar understanding of an economy that has been found in other industrial regions of Italy (Ghezzi, 2007; Yanagisako, 2002; Holmes, 1989), even before the political rise of Berlusconi and the neoliberal turn of Italian politics (Molé, 2012; Stacul, 2007; Boni, 2008). In all these cases, *la 'fabbrica'* is a sign of personal and familial success, modernity and ability. Whereas throughout the rest of Italy, industry was the subject of desire and hope – an unreachable objective for most due to the high start-up costs. In Valenza this dream was at hand. Low starting-up costs, a highly receptive world-wide market, and a high offer of work from outsourcing were the conditions welcoming an artisan once they wanted to set up their own business. Thanks to these conditions, even small studios thrived and made the desire to become a firm-owner affordable and available to anybody with even modest financial resources. Crucial, instead, was the ability to mobilise social connections to create a market for the new studio.

The story of Santuzzo's workshop is paradigmatic of this form of entrepreneurship. Santuzzo is a bench-jeweller who immigrated to Valenza in the mid-1970s, without a formal goldsmith education. He was trained in a workshop as an apprentice and after ten years of working in the city he had developed his skills and saved a tidy sum:

> "It was just a few million '*Lire*' [a few thousand pounds]. More or less the same amount of money that was necessary to buy a small car. I decided to try it. I talked to my employer and expressed my decision. He supported me and promised me some work, at least at the beginning. So I started. I rented a sort of garage, although the owner called it a 'workshop'. I set up four desks with their equipment. Another colleague of mine decided to join me in the enterprise. We hired another pair of boys and we started. We mainly cast jewellery frames and did simple gem-setting. My former employer maintained his promise and gave us some work at the beginning. In the meantime we found new clients and grew. We changed site in the mid-1990s and gained some more people. Already in the 1980s we worked not only as a supplier for Valenza firms, but started marketing our stuff in the rest of Italy, mainly in the South. The business was going well. I was happy. I never, never imagined that I, a son of a Southern peasant, could have made so much money and had a firm. It was like in a dream..."

The majority of firms open in the city today shares a common history with Santuzzo. Opened mostly in the last forty years (Maggiora, 2010: 541-42), they were created with the investment of savings of one or a few goldsmiths, often small capitals.[2] The issue at stake, instead, involved the capacity to find work. As seen in the previous chapter, finding other firms interested in outsourcing and creating a (possibly stable) network with them are crucial for these small workshops that thrive on outsourcing from other firms. In this respect, the role of the new firm-owner's previous employer is crucial. As in the case of Santuzzo, stories of previous employers who encouraged and helped the new firms are very common. This phenomenon, in Valenza, is called '*figliolanza*' [off-springing]. This process, already attested in the late 19th century (Gaggio, 2007: 78), is deeply rooted in the development of the network economy. A firm-owner, against the professional growth of a talented employee, and thus the risk of losing her to the attraction of better work opportunities offered by other firms, would encourage and support her in opening an independent enterprise; the firm-owner would also financially support the new enterprise by offering outsourcing work and, sometimes, credit for the start-up. This process results in the creation, therefore, of a strong link between the two firms, which is based on mutual '*conoscenza*' and

[2] As also seen in the previous chapter, most of the '*fabbriche*' were opened in originally non-production spaces (e.g. flats, former stables, garages or attics) easily available on the market for rent or to let. Moreover, the cost of the required equipment was limited. Finally, in the second half of the 20th century (Gaggio, 2007) banks started lending gold or other precious metals, thus, firms did not have the necessity of buying gold reserves to start their activity but could rely on these loans. In this respect, only a limited amount of capital was required for the start-up.

'*fiducia*' (Chapter 3), and, in the eyes of the firm owner, would guarantee that she continues to enjoy the skills of her former artisan; a service that otherwise might be lost.

Besides the important contribution of former employers, the new firm often requires a broader market to flourish. In this respect, to gain jobs, the new firm, that is, its firm-owner(s), must be known by other firm-owners. The previous employer may facilitate these contacts, but it is the new firm's work that must be appreciated for its quality, that is to say, the new firm's owner as well as their employees must be valued for their products and skills; that is for their '*artigianalità*'. The opening and success of a firm can be read as a further degree in the process of legitimation and integration within the goldsmiths' 'community of practice' (cf. Lave and Wenger, 1991).[3]

Thus, '*artigianalità*' can be considered the nub of the professional life of a goldsmith and the basis of the entire economic structure of this industry. However, as Astolfo hinted, '*artigianalità*' has also played a fundamental role in making the jewellery industry an aggregative and inclusive reality that hinges on the possibility of economic success it provides.

After WWII, the jewellery industry provided generally higher salaries than other secondary sector trades in Valenza and neighbouring cities (Penna Ivaldi, 2008). In particular, from the 1970s to 1990s, when Valenza's industry reached its maximum expansion in terms of number of employees and firms (Maggiora, 2010), the average wage of a goldsmith was about twice the national salary for metalworkers with the same level

---

[3] Although the status of entrepreneur has been reachable, it has proved to be a particularly fragile one. Analysing the censuses of Valenza firms since the mid-1970s (CCAI, 2011), the average life-span of a jewellery firm has been about ten years; five in the case of smaller studios. Fluctuation of the price of precious materials, controversies among partners, legal and fiscal issues, sometimes even good employment offers may lead to firms closing down and former employers turning into employees. Thus, it is not surprising to meet goldsmiths who have experienced that change of roles twice or three times in their lives.
Also taking into consideration what was explained in the previous chapter, the jewellery industry is an area in which entrepreneurship and entrepreneurs cannot be considered a completely separate and distinct body from workers, in contrast with Marx and Engels' (2000 [1848]) theorisation of the distinction between capitalist entrepreneurs and factory workers, echoed and endorsed by Bourdieu (1984). Instead, entrepreneurs and workers appear to be two expressions of a same system of cultural practices connected to production that is articulated through learning and employing manual skills and production knowledge – in other words, '*artigianalità*'.

of education and seniority. In the case of skilful goldsmiths, the wage could increase and reach the same levels as a head physician employed in a public hospital.

Moreover, since the 1960s, Valenza's jewellery industry has rapidly expanded, requiring more trained workers than Valenza's market was offering. The firms, still barely receptive to outsiders in the 1950s (Gaggio, 2007, Penna Ivaldi, 2008), started recruiting newcomers of both genders, even if non-qualified. They were trained in the *'fabbriche'*, providing them with the basics of the goldsmithing art.

Moreover, since the early 1950s, thanks to the creation and expansion of the two professional highschools and the growth of the business, Valenza has become a destination for immigration of people from all around the country and from abroad. Between 1951 and 1971 the city almost doubled in population (from 13,000 to 23,000 inhabitants) and the number of goldsmiths passed from about 1,900 to approximately 5,000 (Maggiora, 2010: 234). This datum, provided by Astolfo, offers an element to understand the role played by this industry in attracting people to Valenza:

> "The jewellery industry appeared to me, and to many other boys and girls who have come to Valenza in the last half-century, as a sort of dream... A promise... Your education was not important, many in my generation never got a highschool degree. It didn't matter if you spoke the local dialect or even Italian. The only thing that seemed to matter was our manual ability to reach an economic success. Our ability to embody the goldsmith's craft."

After that dinner we met numerous times, for a coffee or for a chat. One day, he decided to talk about his history. He came to Valenza in the late 1960s, from a countryside village a few hours from Naples. He came from a family of farm labourers: the third of four siblings. After completing middle school, he was sent to his aunt who lived in a city near Valenza. The aunt, who worked as a civil servant in Valenza, suggested that he attend the local professional school, where he studied and graduated as a gem-setter in the mid-1960s. After that, he found a job in a big firm in the city: a first contract as an apprentice, then a full-time position. In ten years, he told me, he made enough to buy a flat. In the 1970s he married, and in the meantime he had changed firms several times, getting a better pay every time. In the 1980s he decided to open his studio, where he still works.

Remembering this history, the jewellery industry was often referred to as a 'system of hopes': a hope of prosperity for generations of people coming from the countryside, from poverty. Herzfeld (2004) explains the role of artisanship in Rethemos, as the way through which young people from the countryside left the marginal economic and social conditions of rural life to enter into urban life and improve their conditions. However, he noticed that, while they have a richer condition, artisans are a marginal group inside urban Cretan and Greek society; a group unable to reach economic gains and social recognition comparable with State jobs or other forms of entrepreneurship (Herzfeld, 2004: 12-17). This is not the case of Valenza, where goldsmithing had provided most of the workers with comfort and an indisputable public recognition in the city (Chapter 1). At the same time, the jewellery industry appears as an ideal model of life and work impregnated with expectations. Ferguson (1999), noticed that, in Zambia, economic booms and urban industrialism sustained by the mining industry between 1950 and the 1980s, represented to people from the countryside the centre of expectations of modernity and welfare. Pursuing these expectations, they left their original communities and embraced an urban, Westernised, way of life. Not dissimilarly, in Valenza, the jewellery industry attracted people from all around the country, and often from abroad, who saw in the business the possibility of reaching high salaries without the need for a formal high or higher education, about just after a period of apprenticeship completed in the local schools or, often, simply in the workshops. In the case of Valenza, the system of hopes connected to jewellery production was the motor of an inclusive dynamic that led people from Valenza and outside the city to participate in the same business and be valued mostly for their ability to learn and practice skills and express crafts and creativity. It is in this respect that goldsmiths, including Astolfo, saw *'artigianalità'* as the centre of an inclusive dynamic:

> "When we arrived in Valenza we were Neapolitans, Sicilians, Piedmontese, Venetian, white, black, blue or red. However, when you start working, and learning how to do jewellery; when you learn crafts and how to understand production, you become a goldsmith. You are a goldsmith. That's all. In this respect, you can say that the goldsmiths of this city are a community: a community founded on *'artigianalità'*."

'*Artigianalità*' and Valenza

Astolfo's experience closes this analysis and virtually also closed the circle that I opened, showing how *'artigianalità'* is used as trope in an identity rhetoric of authenticity. In this chapter I showed how this concept is used by goldsmiths to express and explain their activities and professional life, the value of their work, the process of making a piece of jewellery, the structure of a goldsmith's career, and the structure of the jewellery industry. These are different trajectories, whose meanings are not interconnected in an analytical chain that links signifier (the word "*artigianalità*") to a signified (a precise, maybe scholarly, definition of craftsmanship). From this survey, in fact, it emerges that there is no such precise definition, but rather a semantic space.

The trajectories of meaning spread out one after the other, sometimes conflicting, sometimes overlapping, sometimes interconnecting, or just standing detached from one another as parallel entities in the discourse. In this non-linear configuration, the trajectories describe an ideal space steeped in a sense of pride and belonging to a community of peers. When goldsmiths talk about *'artigianalità'*, this concept turns into an explanation of the industry from the inside that denotes its positive uniqueness. The distinguishing quality of this uniqueness is *'artigianalità'*. This is the fundamental element that all the trajectories share. However, the quality of this uniqueness is the result of a discursive '*bricolage*': a synthetic process that draws from personal understanding, feelings, memories, fears and expectations and is completed by the articulation of some particular stylemes that frequently return, as '*doxa*' (cf. Bourdieu, 1977: 167-69), in the city discourse: the uniqueness of crafts-based production, the difficult balance between individual's craft and production and creative capacities of a machine, the role of craftsmanship as a hinge of the entire jewellery industry. In this respect, *'artigianalità'* appears as a multiform, inchoate but meaningful object suspended between an individual and collective dimension.

To portray this crucial aspect of the everyday discursive formation of *'artigianalità'*, I took each trajectory as a distinct ethnographic object, and followed and analysed it separately. Where the trajectories diverged, I did not impose a unifying interpretation, rather, I preferred to leave the *aporia* unsolved. I have allowed incoherence among trajectories to emerge in this chapter, since I consider it a fundamental trait that turns *'artigianalità'* into an 'evocative object' (cf. Turkle, 2007).

According to Turkle (2007: 5), 'evocative objects' are objects that are able to mobilise thought and feelings in people. The scholar refers to physical objects, such as a violin or a comic book, however this model can also be applied to a discursive object, such as *'artigianalità'*. It also produces feelings and thoughts in goldsmiths, leading them to disclose their understanding of their work, their experiences, and their expectations. In this respect, the seamlessness of *'artigianalità'* that allows this narrative exercise does not delegitimise any ways of presenting production and work. In so doing, *'artigianalità'* turns out to be the 'keyword' (cf.

Williams, 1983) of the jewellery industry, and its cosmos of people, objects and feelings.

Although trajectories develop as distinct entities, the result of this analysis shows an ideal point of convergence of these trajectories. All the trajectories seem to address the existence of a distinct community distinguishable as Valenza, or the goldsmithing community (of Valenza). They evoke the profile of this entity, articulating and recognizing it on the basis of a shared *'artigianalità'* among its members. Thus, *'artigianalità'* does not only describe a method of work: it describes the locale. It becomes the 'keyword' (cf. Williams, 1983) that opens up a way of understanding Valenza and its community: a community bound together by *'artigianalità'* but whose cohesion is precarious, as precarious as the equilibrium between hand and machine. 'A*rtigianalità'* appears, thus, as a narrative through which the self-defined itself and outlines the profile of a community in which the self finds its peers.

While scholarship on crafts emphasises the aspect of the individual's and the community's experience of production, this analysis points out that *'artigianalità'* is also a way of imagining, defining and creating a community: a precarious cosmos of relations, memories and actions. Implicitly, it follows that jewellery making, in its form as an artisan industrial district, is the very element on which this community is imagined.

This analysis concludes and completes the first part of the book. In these first four chapters I have aimed at presenting the role that the jewellery industry plays in the city and in the life of the goldsmith community. I developed this description, taking as a starting point particular object in the city discourse: established formations, such as the rhetoric of 'the city of goldsmiths', and the concept of *'artigianalità'*, or discursive '*imponderabilia' (*cf. Malinowski, 1932 [1922]: 18), such as the description of the city as a *'fabbrica'* or that of networking as a romantic affair. From these discursive objects, I expounded the link that the jewellery industry has with the city. Moving focus, I argued that the industry is an identity feature of the local discourse, and the principal marker of the city's space and time; I presented the structure of the industry and its sociality; finally, in this chapter, I intended to show how the industry and jewellery-making are experienced and understood by goldsmiths and how, in this understanding, goldsmiths find the elements to imagine themselves as a community. The analysis of *'artigianalità'* has confirmed, from another perspective, the fundamental role played by the industry in creating a 'sense of place' (cf. Field and Basso, 1996) of Valenza.

In these chapters, the crisis has been marginalised so as to bring out this profound relationship between city and industry. Moving my focus on to the changes brought about by the economic downturn, which began in 2008, in the second part of the book I will show how the 'sense of place' (cf. Field and Basso, 1996), the industry and the everyday way of experiencing and imagining the jewellery industry were transformed during my fieldwork, virtually turning a new page for the life of Valenza.

PART II:

'*LA CRISI*'

CHAPTER FIVE

A NON-LINEAR HISTORY OF THE CRISIS

The three years from 2008 to 2010 will be remembered as a particularly dramatic period in the history of Valenza. In those years, the jewellery industry of the city experienced a profound downturn: the worst after the Second World War. While at the beginning of 2008, about 7,000 people were employed in the jewellery industry, by the last quarter of the same year dozens of small workshops had closed and a first wave of temporary personnel suspensions or permanent dismissals had started. From October to December, about 1,000 workers, approximately 15% of the jewellery industry's workforce, were made temporarily redundant or were permanently dismissed. This figure increased during subsequent years. In January 2011, 2,500 goldsmiths were estimated to have been involved in temporary redundancy schemes, and another 1,800 had lost their jobs (Poggio, 2011).

These figures are indicative of a profound change that occurred in Valenza: the deep downturn of the local industry that my informants called *'la Crisi'*, the Crisis with a capital 'C'. In the first part of the book, I have highlighted the link that binds Valenza and its community with the jewellery industry, and the complex and non-univocal nature of this relationship. In the second part that opens with this chapter, I shall move to investigate how *'la Crisi'* impacted on the city and modified the link. In this chapter, I will begin this investigation by presenting the downturn and, in particular, its causes, through the narrations of Valenzani.

All the narrations are the results of the attempts by Valenzani and scholars to make sense of the abrupt local downturn. These narratives, which give an account of the elements of the change in Valenza and in international jewellery production and consumption, respond to this objective through the selection and arrangement of these elements according to coherent plots, following those principles of rationalization of the past into a coherent narration explained by Taleb (2007: 62-84). In the days of my fieldwork, the local debate was mostly dominated by one narration of *'la Crisi'*, which I refer to as the 'key narrative' of this change. The narration was woven by goldsmiths as well as by scholars, mostly economists and sociologists, and made sense of the change by explaining the local transformation as a local consequence of global economic transformations, namely the Credit Crunch, and relegating Valenza goldsmiths to a condition of victims of the de-humanised grand mechanism of the market.

However, other well-grounded and plausible narrations were nested in the city's discourse. These are 'alternative narratives' that focus on spatialities, temporalities, objects and aspects of the jewellery industry that are different from the ones accounted for by the 'key narrative'. These, moreover, portray Valenzani goldsmiths in the role of agents or active participants in the change. In this chapter I will focus on two of these 'alternative narratives': the first describes the change in international consumption in luxury goods that occurred in the 2000s; the second points out the failure on the long run of a model of entrepreneurship based on small supplying firms.

These multiple narrations, in their individual plausibility and legitimacy and collective non-coincidence, shed light on a multiplicity of ways of understanding *'la Crisi'* and the role played by the community in this change. Moreover, they participate in completing a picture of a change that goes beyond linear causality. The downturn emerges as an example of a non-linear history (De Landa, 1997): a tangle of concatenations of events that influence each other in ways that are not simple ascribable to linear causality.

When Deleuze and Guattari (1987) proposed a first attempt at a non-linear history, they saw the world's becoming as being distinguished by a multitude of dynamics that characterised the transformation of matter. The authors proposed to view this complexity as a system of non-mechanistic permutations among objects, which moves through simultaneously independent and interconnected trajectories: the *'plateaux'* and 'assemblages' (Deleuze and Guattari, 1987: 502-06). One of the striking features of this ontological model is the non-reductive spirit that moves it: complexity is made up of an uncountable number of '*plateaux*' and 'assemblages', and every single object can be an element of different *'plateaux'* and 'assemblages'. Translating this complexity into a historiographical effort, Delanda concludes that in a non-linear world there are infinite possible histories of bifurcations, modifications, disaggregations and re-aggregations of aggregates of matter (De Landa, 1997: 15-16). In other words, a non-linear history is an understanding of the world's becoming open to the unpredictability of the process.

In a methodological perspective, to outline a non-linear history by examining and assembling the different narratives that occurred in a community, does not aim to negate this or that history, but to expand the field of enquiry beyond the boundaries fixed by each narrative. Moreover, by highlighting contradictions and mutual interactions, it sheds light on the semantic space that underpins the concept of '*la Crisi* and allows to bring to the fore the cultural tensions triggered by the change. Following this reasoning, this chapter aims to produce a non-linear history of the crisis in order to introduce *'la Crisi'* and to present the ways in which Valenzani understood it and the role that goldsmiths and the city played in it.

Considering a crisis

The English word 'crisis', like the Italian '*crisi*', stems from the Latin word *crisis*, which, in turn, was derived from the ancient Greek, *κρισις*. *Κρισις* meant an irrevocable change or break-up. From that original meaning, the same expanded to encompass any "specific, unexpected, and non-routine [event] or series of events that creates high levels of uncertainty and threat or perceived threat to an organization's high priority goals" (Seeger et al., 1998: 158)

In its current use, in English as well as in Italian, it describes a troublesome moment or a transformation through which a subject (a person, an object, an idea, etc.) passes from a positive stage of existence to a negative one. Thus, to talk about a crisis is to talk about a transformation, the result of which is already known to be negative.

However, to talk about a change implies some relevant epistemological problems concerning the difficulty of translating 'dynamism' (the subject's becoming) into 'staticism' (that of the meaning of the words). In other words, to talk about a crisis implies an intellectual process that passes through the arbitrary definition of some 'touchstones': some fixed elements on which a discourse can be based and an analysis can be articulated. Thus, to define 'a crisis' is an act of classification that, through processing reality through fixed categories, makes the complexity of the world's dynamism sensible and communicable.

Bowker and Star (1999) explored the nature of classification systems and the implications that classifications have on research and, more generally, on the perception of the world. One of the central points of their work is that any classification is far from being a neutral element in research, but by organizing reality through fixed categories, it is fundamentally based on the exclusion and inclusion of specific data. Thus, it determines and is determined by the results of a study. In other words, they explain that

> "Each standard and each category valorises some point of view and silences another. This is not inherently a bad thing – indeed it is inescapable. But it *is* an ethical choice, and as such it is dangerous – not bad, dangerous" (Bowker and Star, 1999: 320-21)

The danger they highlight is the risk of treating a classification as a neutral process and not interrogating their principles and the nature of their outcome.

Faced with a definition of a crisis, therefore, we are led to question this classification and, in Bowker and Star's terms, its 'political aspect', by reconsidering the entire process in the light of the data included and excluded from the final account. Whereas through the concept of economic crisis social transformation is approached through economic categories and reduced into a (social) mechanism based on demand, offer, capital, labour, price, etc., the work of Stewart (1996) shows that much of an industrial decline remains unaccounted for in this econometric formula, in particular with regards to a community's life and perception of change. It is by aiming to voice this unspoken dimension that I approach the case of Valenza.

The emergence of *'la Crisi'*

During the months spent in the field, I witnessed a rapid change in Valenza. A change announced by superficial changes in the ordinary face of the city: the proliferation of "Workshop to let or sale" signs hanging on the doors of condominiums; the plunge in the price of real estate in the city (FIAIP, 2011); the multiplication of shops in the downtown left empty for months. These and other small changes told of a city that was struggling with a difficult time for its economy. The spread and intensification of these signs indicated the worsening of the situation. Overall, this a change was difficult not to notice in a city known for its opulence, its being permeated with hundreds of workshops, and the intense activity of its artisans. In the course of months, I observed the fading away of that city. Using a metaphorical expression used by the goldsmiths themselves, "I saw the chimneys stop smoking." This was *'la Crisi'*.

From December 2008, in Valenza's discourse, the word '*crisi*' became the 'keyword' (cf. Williams, 1983) of this change and the way to talk about it. Although the change in the market appeared starkly in its abruptness and strength from the early days of October 2008, it was only in December that the press, and more generally, public opinion began to deal with this topic. In the autumn, discussions about the market downturn as well as its local effects were avoided by goldsmiths. As a fifty-year-old gem setter, whom I interviewed in April 2009, explained:

> "[In autumn 2008], *'la Crisi'* was the big elephant in the room that nobody wants to talk about. We suffered but we did not talk. Why? We did not want to publicly admit the problem. We did not want to talk because we did not want to lose face in front of the other goldsmiths. It was surreal. In those months, none of us was selling, but we continued to produce just to protect our face. It was a sort of taboo... When the first firms started closing and the situation of the market was not improving, we timidly began speaking..."

In spite of this reluctance and silence, the word *'crisi'* started circulating among the goldsmith community to define the market situation, the difficulties of selling in Italy as well as abroad, and being paid on time. However, the use of the word was mainly limited to informal discussion. When directly asked in public, goldsmiths, both firm-owners and workers, instead tended to minimise the situation. The market downturn and more specifically its effects on the locale were described as a temporary phase, a *'molla'* in the local dialect. However, *'molla'* [slackening] is a technical word in goldsmithing jargon (Chapter 2). It refers to a normal market cycle during which a market contraction, the *'molla'*, is followed by a period of expansion, the *'bonna'* [good times]. In other words *'molla'* involves *'bonna'*, describing a cycle that continues without interruption. Hence this terminology implies a fundamental security and does not refer to an extraordinary transformation, a radical change in the market that requires profound adjustments in the local industry. To portray this exceptional event Valenzani as well as the press had used another word: *'crisi'*. By examining historical accounts and local newspapers, it appears that, in the 20th century, *'crisi'* was used only a few times (e.g. Rubino, 1992; Bottino, 1984), and always to describe moments of extreme weakness in specific sectors of the local economy. In particular, *'crisi'* was linked to the irreversible decline of the footwear industry.

Valenza's footwear industry was mainly specialised in medium quality products for the internal market, as seen in the introduction. It was a flourishing trade and the prime industry in the city until the 1950s, when it declined due to competition from new contenders, such as the Marche firms (Blim, 1990). During the 1960s, the industry began its *'crisi'*: a rapid decline that, in less than ten years, caused a milieu of over 200 firms to shrink into a handful of medium-small workshops that survived until the 1990s (Maggiora, 2010, Penna Ivaldi, 2008).

Fifty years after the demise of the footwear industry, the word *'crisi'* is still permeated by a sense of fatalism, and generally describes a turning point leading to a negative period, the duration of which is as unpredictable as the final effects on the locale.

In the early days of December 2008, the signs of the economic downturn appeared more and more clearly. In November, an initial group of large firms had started laying off their personnel: by the end of the year, about five hundred workers had been made redundant (Zemide, 2009a). Faced with these signs, the silence was infringed. The 19th December, for the first time, in a four-column interview in the *il Piccolo* newspaper (Zemide, 2008), the mayor of Valenza, Gianni Raselli, openly referred to the turn of events as '*la Crisi*'. After that article, '*la Crisi*' spread in the local discourse (see Chapter 8), and turned into the focus of the collective narration through which Valenza made sense of this change and the work of scholars documented it.

I have encountered this narration since my first day of fieldwork: the 21st of December 2008.

Encountering '*la Crisi*'

21st December: a few days to Christmas. Once again, I was back in Italy. This time it was for research: four weeks dedicated to the collection of data and redefining my research project. I had a place to stay in the outskirts of Valenza, in a rural village named Lu, about a fifteen minute drive from Valenza. After the 1960s, driven by the low price of houses, the short distance from Valenza and the beauty of the hilly, rural landscape, a number of Valenza goldsmiths moved into this community; there, some of them had also opened their workshops there and became deeply integrated into Valenza's industrial network (Benzi and Fugagnoli, 2004a). After three decades, Lu had become a Valenza residence neighbourhood and a production node within the jewellery network (Fontefrancesco, 2006a: 33-37).

On the evening of the first day of fieldwork, I decided to go to one of the village's two cafés to listen to some gossip and see if I was able to meet some of the goldsmiths to get some preliminary information about the current economic situation. The two establishments were located along the provincial road, a few yards from the village's main square. They faced each other: on one side of the road, Bar Nuovo, on the other Bar Sempione.

It was a frosty night and almost nobody stood outside the cafés. There was just one exception. In front of the main door of Bar Nuovo, Andrea was smoking a cigarette. About forty years old, short black hair and tanned skin, he was muffled up in a black padded jacket to protect himself from the bite of the cold nocturnal wind. Taking short drags on his cigarette, he was lost in thought. He was staring at the street absent-mindedly and did not notice me approaching him. Coming closer, I hailed him. In the past, I had played with him for years in Lu's football team. At that time I have been just a high school student, and he had already worked for twenty years in the jewellery trade as a goldsmith, and then for a few years as an entrepreneur after he and a couple of partners had opened a firm located in the very centre of Valenza in the late 2000s. After almost ten years, he was still running that enterprise.

My '*ciao*' recalled him from his thoughts. His frown relaxed a bit after seeing me. He engaged me in conversation, while he was finishing his Marlboro cigarette. Outside the Café, we chatted for a while before we ended up talking about my research and interest in the change in Valenza's jewellery trade. While I was explaining the topic of my work, my intention to study the changes of the jewellery industry, he again grew sullen. Then, with a stern voice, he observed that,

> "Michele, do you want to know what is happening to Valenza's jewellery industry? It is very easy. We are experiencing a terrible crisis. We are experiencing *'la Crisi'*. This global economic crisis is killing us. All these stories of derivatives and banks have become our crisis. It created a climate of complete insecurity that blocked all the selling abroad and in Italy. It has been two months since the market halted, and I am afraid that it will take time, a lot of time before everything will be back to normal. This is what is it happening."

Those few words, slowly delivered in an attempt to hold his anger and frustration, were my first encounter with what, after three years of fieldwork, appeared to have been the most common way of narrating the *'crisi'* of the jewellery industry, the negative economic transformation that occurred in the city.

Local authorities, jewellery entrepreneurs, artisans, retailers, civil servants and highschool students presented the crisis with the same plot, the same rhetorical mechanism that links the local, the present and future of a simple although well-known Piedmontese town, to the changes in the global, the international market. This account of the downturn aligned events that had happened and were happening in the city with facts occurring outside the community. If the nature of the globalised world can be described as a system of disconnected spatialities and temporalities, as proposed by Ferguson (2002), this narration concatenates realities into a precise mechanism that resulted in, using the metaphor suggested to me by one of my informants:

> "A tsunami that struck Valenza: a giant wave coming from outside that devastated our city."

In order to describe this devastation, they drew from their experience and the wealth of stories they had been told. They pointed out the shutting down of 'hundreds' of firms, or the precarisation of their jobs, the loss of profit; they listed the vicissitudes of friends or relatives who experienced the "bite of the crisis on [their] very skin", or talked about their direct experience of being fired, having to close a firm or seeing their positions being jeopardised by '*la Crisi*'. Although, in most cases, the crisis was not a quantified phenomenon in their accounts, it was explained through numbers and figures drawing from the quantitative research released in 2009.

'*La Crisi*' in figures

In fact, after that year, '*la Crisi*' became the subject of a small set of economic studies, well known among the goldsmiths I met irrespective of their level of education. In particular, Osservatorio Internazionale del Distretto Orafo di Valenza [Valenza District International Monitor Unit] was the principal institution involved in this research. The first academic account of this crisis is dated May 2009. During the conference *V+ 2009*, Paradiso (2009) proposed an initial analysis of this phenomenon, by pointing out the general downturn in demand for jewellery that characterised the main international markets from 2008 (Paradiso, 2009: 18) as a cause of Valenza's drop in exports, calculated to be -9% during 2008 (Paradiso, 2009: 6). From this drop followed the aforementioned increment of people enlisted in programs of temporary redundancy and who lost their jobs work.

In the course of the following months, new studies were released that further detailed the crisis from an econometric perspective. In the pages of the Osservatorio's newsletter, Gereffi et al. (2010:7), considered data concerning the year 2009, noticing the worsening of the crisis in the further reduction of exports (-30%). In the same months, the Intesa-San Paolo Banking Group Research team quantified Valenza's crisis as a general decrease of 31% of the city's entire turnover, the worst performance among all the Italian jewellery districts (Guelpa, 2010: 17). This research, however, also points out a general revival of the market in the second part of 2010, of over 30% with respect to the 2009 turnover (Guelpa, 2010: 17). The report seems to be optimistic about the future of the Italian trade, but does not explore in depth the actual case of the jewellery industry.

From a different perspective, in 2011, the Osservatorio Provinciale del Mercato del Lavoro [Job Market Provincial Monitor Unit], a research department of the Alessandria Provincial Council, published a new account of Valenza's crisis exploring the transformation of the local job market. It clearly appeared that as a consequence of the recession in the jewellery industry, the local job market experienced a plunge. From the study it emerges that in the course of 2009-2010 the number of unemployed persons in Valenza dramatically increased, reaching 1,854 people (OPML, 2011: 2) out of the about 20,100 inhabitants of Valenza at the end of 2010: 609 goldsmiths were definitively dismissed in 2009 (OPML, 2011: 15) and another 337 in 2010 (OPML, 2011: 13). In this respect, the downturn of the jewellery industry was indicated as contributing to the rise in Valenza's unemployment rate. This reached 9.2% in 2010: a percentage higher than the regional unemployment rate, stable at 8% over the past three years (UP, 2010: 3). This intensification, they point out, is linked to a change that occurred in the entrepreneurial milieu of the city: from 2008 to 2010, several hundred workshops[1] ceased their activities (OPML, 2011: 3-5).

These studies were known by my informants. University graduates as well as artisans with no highschool education referred to them in their speech, to enrich their accounts and endow their words with authoritativeness. Such use can be explained by considering that the studies had been presented and commented on in public meetings and conferences (e.g. the *V+* conference in May 2009) and in newspapers. So, even though an artisan might have not read the reports, they were informed about their contents, thus able to use them in their speech. In this way, the studies become part of the main narration. Together with the individuals' experience, they contribute to expanding, and giving better detail to its plot. A particular plot that subordinates local change to global transformation and places the epicentre of the local change in the financial crisis that between September and October 2008 brought the world's finance, and more broadly, economy, to what Attali (2009 [2008]: 8) defined as "the brink of catastrophe."

---

[1] Although the report does not give details about the precise size of this wave of closures, from the comparison of the annual census of Valenza jewellery firms *Valenza nei Marchi*, from 2008 – census of 2007 – to 2011 – census of 2010– (Bellini, 2008; 2009; 2010; 2011), it appears that one hundred hallmark-holding firms closed. This datum, however, does not account for the small workshops that worked as suppliers of other enterprises, generally carrying out only specific phases of the production.

Connecting the global to the local: the armillary sphere

The history of the Credit Crunch, *per se*, concerns gold and jewellery very little. Instead, it is a history of the growth of two speculative bubbles – derivatives and the real estate market – and their bursting. Tett (2009a) offered a detailed socioeconomic account of this history, portraying the growth of the bubbles through the 1990s and 2000s, their merging through the invention of sub-prime mortgage derivatives, the cracking of these markets in 2006 and 2007, and their final burst in autumn 2008, with the default of international banks, such as Lehman Bros., and investment groups, such as AIG. Between September and October 2008 about US $40 trillion was lost (Robbins, 2009: 11). State interventions were able to prevent the banking system from experiencing a complete meltdown. However, the effects of the financial crisis rapidly propagated beyond the borders of the financial and real estate markets, as the New York Times recently summarised:

> "While financial Armageddon was avoided, the crisis spread around the globe, toppling banks across Europe and driving countries from Iceland to Pakistan to seek emergency aid from the International Monetary Fund. A vicious circle of tightening credit, reduced demand and rapid job cuts took hold, and the world fell into recession." (New York Times, 2011)

Since 2008, a vast body of literature has been written about the effects of the Credit Crunch, and the effect of this financial crisis on the stock exchange and goods markets. In particular, it has been noted that, after autumn 2008, there was a reduction in general (goods) consumption, in the USA (e.g. Lee et al., 2010) as well as in Europe (e.g. Gros and Alcidi, 2010). This recession appears to have also undermined international jewellery markets (for a precise analysis of European performances see: Searce, 2009; a quantitative analysis of the USA market is provided in: Gereffi et al., 2010) and consequentially Valenza (Gereffi et al., 2010; Paradiso, 2009).

This understanding, which is part of Valenzani's own narrative as the "tsunami" metaphor shows, connects the local to the global, through a series of mechanical effects, and transforms the local crisis into a cascade effect of the global downturn, a dramatic adjustment to a change in consumption. The city's downturn appears as the result of a chain of events originating elsewhere, above the level of the community. Its epicentre was within the sphere of finance, and it propagated out, reaching the jewellery trade, and then Valenza and its industry. Thus, the very description of the crisis, the manifestation and causation of the local downturn sheds light on a concentric conception of the world economy that is centred on the micro-level of the single firm and developed in expanding layers: the local industry of Valenza, the international jewellery trade, global finance: a conception strikingly similar to the theorisation of global economy recently proposed by Gudeman (2010).

In 2010, in his analysis of the world economy in the light of the Credit Crunch, Gudeman proposed a descriptive interpretative model based on the current integrated relationship between finance and other sectors of the economy. Starting from the heuristic model that he initially proposed in *Conversations in Columbia (*1990), and then revisited and expanded over the course of his career (e.g. Gudeman, 2001; 2005; 2008), he recently interpreted the modern economy as the integration of five, different value spheres:

> "Economists may see economies as flat or smooth plains consisting of markets and market-like behaviour that lead to equilibrium situations, but I think they consist of overlapping and conflicting spheres of value and practices that include markets. I label these fuzzy-edged spaces House, Community, Commerce, Finance, and Finance of Finance or Meta-Finance. The domains are separate but mingle; individuals and cultures emphasize them differently; their relative prominence changes over time; and they represent competing interests and perspectives. These five domains, in order, enjoy increasing reach in physical and social space and in the inclusiveness of material activities, services and institutions. They are increasingly abstracted from the material economy of everyday life, and increasingly liquid: the speed and number of transactions multiply in the upper spheres of finance and meta-finance. This liquidity and ability to shift financial resources and insert them in different parts of the economy gives the upper spheres greater control of the economy and opportunities for sequestering value from elsewhere. For example, liquid resources can quickly flow to situations of arbitrage, closing pricing gaps before others, and can (with risk) underwrite commercial innovations." (Gudeman 2010: 4)

In contrast to the concept of the sphere of exchange introduced by Bohannan (1955) and revised by Douglas and Isherwood (1979), the definition of spheres of value differs in terms of the variety of arenas of exchanges, a higher level of abstraction, a wider geographical extent, difference in the principles underpinning the exchanges and a diversity in the substance of the exchanged objects. However, as it was in the 'spheres of exchangeable goods' of the Tivs (Bohannan, 1955: 53), the spheres of value are hierarchised by the different values given to the exchanged goods and by the capacity of the exchanges occurring in higher spheres to impact, 'cascade' down to, other spheres, affecting their exchanges and the very possibility of exchange. The world economy takes on the appearance of the movements of the spheres of an armillary sphere[2].

Without doubt, the idealisation proposed by Gudeman has the merit of embracing the world economy in a unified and integrated system. However, this model tends to result in an essentialisation of the global and local economy into a sort of global clockwork. Moreover, Gudeman's model presents another problematic aspect in its implicit subordination of local culture and the lives of individuals to the global economy and a dehumanised market dynamic, in spite of the theorised self-reliance of household and community (Gudeman, 2001, 2005). This subordination is a key that has been used by the anthropologist to explain the social changes that the Credit Crunch produces on local areas. The crisis did indeed have an important, indirect effect. It exposed the network of implication that links industry to finance, politics and (local) culture. It also brought about the scenario of the redefinition of many local, cultural paradigms, such as local identity. In particular, the case of the Icelandic default demonstrated how a global downturn can have direct repercussions on local economies and societies. As explained by Loftsdóttir (2010), the global crisis that brought the Nordic countries to bankruptcy was the agent of a reshaping of collective identity through a communal shift in meaning of public symbols, such as the image of the Viking, and the trigger of a political debate about the future of the community. The Icelandic case appears to follow Gudeman's model of a cascade effect from the meta-finance level down to the community sphere. However, what it also demonstrates is the ability of a population to embrace different kinds of economies, and rethink their modes of participation in the markets (Loftsdóttir, 2010: 12-13). In other words, it shows the existence and relevance of a reversed cascade effect, that is, the possibility for a local community to affect 'higher' spheres. This is not clearly acknowledged in Gudeman's account. However, since Hertz' (1998) work on the Shanghai stock exchange, the anthropology of finance has demonstrated the interdependence between local culture and global finance (Maurer, 2005). In Gudeman's work, this

---

[2] The armillary sphere is a medieval astrological tool based on a geocentric universe. The theoretical model of this tool lies on the essentialisation of the universe in concentric spheres, the heavens. A physical representation of this model, the armillary sphere consisted of different concentric, mobile bands – the heavens – that surround a fixed sphere, the earth. It was used to predict the movements of the heavens for the formulations of horoscopes. The armillary sphere is here taken as a metaphor for a system of thought in which human actions are seen as dependent on the movement of higher, essentialised, almost abstract, entities that dominate humans' life and future.

lack, or at least the lack of a clear statement of its existence risks perpetrating a world view that marginalises the role of individuals, implicitly depicting them as victims of the economic system rather than its players (a thesis which was particularly stressed in less recent works, such as: Gudeman, 2001, Gudeman and Rivera, 1990), and dis-empowering individual agency, delocalising agency outside the community into 'higher' spheres. In other words, by interrogating the world through this model, a researcher may end up with a linear account in which individual history is subsumed by a plot of dependency and submission to global, financial markets. However, the acknowledgment of the actual active role played by individuals and communities in their everyday participation in the economy – even with unintentional and indirect actions, such as opening a line of credit with a bank (Langley, 2008) – challenges the very hierarchisation of the sphere. It ushers in a conception of the economy as a flat multiplicity (Deleuze and Guattari, 1987: 9) in which different markets, different regimes of value and practices of exchange coexist and collaborate through a model that is not a linear cascade effect, as suggested by Gudeman, but rather a non-linear permutation (De Landa, 2006: 9).

Despite these limits, Gudeman's analysis presents fundamental similarities with the understating of global economy conveyed by the main history of Valenzani. These similarities make Gudeman's theory an important ethnographic resource for understanding how Valenzani think about the economy and negotiate their place in it.

Considering closely the Valenza conception, we notice that it, like Gudeman's, describes the world economy as, a concatenation of essentialised objects that "attributes [the aspect of] an unchanging, primordial ontology to what are historically contingent products of human or other forms of agency" (Herzfeld, 2010: 235) In other words, the economy appears as an immanent, metaphysical machine in which local producers appear as subjects of its dehumanised running, rather than its actors and motors. Thus, this interpretation of the economy ushers in a particular anthropological understanding of the locale. Local goldsmiths are victims of global transformations; innocent subjects who have to cope with the sudden downturn of the markets and the (consequential) change in consumers' attitudes, finding themselves unable to face these changes. Thus, through this hierarchisation, the narration of the city leads to the victimisation of the innocent locale. In fact, if the crisis is represented as a sort of accident for which the community does not, and cannot have any responsibility, then the artisans emerge as innocent victims of chance.

This mode of understanding reflects a particular kind of feeling that goldsmiths showed when thinking and talking about the downturn. It portrays the sense of powerlessness that erupted in the everyday life of artisans and entrepreneurs, cracking the mask of self-reliance, boldness and swiftness that goldsmiths used with customers, tourists and, more generally, non-goldsmiths, when they talked about the change that was occurring in the city. In the conversations in front of cafés, or speaking in an office on a working day, or, sharing Sunday lunch, this narration, as an 'ordinary affect' (cf. Stewart, 2007: 4), traces a network of powerlessness, and describes a common way of perceiving the downturn as an epochal change from which no possible escape is given to the individual.

If the particular vision of the world economy portrayed by the narration subordinates the local to the global, the agency and, consequentially, any responsibility over the change are not attributed to local actors. Thus, the peripheralisation of the local guarantees the innocence of a community. On the basis of this innocence, through and within the narration, the community re-negotiates its position in the world. It becomes the transformative object able to turn shuttered firms and lost positions into objects similar to the imperial debris described by Stoler: the residue of a past on which people draw "to make claims on [the] future" (Stoler, 2008: 202). All these claims shared the idea of the substantive innocence of the goldsmith community in relation to this change, often compared to a natural disaster by my informants; by virtue of this innocence, they were believing in the duty of the State to bring succour to a community in need. On the individual level, this process shows a system of hope in the ability of public bodies to intervene and relieve the situation of need and uncertainty. On the collective level, it becomes the rhetoric underpinning a number of initiatives promoted after 2008 by local professional associations and spontaneous groups of artisans. These initiatives campaigned for public intervention to support Valenza and the jewellery business through the creation of exceptional funds for firms in financial difficulties or special social cushions for temporary redundancy (e.g. Comune di Valenza, 2009a).

Non-linearizing history

Through this narration the need for understanding the change is answered. In so doing, the world is explained, and an ideal emotional place, in which the goldsmith community is located, is created. It is an imperfect answer, unable to respond to questions such as why Valenza suffered from the downturn more than other Italian centres, but good enough to generate an ethical and an affective key for a community to read the change of its city.

A history, a narration about the past, is produced, and in so doing, information is selected and organised. Elements considered significant are included, while those considered insignificant are expunged. In Strathern's words (1996), it is a "cut in the network" of memory through which some elements end up being remembered and others forgotten. The tension between memory and oblivion that was clearly theorised by Ricoeur (2000: 108-10) is manifested. The complexity of the becoming of the world is reduced to an understandable, to some extent comfortable, narration, but in so doing, something is left out of the account; something is forgotten, left at the margins of attention. Although this selection can happen on an unconscious level, this does not exempt us from questioning this process. Following Foucault's challenge (2003), in our efforts to understand a social transformation, such as Valenza's crisis, and a cultural process, such as the way of understanding the crisis, we are pushed to investigate what has been remembered and what has fallen into oblivion.

In the following paragraphs I will pursue this heuristic imperative by presenting two 'alternative narratives' that interweave with the chain of events portrayed by the main one: the history of the change in jewellery consumption and the history of the difficult approach to 'globalisation' that Valenza firms have had since the late 1990s. I choose these two narratives because they are known to Valenza goldsmiths, who sometimes recall them when thinking about their work. However, although narrated, these other historical accounts are generally not related to the 'key narrative' of the crisis. They are kept apart, isolated, as if they were somehow an extraneous chain of events unrelated to the present economic and social conditions of the city. In this case, however, I want to show the interconnection between these different lines of events, and in this perspective, recuperate the non-linearity of the crisis.

"Therefore I decided on a travel package...": A change in consumption

It was the 25th April 2009. In front of the Giovanni Pascoli Primary School, the City Council had organised a public concert to celebrate Liberation Day. It was a hot day, and many people came to attend the free show. A few dozen people were sat in front of the stage, in the chairs provided by the municipality, but most were lying on the grass of the park in front of the school, in the shade of horse chestnut trees. I was sat with Alfonso, a fifty-year-old artisan. He was the eldest son of a Sicilian couple who migrated to Valenza in the 1950s, when he was just a child. He grew up in Valenza, and had barely any memories of his Sicilian youth. After middle school, he began working as a goldsmith. In the late 1990s he opened a workshop with some friends. The workshop was still active, but they were struggling to maintain it. Thus, after almost forty years of work, he was dreaming of the day he would turn sixty, so that he could retire. He was joking about this hidden desire, but, he was arguing that the business had become increasingly difficult in the past few years:

> "You know, it is always more difficult. It is not just this damned crisis... It is something else. It is just that people seem to no longer be interested in jewellery. It is not a recent phenomenon. It started a long time ago. People started preferring other stuff for their girlfriends and holidays. Sometimes cheaper stuff, many times just other stuff... I don't know... I don't know... And the increasing cost of gold is not helping us... Not at all... The cost of even the simplest gold trifle quadrupled in the past ten years!"

Alfredo continued to tell me about this change for a few more minutes, before he was called by other friends of his and had to leave the party. He remembered when he was young, back in the 1970s and 1980s, and everybody was used to giving jewellery for any mundane event, while "nowadays... No more, no more."

His rosy memories are maybe not the most accurate historic sources, but it occurred other times during my fieldwork that people, not just goldsmiths, showed me a change in what are referred to as, in economic jargon, patterns of jewellery consumption. However, this is a change that has been also noticed by scholars observing trends in luxury markets.

Studying the worldwide trend of this market, Fox (2009: 2-5) has noticed that it experienced a constant growth during the 2000s, in spite of economic and political crises. However, if we look into the data, we notice that different products performed in different ways. In particular, the jewellery market shrank (Gereffi et al., 2010: 2-3): it is significant to notice, for example, that the quantity of gold manufactured per year from 2000 dropped by 45% during the decade (Gereffi et al., 2010: 2 based on World Gold Council's data). In relation to Western markets, Carcano (2007a) has proposed to see this downturn as a result of a diversification of consumption that had led consumers to prefer other luxury goods, such as food and holidays, to traditional prestige products, following a trajectory arguably caused by the advent, in the late 20th century, of a new morality of consumption more interested in the physical and mental welfare, as theorised by Hilton (2004: 118). Although Carcano offers an interesting theoretical outline of a change, it gives little account of the actual changes in consumption practices, that is, the role that jewellery plays in society.

Anthropologists have pointed out that jewellery embodies well the model of luxury goods proposed by Appadurai (1986: 38): objects whose sources of value are scarcity and superior aesthetic features. In particular, in the modern world, it can play an important role in creating parental ties and maintaining gender relations, as shown by Chan (2006), as well as cohesion within the family network, as explained by Donati (2000). In particular, it is a fundamental part of gift-giving practices during courtship, generally by the man to the woman, to strengthen the link between partners, and among the members of a family and its close friends to celebrate particular occasions, such as the completion of some social rite of passage (e.g. marriage, the completion of a University degree, and the birth of a child). The high price and the (relative) difficulty in procuring these items mean they are considered an 'important' gift, a prestigious gift. In these instances, the gift-giving seems to carry out two, distinct functions. On one hand, through gift-giving, the jewellery is transformed into an 'evocative object' (cf. Turkle, 2007) for the receiver, since, as Mauss (1967 [1925]) noticed, the gift links the object to the person and to the situation of the gift. Thus, it becomes a device able to remind the receiver of an event, the giver, and more broadly a social network. On the other hand, this practice of gift-giving can also be seen as a practice of wealth redistribution within a network, the enlarged kin-network, aimed at reinforcing the links between its different members. These practices that I noticed during my fieldwork appear to occur in most Western countries, where they are some of the principal reasons behind the purchase of jewellery (Carcano, 2007a). However, these practices are changing. Following Miller (2012: 56-57) jewellery consumption still maintains a dialectical nature, but the very social meaning of jewellery is changing. Although my fieldwork was not primarily focused on jewellery consumption, during my research I had the chance to collect experiences that can illuminate this change. Thus, I would like to present three short 'tales of the field' (cf. Van Maanen, 1988) and from them infer some possible conclusions about the change in the social life of jewellery that may have affected Valenza's industry.

The first tale takes place in the living room of a flat on the outskirts of Alessandria, 15 km from Valenza. Alessandro is a goldsmithing firm's clerk in his thirties. He is the son of a family of Valenza goldsmiths who has decided not to continue in the family business. In 2008, he left Valenza and moved to Alessandria to live with his girlfriend. In March

2009, it was their fifth anniversary. Hence, he decided to spend some money to give a 'decent' present to his partner.

> "I spent some time before deciding what to give her. My father is in the jewellery business, and it would have been quite easy for me to find a ring or any other good piece of jewellery and get a good price. I know that my father, when he was young, may have given my mother a ring or something like that. However, I think a piece of jewellery would not have been a good idea... It's not because it is a 'banal' choice. That's not the point. I wanted to give her something unique... Something that we could share to some extent... A gift that could create an unforgettable moment in our lives... Therefore I decided on a travel package, a week in Portugal..."

The second tale is located in a similarly domestic setting, in the country house of a Milanese family, located on the hills surrounding Valenza. Lucia is 45. She is an executive manager in a private bank in Milan, the same bank in which she was employed in the mid-1990s after university. She has a ten years old son who received his first communion, in May 2007.

> "Well, I am not really religious, but the first communion is still an important holiday for my family. When I did mine, almost forty years ago, all my relatives gave me some piece of jewellery. They were presented that had to last a long time. I remember, I received a beautiful small medal I wore for almost twenty years... Well, when I had to choose the present for my son I preferred to stick to tradition, but many of our relatives opted for technological stuff: some video games, and a mobile phone... They explained their decision to me saying they found it more appropriate to give him something he can use... Something more 'practical'..."

The last episode, finally, occurs in a park in the centre of Valenza. Marco is a young man of 25. He was born in a village twenty kilometres north of Alessandria, not far from Valenza. After completing his secondary school studies in Valenza, he moved to Milan where he completed, in June 2009, his Bachelor Degree in Political Science. After some months being unemployed, in October, he found a job as an accountant in a supermarket in Milan. He wanted to celebrate this event with his girlfriend, a couple years younger than him, and still a university student.

> "I didn't have much money in my pocket, but I really wanted to celebrate this contract. I wanted to do something special. Ok, first of all a dinner in a good restaurant... Then... Well, first of all I thought of a ring she liked... It was a simple ring...Not the big stuff I was used to seeing in Valenza... But when I saw the price... Damn... I opted for a weekend in a small village on

> the Liguria coast. There were not many people. It was sunny and warm. We were happy, and I saved at least one hundred Euros..."

These three episodes are paradigmatic fragments of a research experience that, against the everyday intense work of the goldsmiths, noted a slow reduction and disappearance of jewellery consumption in the context of practices of gift-giving. While the memory of such customs was still living in the informants' minds, such as with Lucia, these practices have been eroded and substituted by the use of new, other objects, such as holiday packages, in the case of Alessandro, and electronic devices, as in the case of Lucia. In the light of Parry and Block's (1989: 23-24) theory of value, we could conclude that jewellery consumption is being replaced by that of goods that better fit the individuals' needs of the short-term transactional order, while risking being unable to answer to those of the long-term cycle, which are the reproductive (in a broad sense) needs of the society, in this case the relational network, in which the exchange is embedded. While we may connect this change to the inability of Western societies of thinking and caring about their future, as proposed by Connerton (2009) in his gloomy account about Modernity and its effects, one of the explanations I was given for this change entirely relates to the economic issue of price, as in the case of Alfonso and Marco.

In the last decade, the price of noble metals and gems boomed. For example, the prices of silver, passing from 4.8 £/Oz. in 2001 to 16.5 in 2010, and gold, from 270 £/Oz. in 2001 to 1,200 in 2010, have quadrupled, while platinum increased from 610 £/Oz. in 2001 to 1,500 £/Oz. in 2010 (www.kitco.com). While this increase has been explained as a response by investors to the extreme fluctuations of the stock-exchange in the last decade (GWC, 2011: 5-9), this boom affected the price of jewellery made from these materials, as with the jewellery of Valenza, as remembered by Alfonso. This increase caused the rise of jewellery prices to a level that would have become too expensive for a large proportion of the public. Although somehow sensible, this explanation leads to a further reflection.

In the late 1990s, Kemp (1998) demonstrated that the social prestige of a luxury good is positively reinforced by the increase in price. Reconsidering Kemp's theory, in light of the ethnographic evidence and the drop in demand following the rise of jewellery prices, we may be led to argue that something decreased the value of this class of products. In other words, reading the change through Graeber's (2001: 47) theory of value, jewellery seems to have lost (part of) its symbolic power to represent social relations in Western society, such as social prestige, wealth, affection, etc. This cultural change may explain why, after the rise in the price of precious materials, people began to prefer other goods, and, on those occasions when they had to buy jewellery, they opted for cheaper productions, such as jewellery made in extra-European countries, e.g. China, India, Turkey and Thailand, or costume jewellery made with non-noble alloys (e.g. CPI, 2009). This diversification in consumption ended up penalizing the Italian, hence Valenza, industry and resulted in its market quota being eroded by Asian contenders, as was indicated recently by Gereffi (2010: 2-4). Moreover, an explanation rooted in the analysis of consumption may offer elements to answer the question left unsolved by the 'key narrative' of the crisis: the question of why, during the period 2008-2010, it was Valenza, the only Italian centre almost exclusively specialised in high-quality and high-price jewellery making, that most suffered from the downturn (Guelpa, 2010: 17).

A golden age and its decline

There is another 'alternative narrative' that often recurred in conversations with Valenzani. Echoing a broader national debate about the decline of Italian small and medium enterprises during the 2000s (e.g. Di Quirico, 2010; Colli, 2010; Rabellotti et al., 2009; Festa and Sapelli, 2009), my informants depicted '*la Crisi*' as the last dramatic episode of the decline of Valenza's jewellery industry, and its model of entrepreneurship based on small firms, after its golden age in the 1980s and 1990s. In so doing they pointed out the inability of local entrepreneurs, during the heydays of the jewellery industry, of developing the knowledge and tools necessary to compete and thrive in an international market that has grown more and more competitive since the 1990s.

Valenza's industry met with an overall steady growth throughout the 20th century, reaching the maximum peak between the 1980s and 1990s (Maggiora, 2010: 343-66). This period, which in the entire country represented the golden age of a particular form of industrialism based on milieus of small and medium export-oriented firms (e.g. Nesi, 2010: 26-27; Festa and Sapelli, 2009), is described as a particular context of abundance and easiness for the local businesses (Nesi, 2010: 26-27; Blim, 1990; Yanagisako, 2002; Ghezzi, 2007; Gaggio, 2007: 249-265; see also: Bosco, 2004); a period that I want to describe through the words of one of my informants, Claudio.

Claudio was a goldsmith and modeller in his fifties. He was born in Alessandria, but, pushed by his family, he started working as an apprentice in Valenza in the late 1970s. First of all, he worked as an employed artisan; he mastered the goldsmith's craft and, in the mid-1980s, opened a small workshop with four employees whose productions were mostly sold on the national market. In the mid-2000s he closed the workshop, and nowadays he is working as a freelancer modeller for many different firms.

I met him many times during my fieldwork, since he is the father of one of my schoolmates and friends. One night in March 2010, after I came to his place, actually looking for his son (only to discover that he was not in the city), in his kitchen and over of a bottle of Barbera wine, a seasoned sausage and a loaf of bread, he decided, for the first time after almost ten years of mutual acquaintance, to talk with me about his life and professional experience. With his biography and experience, Claudio is a representative figure of the Valenza milieu and the hundreds of small entrepreneurs who lived through the history of the last forty years in the city. Above all, he was one of the most passionate, and at the same time clear tellers of this story of success and downfall, that started with a golden age of prosperity:

> "It did not matter how much of a 'dog' [unskilled] you were with the [job's] tools, there was always work for everybody. If someone was a bit good in his work, he could make millions every month with his [regular] work, some overtime and a bit of [informal] work at home. With the money I made with the firm in those years, I bought my house, a house in the Alps, another in Liguria, on the coast. I was used to changing my motorcycle every year and the car every two or three... They were good times... Very good times."

Thus, Valenza entrepreneurs, as Claudio described them, shared a common characteristic with those of San Lorenzo. Most jewellery entrepreneurs, like their Marche counterparts, tended to invest their firms' profits outside the firm, gambling on the stock exchange or buying real estate and leisure goods; only a few entrepreneurs reinvested at least some of their profits to develop a marketing network, buy new technologies and equipment, or expand the firm itself. While Blim (1990: 194-6) explained this tendency through the entrepreneurs' desire to improve their standards of life and show off their achieved status, Claudio pointed out another fundamental reason that we should take into account:

> "In truth, nobody was reinvesting [the profits in their business], but I have a question for you, lad. Why should we have had to? There were plenty of jobs at that time. There was even too much to do. Why should we have had to look for other work? Now I can see the shortsightedness of that choice, but at that time, who could have said that the prosperity was going to end?"

The success – arguably over-success – that these firms knew actually became a deterrent against investment and research. Basic economic considerations, not just the desire to show off the attainment of a new economic status, led to the diversion of capital away from firms and towards other fields of investment or expenditure. Thus, this over-success, while it was at the heart of a rise in the standards of living of the Valenza population, also inevitably stiffened the economic dynamism and entrepreneurial potentialities of the district, making it unprepared for a potential worsening of market conditions, as observed by Benzi (2004a).

However, the prosperity eventually ended in the 2000s. The main reason entrepreneurs gave for this was the shift in the Italian government's commercial and monetary policy.

During its 10th legislature (1987-1992), the Italian parliament launched policies aimed at liberalising the national market after almost fifty years of political actions supporting national production against international competition. Some important steps of this process were the signing of the *Convention Implementing the Schengen Agreement*, in November 1990, concerning the free transit of goods and people in and across the borders of the member countries (since 1997, all the European Union members, plus Norway and Iceland), and the participation in the adoption of the Euro currency, in December 1995. These choices marked a turn in Italian economic history. They marked the end of that protected micro-cosmos that had been Italy in the past decades, and forced national industry to face the challenge of a globalised market and an international competition without those securities that had guaranteed Italian production a competitive advantage against other countries' productions: a severe industrial protection aiming to help, almost force, consumption of national products in Italy, and a periodical devaluation of the currency that guaranteed further marketability to Italian products in large international markets such as the USA or Germany.

This protectionist political framework had also supported Valenza's jewellery trade and helped its boom, by almost closing the Italian market to foreign productions, and offering a commercial advantage to its products in international markets thanks to the low value of the national currency. Thus, in Italy as well as abroad, Valenza's industries were able to dominate the haute and medium jewellery markets, although my informants, as well as scholars who wrote extensively about the city, such as Lenti (1994; 2010), Gaggio (2007) and Paradiso (2008a; 2008b; 2008c) tended to identify Valenza only with high-quality productions. However, it is important to remember that a large proportion of firms thrived on medium-quality, un-branded jewellery, such as wedding rings, trilogy rings and tennis bracelets, that were economically aimed at a middle-class market and intended for everyday use. The quality of their manufacture and, most importantly, their low price due to the low value of Italian currency were at the basis of the success of these Valenza products in markets such as the USA and Germany.

Until the 1990s, this market flourished so well that a large number of Valenza firms did not find it necessary to invest in a marketing strategy to create recognizable brands or to further expand their commercial system by exploring new markets or enlarging their commercial networks in previously-explored ones: only a handful of enterprises, generally large-scale ones, such as Damiani (www.damiani.it) or Pasquale Bruni (www.pasqualebruni.it), moved in this direction. However, since the late 1990s, new contenders have emerged in the international market. Asian countries, such as China, India, Thailand and Turkey, became international players on the jewellery market and eroded the quotas of Italian exports (Carcano, 2007b) and, thus, Valenza's. In particular, they colonised the market of un-branded, low- and medium-price products, by offering cheaper products than the Italian ones, as Carcano (2007a: 45-51) highlighted.

Over the course of the 2000s, Valenza lost market shares against international competition. In those years, the performance of Valenza entrepreneurs was further undermined by a series of events that affected demand across the entire world and, in particular, in specific important markets, such as the USA's after the dot-com bubble's bursting in 2000 and the 9/11 terrorist attacks, the United Arab Emirates' after the 9/11 attacks and invasion of Iraq in 2003, and Hong Kong and Singapore's after the SARS epidemic in 2003 (Paradiso, 2007; Gereffi et al., 2008: 2).

These changes and difficulties triggered a local transformation. After fifty years of constant growth of turnover and number of firms, in the last ten years the number of enterprises and the number of people employed in the trade decreased. Maggiora (2010: 529), in his history of Valenza, roughly calculated a constant regression of the industry, expressed by the decrease in firm population by over 300 enterprises and the loss of over 2,000 jobs during the 2000s. Unfortunately, his calculations are not accurate. However, they describe a scenario of a long recession, the same landscape described by Claudio, which contrasts and completes the account of the 'key narrative' of the present crisis.

Over the course of the second half of the 2000s, AOV, together with other institutions, launched long-term programs to make up for some of the fragilities of the local milieu, such as the lack of brand strategies. They invested in building a new exhibition centre to host the annual international jewellery exhibition, *Valenza Gioielli*, and other events concerning the jewellery industry, and created a collective brand for Valenza firms to promote their productions: the new exhibition centre, Expo Piemonte, was inaugurated in 2009; in the same year, the collective brand gained widespread use in 2009 (Fontefrancesco, 2012). Thus, at the turn of the decade, it is difficult to foresee the actual effect of these initiatives. In particular, it was difficult to imagine for a goldsmith in his fifties, who, one evening in March, concluded:

> "My dear lad, the last two years were horrible. It is true. But I have seen, during an entire decade, our city [industry] becoming thinner and thinner. The fat cows ended long ago, and even our fat was gone, really, before this last, harsh crisis started. However, if this crisis is so hard, if you want to understand this crisis, you must not forget the past decades and what happened then. As for the present and the future, God knows what's going on."

A Non-linear history

Claudio, Alfredo, Alessandro, Lucia and Marco, with their words and experience, contribute to make new stories emerge: 'alternative narratives', new assemblies of events that intersect, expand, and redirect the 'key narrative' of the crisis. The existence of these stories and many others that I encountered in the field is not taken here as a disproof of the main one, as an antithesis in a dialectical process. Rather, it is considered as a fundamental element to go beyond the traditional heuristic process that compares different accounts and points of view, seeking the ultimate (unspoken) truth in an essentialist process that ends up fabricating it. In order to avoid essentialism, thus, we are brought to embrace the multitude of truths and consider the semantic space these narratives describe. Our interest is not in negating this or that history, but to study their assembly, contradictions and mutual interactions in their description of worlds, people, objects and actions.

Following this reasoning, we can go back to our 'alternative narratives'. Both of them introduce into the discussion new protagonists, new economic and cultural transformations, in order to make sense of and deal with the world. They throw into discussion their global-local conceptualisation that underpins the 'key narrative', and relocate agency among different actors.

On the one hand, the history of the change of consumption that Alessandro, Lucia and Marco helped to narrate translates the armillary sphere of the 'key narrative' into what may be referred to as, in Deleuze and Guattari's (1987: 9) terms, a flat geography of individuals who, through their actions, affect other individuals, describing relational and economic networks. They create a (transnational) assembly that in its flatness makes the distinction between local and global lose meaning and evocative effectiveness. Within this assembly, moreover, the agency itself is redistributed to its very constituents who, with their actions, affect and are affected by the market.

On the other hand, while the world represented in this history of a golden age and its decline is dichotomised between the local sphere of the city, and a global sphere of the market, there is also a recognisable tension between these two spheres that is not just ascribable to a relationship of dominance of one over the other. It is a dialogical relationship in which, at the end of the day, the locale is the artificer of its own future. Consequently, we see that in the 'alternative narrative', the agency is often granted to Valenza entrepreneurs, and more broadly, to the local sphere, while the 'key narrative' negated it.

These narrations, thus, are emblematic of different ways of interpreting the world and the role that an individual and a community have in living and acting. These are parallel, competing paradigms that coexist in the living fabric of Valenza. The aim of this chapter has been to describe the emic understanding of the causes of the city economic crisis. In so doing, facing the multiplicity of narratives that occurs in Valenza, I did not aim at bringing it to a synthesis, writing a new 'meta-narrative'. Instead, it is crucial to disclose their coexistence, interactions, reinforcement and contradictions, since this is the semantic complexity that the concept of '*la Crisi*' evokes, within which Valenzani define their agency, and more broadly their place in the world.

In our case, the non-linearisation of the history of the downturn sheds light on the actual consistency of the sense of innocence identified by the 'key narrative'. The main narration seems to offer some shelter or relief from the severity of the situation, by relieving goldsmiths of responsibility; however, the narration of the end of the golden age goes exactly in the opposite direction, pointing out their responsibility deriving from entrepreneurial choices. The dialectics between the agency and patiency are unsolved in goldsmiths' everyday lives and when referring to themselves. In their testimonies, the two narrations are interwoven, often juxtaposed in sentences that sound like:

> "This crisis is not our fault, not at all, but… but we never really thought that something like that might happen and we did not prepare for the occurrence."[3]

From these words and many other similar expressions, goldsmiths extract a way of feeling far from being pacified in their resignation to impotence. The juxtaposition creates space for individual and collective uncertainty: a way of feeling suspended between guilt and innocence, between agency and impotence.

At the same time, the 'alternative narratives' also show different ways of understanding the global and the local, the validity of these categories, and the way in which people interact. From their accounts emerge a multitude of ways of understanding that co-occur in the city discourse: a difference that indicates a complexity in ways of understanding the economy and society that goes far beyond the rigid borders of a theory *à la* Gudeman such as the one that underpins the 'key narrative'.

Despites these divergences, the 'alternative narratives', their existence and the very possibility of existence do not negate the narration of the 'key narrative', rather, they enlarge its scope to include silenced elements. 'Key narrative' and 'alternative narratives' are part of the same dialogical process that is (at least potentially) able to describe social reality in its complexity. Thus, if we think of the various histories as lines, we can see Valenza's downturn, and more broadly any historic event, as a device, in Deleuzian terms. According to the French philosopher, a device is, in fact:

> "A tangle, a multi-linear ensemble. It is composed of different sorts of lines. And these lines do not frame systems that would be homogeneous as such (e.g., the object, the subject, the language). Instead, they follow directions, they trace processes that are always at disequilibrium, sometimes coming close to each other and sometimes getting distant from each other. Each line is broken, is subjected to variations in direction, bifurcating and splitting, subjected to derivations." (Deleuze, 1989: 185)

To accept history as a tangle of lines is to move a step towards a non-linear conception of the past. This conception goes in the direction of enriching the understanding of society and its transformation by showing social becoming as a process based on a multitude of causalities and on which are based a multiplicity of possible epistemologies. In this perspective, we can reconsider the case of Valenza and see how these lines

[3] From an interview that took place in June 2009. The informant is a forty-year-old gem-setter, formerly owner of an individual enterprise, which eventually closed in the December of the same year.

create different 'assemblages' of events that interact with each other. Together, they offer a retrospective, non-linear account of the change, able to shed light on individuals' efforts to make sense of their world and their being in the world.

To read historical events as a tangle of lines also implies a reconsideration of the event itself: no longer just a point of articulation in a linear process, an event becomes a moment of irradiation of multiple lines, multiple transformative processes that involve different actors in different ways. In other words, *'la Crisi'* loses its apparent coherence and unfolds in multiple concatenations and ways of understanding, experiencing and being the change. Of this multifaceted subject, in this chapter, I have explored different causes that underpinned it and some of its effects. Starting from this basis and continuing my exploration of the ways in which *'la Crisi'* was experienced in Valenza and affected the city, in the following chapters, I will unravel this tangle of transformations, and demonstrate how the downturn has triggered a process of redefinition of both local industry, and the individual sense of belonging to Valenza, by starting to explore the experience of unemployment and unbecoming experienced by those goldsmiths whose jobs were victimised in the downturn.

Fig. 10: Children playing with the roundabout

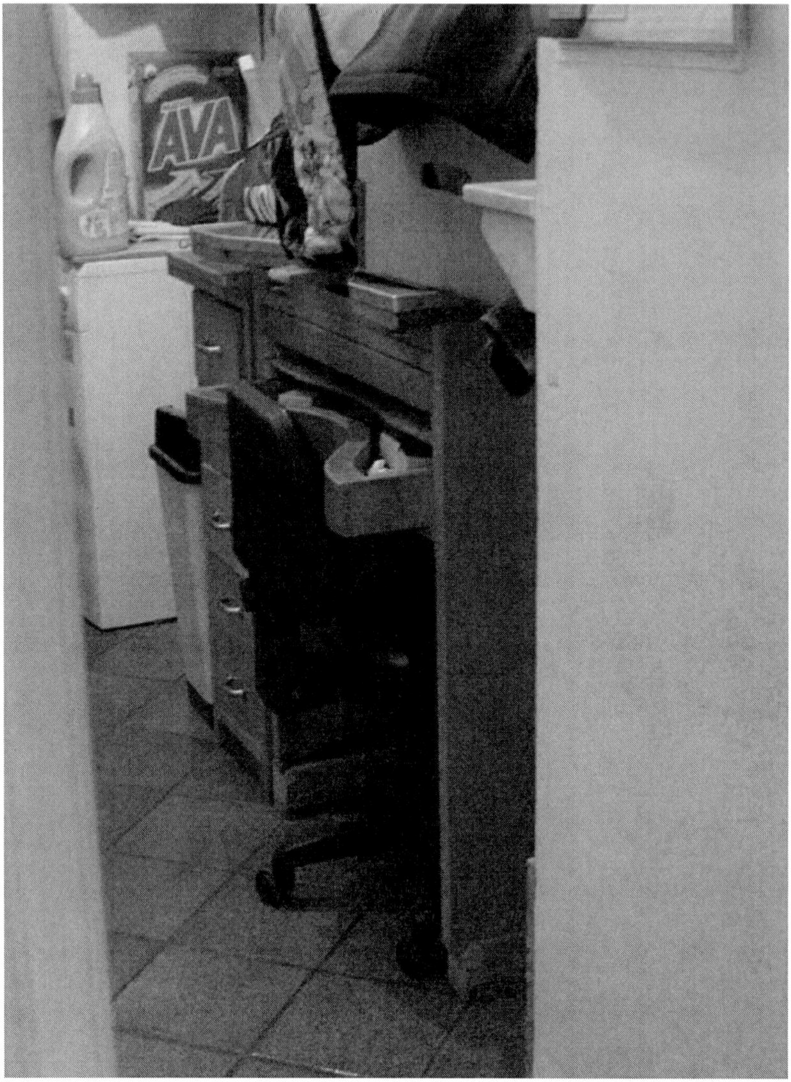

Fig: 11: Domestic ruin: a goldsmith workbench

CHAPTER SIX

JOB LOSS: UNBECOMING A GOLDSMITH

A few hundred metres from Piazza Duomo, there is a small park located in front of a nursery school. It is a few hundred square metres wide, delineated by large grass flowerbeds and trees. At its centre, there is a peculiar, modern merry-go-round: a round platform on which pipes and wood panels are installed. It looks like a cross between a flying saucer and a boat. Every day, from Monday to Friday at 5 pm, the kids left the school to play with this structure while their relatives wait, sitting on one of the benches.

It was an afternoon in late March 2010. In the preceding few weeks, I had become accustomed to coming here around 5 pm to take a break. I would sit on a bench reading the daily newspaper or spending time doing nothing, while as a few dozen howling kids and some adults, mostly their mothers, nannies or grandparents, passed by in front of me.

In the days leading up to the scene, I noticed an exception to this picture. A tall man, about forty, had begun to regularly come here with his son and let him play a bit with the other kids. Today, he sat on the same bench as me. In front of us, five or six kids were playing with the roundabout: first, they were playing at pirates – acting like buccaneers and using the structure as if it were a galleon; a few minutes later, astronauts – they became spacemen, and the structure, a UFO; then cowboys – they were soldiers and Indians, and the structure, a fort. Then, I lost count of their uninterrupted flow of change and becoming.

I was watching this spectacle when the man asked me whether I was the father of some of the kids. I answered that I was a student taking a break from work. We started chatting, and he explained that he was a bench-jeweller and had been following the *'cassa integrazione'* scheme - a welfare programme for temporary redundancy, which I will analyse later in the chapter - since the previous November. He worked part-time in the firm until January, when he was definitively dismissed. Then he continued:

> "It has been months since I last visited my *'fabbrica'* [the workshop where he worked] or even walked around it. I do not know what to do. It is just a pain. After being sacked, I tried to work a bit at home, keep my hands busy... But... I stopped... I did not know why... I was doing it because I am a goldsmith... But I am not even one of those anymore... I feel I am in a 'Limbo' in which I am stuck..."

He stopped. He was visibly affected, almost moved to tears. He bowed his head, staring at his feet. Then, looking out in front of him, towards the kids, he commented:

> "I would like to be like them and be able to change roles with the same rapidity they do. I... Instead I am trapped in what I am and what I do... I used to do. I am a goldsmith... A goldsmith without work... I am just nothing... Someone who waits [*ch'aspetta*] to understand what he is and is not anymore... What he can become..."

Then he looked at me with an expression of embarrassment. Hastily, he took leave of me, called his son, and quickly went away without looking back at me, or the merry-go-round. When they disappeared beyond the corner of the street, I took note of his words, and completed this account the same night.

***

After that time, for almost a month I regularly saw the goldsmith in the square. Every time, he openly avoided or ignored me. I do not know his fate, or his name. However, his fragmented history and words vividly open up a fundamental dimension of unemployment in Valenza. The words of the informant complete the picture outlined the statistical data I mentioned before: a picture of an advanced precariousness of working (Molé, 2012) conditions and rampant unemployment.

In the previous chapter, by narrating a non-linear history of *'la Crisi',* I highlighted some of the possible causes of the downturn and ways of understanding it. Following that, in this and the next chapters, I intend to analyse the principal effects that the downturn had on the goldsmithing community, the industry and the city. Embedded into this framework, this chapter explores the effect of a job loss and the social and cultural processes triggered by this vicissitude, which owners of small firms as well as employed goldsmiths who lost their jobs had to face in a context of a rapid shrinking of the industry. While in Chapter 4 I investigated *'artigianalità'* and the process through which apprentices pursue this ideal and reach this particular understanding of work and the world, becoming goldsmiths and members of the goldsmithing 'community of practice' (cf. Wenger, 1998; Lave and Wenger, 1991), in this chapter, by exploring the tangle of feelings and ways of understanding society and (past) work shown by (former) goldsmiths I will explore the process through which individuals reconsider their belonging to this community and their understanding of their profession, city and personal future.

In so doing, I will base my analysis on a heuristic body developed in anthropology in the last fifty years (Jancius, 2006; Perelman, 2008: 11). Anthropologists have seen in unemployment an experience of marginalisation and redefinition of the individual's social status and identity (Perelman, 2008: 10-11). In so doing, scholars, such as Newman (1989), Diedrich (2004), Jancius (2006), Hall (2006), have used Van Gennep's liminal phase concept to describe this experience. This concept, however, brings with it implications that are difficult to apply to the case of unemployment met in Valenza. Abandoning this model, I argue that unemployment represents for goldsmiths a 'Limbo': an existential condition underpinned by the ambiguity of being and at the same time not-being a goldsmith. Moreover, considering the process of self-redefinition, I aim to propose an interpretation of this process as an opening to becoming based on un-becoming a goldsmith. In this respect, besides confirming Perelman's thesis about the potentialities of ethnographic studies of unemployment to offer a "diverse picture of what it means to be a worker" (Perelman, 2008: 11), this analysis will offer elements to comprehend the practical possibility for an individual to depart from a 'community of practice' (cf. Lave and Wenger, 1991).

Valenza and unemployment

Since the end of 2008, job losses have been one of the most publicly debated aspects of Valenza's downturn. Private institutions, such as the bank foundation Fondazione Cassa di Risparmio di Alessandria, professional associations, such as AOV and CNA, and public government bodies, such as the City Council and Piedmont Regional Council, were the protagonists of a heated debate aimed at defining strategies to stem what appeared to be an "employment emergency" (e.g. Zemide, 2009a, Rossi, 2009a).

To cope with the recession in the jewellery market, local firms started a progressive cut of personnel through dismissal or employing *'cassa integrazione'* temporary redundancy schemes offered by Italian law. *'Cassa integrazione'* is a vernacular expression used to refer to a social security cushioning scheme based on a national security reserve, the *Cassa*

Integrazione Guadagni [Profit Integration Reserve], instituted by the State after ex-*Decreto Legislativo provvisorio del Capo dello Stato* 869/1947[1]. The funds in this reserve[2] are used to finance special benefits that are granted to all the workers whom a firm, during a negative economic period, has partially or completely suspended from their duty. To be eligible for these funds, the suspension must not exceed 2,080 work-hours (52 weeks) over two years, and cannot be protracted for periods longer than 13 consecutive weeks (three months)[3]. The benefit consists of 80% of the normal pay, up to a ceiling that is established every year by the National Government: in 2010, the standard ceiling was € 892.96 per month, and € 1,073.25, in the case of salaries that exceeded € 1,931.86.

However, in the case of the jewellery industry, the national law only provides this scheme for firms larger than 15 employees. Thus, most of the Valenza jewellery firms were excluded. To protect workers in small firms as well, in January, the Piedmont Regional Council and Alessandria Provincial Council allocated special resources to create a *Cassa integrazione Straordinaria* for small enterprises. Thanks to this special reserve, artisan studios were also able to start programs of temporary redundancy.

'*Cassa integrazione*' turned into a tool widely used by firms to reduce their costs, waiting for a revival of the market. Between 2009 and 2010, about 4,000 workers, 80% of the local workforce, were involved in these schemes (Poggio, 2011): about half of the estimated number are workers who were only partially suspended from their activities, *de facto* turning a full-time occupation into a part-time job; the other half is workers completely suspended from the activity.

Over this two years the possibilities offered by '*cassa integrazione*' helped to delay a possible wave of dismissals that appeared inevitable to local politicians and entrepreneurs (Rossi, 2009a), in mid-2009. However it did not stop the wave completely. In 2009, 800 goldsmiths (including former firm-owners) lost their jobs; another 500 in 2010, while only 9

---

[1] The legislative framework of '*cassa integrazione*' was later reformed many times. In particular I would like to note Legge 498/1951, and Legge 223/1991: the former, the first complete framework of the law; the latter, its latest, most comprehensive reform.

[2] This is financed by the State and all Italian enterprises, which have to contribute to it by depositing a percentage (from 0.75 to 9%, ex-Legge164/1975 art. 12) of the workers' gross salaries.

[3] The modularity of '*cassa integrazione*' mirrors the original objective of the law that instituted these schemes to allow the employers to reduce the amount of workforce employed in production without forcing the workers into long periods of inactivity.

workers were employed in the industry in the same period (OPML, 2011: 7). To complete the picture of the uncertain condition of employment in the city, it is estimated that, on the 1st of January 2011, 1,800 goldsmiths (Poggio, 2011) were still involved in *'cassa integrazione'* schemes.

These data show a picture of an advanced precarisation[4] of an industry, of which, one of the key consequences is rampant unemployment. To understand the social and cultural consequence that unemployment may have, anthropology has offered some conceptual tools developed since the 1960s and the research concerning the 'culture of poverty'[5].

Growing more and more interested in the individual dimension of living in urban and industrialised communities (Kemper and Rollwagen, 1996), anthropologists investigated the social and cultural repercussions of the loss of work on the individual and social groups. Thus, unlike a purely psychological interpretation of the post-employed condition, anthropologists emphasised the interconnection between social context and individuals' emotions and actions (cf. Tiffany et al., 1970), exploring the social and personal repercussions of a job loss, such as the undermining of individuals' social status in connection with their self-esteem (Wadel, 1973). In so doing, they brought out the social meaning that unemployment has in modern societies. In fact, they noticed that this work condition is often

[4] 'Precarisation' has recentely entered in the current lexicon of social sciences (Hesmondhalgh and Baker, 2008; Neilson and Rossiter, 2005; Standing 2011). Since the late 1990s, it has employed in the political debates of European states, such as Italy (Lazzarato, 2004; Molé, 2012), France (Appay, 2010), and Spain (Casas-Cortés, 2009; Ruido and Rowan, 2007). It refers to the recent transformation of work into a flexible and insecure work activity (Ruido and Rowan, 2007; Neilson and Rossiter, 2005; Hesmondhalgh and Baker, 2008). As Neilson and Rossiter noticed: "In its most ambitious formulation [precarisation] would encompass not only the condition of precarious workers but a more general existential state, understood at once as a source of 'political subjection, of economic exploitation and of opportunities to be grasped'" (Neilson and Rossiter, 2008: 52).

[5] Attitudes, such as the sense of helplessness and marginality, and the lack of a sense of history and belonging (cf. Lewis, 1963: 17), arguably distinguish socially marginal groups (see also: Lewis, 1961; 1966). Although still employed in scholarship, mainly by American sociologists, since the end of the 1960s (Valentine, 1968) the concept of 'culture of poverty' has been widely criticised in social sciences and anthropology. In particular, due to its emphasis on the role of social groups and individuals in self-determining their marginal state, the concept has been criticised by scholars who have highlighted its determinism that dovetails with a neoliberal understanding of the world and social phenomena (for a synthesis of the disciplinary debate: Villemez, 2000).

considered to be a negatively-marked social status that causes the social marginalisation of the individual: using Goffman's (1963) terminology, unemployment is presented as a 'stigma'. While the stigmatisation of unemployment has emerged as a general trend in industrialised countries, the strength of this stigma is not universal or universalisable, since it varies on the basis of the social context in which unemployment occurs[6] and on the gender of the individual who has lost their job[7]. The dynamics of marginalisation that engage the dismissed person vary as well and involve the agency of both the individual and their community[8].

Contextually to marginalisation, anthropologists have pointed out the collective and individuals' transformational aspect of unemployment. In fact, the unemployed person must define new categories so as to accept and understand their new social condition (Leana and Feldmann, 1988: 379-80; Perelman, 2008: 11): a process that passes through a profound and perturbing reconsideration of the system of practices and beliefs to which they previously adhered for their job (Newman 1981:319) and can result in removing old systems of practices and beliefs, as well as reinforcing them,

---

[6] Little (1976) pointed out a sharp contrast between the negative view of the loss of work in American lower classes and the more positive one that characterised middle class informants who saw in unemployment the possibility to cultivate their personal interests and family relations. Howe (1990), however, showed that, in the case of Northern Ireland, the intensity of stigma is strictly related to the endemic nature of unemployment in a community.

[7] Leana and Feldmann took into particular consideration the problem of unemployment among women, in open criticism of previous studies where this work condition was "seen as less central to women's identities than it is to men's" (Leana and Feldmann, 1992: 103-04). Instead, the scholars pointed out that: "these traditional assumptions and stereotypes do not accurately represent many working women – those who are primary wage earners, those who are the sole support for dependent children, those who are recent entrants into non-traditional jobs, and those, for whatever reason, who value and enjoy their work. For these women job loss may be even more devastating than it is for their male counterpart, since women generally fare worse than men in terms of both their financial resources and their abilities to replace lost jobs. Moreover, many recent research studies have reported that unemployed women generally have a more difficult time obtaining satisfactory employment than their male counterparts, and that females, once laid off, are twice as likely as their male counterparts to be unemployed for longer than a year." (Leana and Feldmann, 1992: 104).

[8] The marginalisation that follows from being fired is not only caused by the community's refusal of the unemployed person, but can also result from an independent and voluntary withdrawal of the individual from their community, as appeared in the case of American middle-class unemployed people (e.g. Burman, 1988; Newman, 1989).

as Wilensky (1959: 228) already noted in the late 1950s. Thus, this struggle[9] results in an overall process of disengagement of the individual from a profession and social environment of work; a process that is a prelude to any possible future reemployment in different trades.

Thus, in the light of Lave and Wenger's (1991; see also Wenger, 1998) theories, it seems possible to define unemployment as the potential moment when an individual is called to abandon a 'community of practice' and redefine herself. While Lave and Wegner did analyse the mechanism of engagement with such communities, unfortunately they did not explore the practices necessary to abandon them. Since, as we have seen in chapter 4, the goldsmithing community can be considered a 'community of practice' (cf. Lave and Wenger, 1991) founded on the ideal of *'artigianalità'*, an analysis of goldsmiths' unemployment can provide elements to fill this gap by investigating how goldsmiths relate to their skills and knowledge once they are marginalised from production.

To do so, however, it is necessary to explore and define the experience of unemployment, which combines aspects of marginalisation and self-redefinition. Towards this goal, anthropologists, such as Newman (1989), Diedrich (2004), Jancius (2006), and Hall (2006), have looked to Van Gennep's (1960) concepts of *liminal stage*. This concept conveys the idea of this double change, since it describes the moment in which individuals are cast off from their (previous) community and required to develop a new world view to be reintegrated into their society and make sense of their new condition (Newman, 1989: 91-92). Although this concept portrays a condition of being 'between and betwixt' (cf. Turner, 1967) that underpins the experience of unemployment, it also conveys a burden of

---

[9] Ferguson in his ethnography of the Zambian Copperbelt (Ferguson, 1999) has established a clear connection between these two aspects of unemployment. In his work, job loss and worsening of work conditions are read in correlation with the failure of the individual's expectations for a model of a new, 'modern' style of life, and a difficult relationship with their native community. The urban social distress that followed the economic downturn of the local industry appears as the difficult process that individuals had to undergo in order to cope after the shattering of their hopes and the worsening of their living conditions. This process results in a tormented reconsideration of a model of life related to an ideal of modernity that the individuals pursued and in which they believed. To do so, the individuals are obliged to rethink their life in the city and reconsider their relationship with their original community. Thus, unemployment, and more broadly, the worsening of work conditions, results in an inner and collective game played on the basis of the ideals of life and through the individual relationships with different social networks. This tension sheds light on a world view based on an accentuated symbolic dualism between urban and rural.

implications that cannot apply to the case of job-loss (e.g. Turner, 1967; 1977). First of all, a liminal phase is a ritualised intermediary condition, the temporal boundaries of which are known and determined, that implies the possibility of the individual's reintegration in a pre-fixed role. Unemployment is, instead, a condition whose temporal extension is unfixed, unpredictable and potentially everlasting. Moreover, it is also unknown what job an individual may take when concluding her unemployment: it could be a similar position to the one she had in the past, or a completely new one. In other words, unemployment emerges as a condition of uncertainty in which the individual is set aside from a previous known state (past employment) and an unknown future (future employment) structurally different from a rite of passage. Thus, in the following pages employing the terminology used by my informants, I will instead consider this transitional state as a 'Limbo': a concept that in its etymology offers a better insight into the actual tension that characterises this experience and its expression through waiting.

Limbo and waiting

The word 'Limbo' is often used by anthropologists to refer to a condition of suspension that may involve different epistemological frames such as time (e.g. Fabian, 1983) or law (e.g. Markowitz, 1996). This meaning corresponds to the common usage of this term in English, but does not accurately reflect its etymology. The term appeared in English in the 14th century. It derives from the Italian 'Limbo', accepted into English after the success of Dante's *Comedia*. In Dante's work, 'Limbo' is not merely a suspended condition. As Lee concisely explains:

> "For Dante and for the Medieval world, 'Limbo' was the borderland or outermost circle of Hell. Here were consigned those who had had no chance of salvation – ancients, children and fools." (Lee, 1963: 3)

In other words, 'Limbo' is a form of damnation where hellish torment does not correspond to a physical torture, rather to a condition of eternal waiting (for salvation), and a waiting that is eternally frustrated (for the damned).

In this respect, to classify any social condition as a 'Limbo' is not a neutral acknowledgement of a suspension of ordinary conditions. Reconsidering its literary etymology, it is a suspension between guilt and innocence that is imbued with an implicit sense of frustration and defeat. More broadly, reconsidering Dante's verses it appears that 'Limbo' delineates a space/time and a human condition where individuals attempt to make sense of their past by outstretching towards a future that is (apparently) unreachable and unachievable because (it seems that) it will never happen. This propensity to consider becoming is exemplified in Dante's work and by my informants by a sense of waiting and uncertainty.

Waiting is an attitude that is often described by the ethnographers of unemployment, and appears to be an unspoken link between all the different contexts. In fact, the dwellers of Parisians peripheries wait (Champagne, 1999 [1990]; Pinto, 1999 [1990]); Leipzig's workers wait (Jancius, 2006); Philadelphian sacked persons wait (O'Brien, 2006); former miners in Kitwe (Ferguson, 1999) as well those in Western Virginia (Stewart, 1996) wait for a shift in the economy, a State intervention, or just for an unspecified chance for improvement. Different attitudes may be put in place during this wait, but still, the condition of unemployment appears to be a long wait characterised, Stewart explains, by:

> "Its incessant compulsion to story things that happen to interrupt the progress of events; its endless process of re-membering [*sic*], re-telling, and imagining things; its tactile mimesis of decomposing objects and luminous signs that speak to people to the possibilities of something more [...]" (Stewart, 1996: 8)

The display of stories and feelings that the wait brings along, thus, voices the condition of suspension, the 'Limbo', derived from unemployment. This narrative landscape, which these stories and feelings constitute, is unfolded to express and to exorcise the 'absent presence' (cf. Stewart, 1996: 18) of (former) work. By narrating, the ex-mining community's members, in Stewart's account, not only made sense of their world by turning a landscape of industrial ruins into a meaningful landscape of signs, but, by addressing its absence, explain what the mining industry used to be for them, and outline the individual's and community's becoming.

Similarly to the ex-miners, goldsmiths have established a narrative landscape based on the sense of waiting. Unemployed goldsmiths' Valenza is a landscape dominated by a verb: '*aspettare*', to wait. Like 'to wait' in English, this is a common verb, part of the basic vocabulary of Italian. It is a verb whose meaning is suspended between activity and passivity: it describes the attitude, on the one hand, of delaying an action from happening, on the other, of remaining inactive in one place expecting something. This has been the verb most frequently used to explain the condition of unemployment by goldsmiths, as I discovered in the early days of my research, as this extract from my field-notes shows.

***

One morning in December 2008, a few days after the beginning of my fieldwork, I was having a coffee in one of the busiest cafés of the city. The place was crowded. Many people, mainly men, were chatting, sitting at the tables or standing at the counter. In a corner, I saw a former schoolmate of mine, Matteo, who was sitting at a table reading the *Gazzetta dello Sport*, the main national daily sports paper.

At 17, he left school at the end of the third year. During that summer, in 1999, he was hired as an apprentice gem setter in a small workshop not far from the historic centre of Valenza. It had been at least a couple of years since I had last met him. Surprised to see him there, I approached him, hailing him. He raised his head from the newspaper. His face was haggard, and the thin-lipped smile he made did not hide the uneasiness in his eyes.

> "Oh! Nice to see you!"
> He said, then added, with a sarcastic tone:
> "What am I doing? I'm waiting... What do you think?"
> "For whom?"
> "Just my boss, or anyone else, to call me saying there is enough work and he needs me back to work, Michele. It's a hard time... I received the letter of dismissal a few weeks ago and now... Now, I wait."

***

Matteo is just one of the many hundreds of people who, since October 2008, had lost their jobs in the jewellery industry and were obliged to find a new occupation in another field. Although just one person among the many, his words and experience help to better frame the meaning of the goldsmiths' waiting.

At first glance, they would suggest that the act of waiting is the physical manifestation of a passive attitude of a person traumatised by the experience of the loss of his job and unable to react. In this scenario, 'to wait' would coincide with a state of passivity and mental distress that has been associated with the state of unemployment (e.g. Kessler et al., 1989: 651-52). The episode in the café fits with this understanding rooted in psychological literature.

Without negating the social suffering that being dismissed involved, this interpretation, however, seems to exclude an active attitude that Matteo, as well as the other goldsmiths I interviewed, expressed and demonstrated. After our first meeting, I was able to discover another story behind Matteo's waiting. After the notification, Matteo started contacting other firms in Valenza and in the surrounding towns to see if there were any jewellery producers interested in hiring him, even if only part-time. I followed him in his search for some days, moving from one workshop to another. In most cases, the firm owners did not refuse Matteo's application and *curriculum vitae*, nor did they overtly admit their lack of need for a new worker. In most cases they answered with laconic expressions that left some ray of hope, such as "I'll let you know".

> "The first that gave me such an answer was actually my former boss. He fired me and at the same time let me understand that as soon as the turnover grew again he would call me again. Bullshit. In that situation, when no-one clearly says you are useless, what can you do? You wait and continue your search, hoping that someone is going to call you."

In this context, thus, *'aspettare'* is not a passive process antithetical in the search for work, but a struggle for a self-redefinition. At the same time, however, *'aspettare'* voices a fatalistic attitude towards the world that is founded on the individual's recognition of the limitations of their capacity to determine their own destiny. With a similar connotation, the verb often recurred in many of my interviews. It was not only used by unemployed artisans, but also by employed goldsmiths and jewellery entrepreneurs who described their uncertain life in the period of economic difficulty. Thus, this particular meaning given to the verb represents a macro-phenomenon of the local discourse in which the experience of Matteo, and the meaning of the experience of unemployment, must be framed. In the case of other jewellery artisans who were able to maintain their jobs (for longer), this feeling became intertwined with a broader sense of precariousness and insecurity for the trade. In this case as well, however, waiting is not a passive action. Thus, among Valenza goldsmiths, waiting and the sense of insecurity to which it is associated unveil an uneven hierarchy of power in the jewellery economy where the position of the artisan is subordinate to the market changes and the decisions that other players make. Where employed goldsmiths saw their lives and occupations inevitably determined by the choices and needs of their employers, an employer can see their future hinging on the evolution of the market and feel powerless in front of the change. In this respect, a 'pyramid of power' (cf. Gaggio, 2006) emerges: a system of economic subordination that overlaps with the model described by Gereffi (Gereffi, 2007) and explained in Chapter 4. In fact, it emerged from the interviews that while the employed artisans feel their life lying in the hands of their employers, the supplier firm-owners know that the future of their firm is based on the decisions and the production strategies employed by their customers, and the owner of firms with direct access to the market see their insecurity arise from the market and the reduction of demand.

As in the case of Matteo, also in the other interviews '*aspettare*' assumed the same connotation, appearing as a discursive formation describing an interstitial status between agency and passivity, in an economic and social context where the individual's destiny appears to rely on agents outside the individual's actions: market forces, the wills/whims of firm-owners, *et cetera*. Thus, as far as '*aspettare*' emerges as the descriptive verb of a condition that closely recalls the condition of Dante's 'Limbo', it follows that it is in this 'Limbo', within this waiting, that is enacted the redefinition of the self.

Removing ruins

As previously mentioned, anthropologists have seen in unemployment a period of self-redefinition, in which the aspects concerning professionalism and the relationship of the individual with their work and social networks are revaluated and redirected. However, in my interviews this reconfiguration has not been presented as just an adaptation of something pre-existing, since the very substance of the past seems to disappear, leaving the individual in 'Limbo'.

In the interviews, goldsmiths pointed out the job - loss resulted in a radical transformation of the individuals' world. This change appears to culminate in a profound shift in perception of time, space and sociality. The goldsmiths themselves often highlighted this transformation. This is the case of Giancarlo, a gem-setter in his thirties whom I met in January 2011. After almost fifteen years of work, he had lost his job in July 2010, after the firm in which he had worked for almost ten years optimized its personnel:

> "Unemployment is like a 'Limbo'. Your daily routine is completely upset. You would like to go to work, just because it is normal for you to go to your workshop every morning, but you cannot do it... Or rather, you can, but it is useless and painful, since it will remind you that you no longer have a job. Then, you find yourself thinking: what do I do now? You have no idea... Then, you realise that you live in a suspension. The time flows but, after a few days without work, it seems to have stopped. You look at the clock, you see the hands turn and you don't know why... Time appears suspended... And you understand your life, your time and the space around you, in a different way."

The rupture in daily routine and the vanishing of work opens a new scenario for the individual. It is an existential landscape that was generally described as '*vuoto*' [empty], '*svuotato*' [hollowed], '*solitario*' [lonely], and '*spoglio*' [bare].

In this context, the self-redefinition is seen as a transition through this 'Limbo', or its taming through filling the emptiness with activities and new routines. In order to fill the gap opened by the disappearance of work and the sense of emptiness that it brought along, establishing a new daily routine becomes urgent. Echoing the experience of American middle class informants reported by Lee (1985), many of them found in their hobbies, house and family care a way to overcome this problem. Others established new habits. For example, Matteo told me that, after the loss of his job:

> "When I was working, my life has been just my home, my car and my workshop. These were the principal places where I spent my life... Since I lost my job, well, I have discovered and started frequenting new places. The café for example..."

In establishing a new routine, goldsmiths transform their experience of time and space. They create a new geography for everyday life. Public space, as well as domestic space, is reinvented, implicitly to accommodate the suffering brought on by the loss. In Deleuzian terms (Deleuze, 1997: 61), goldsmiths engaged in a broad generative attempt to create a new 'map' for their reality: a new layer of meaning to make sense of a world without a (goldsmithing) job. This process passes through a different allocation of time, and a new form of engagement with a space that passes through the reshaping of the physical and social space of the individual as well. In other words, the 'Limbo' is traversed by removing from daily life the ruins of their time as a goldsmith.

Stoler pointed out that 'ruins', "monumental 'leftover[s]' or relics" (Stoler, 2008: 194) of past times that characterised the landscape are objects endowed with the analytical and evocative power of making the past live in the present, that is, to make the past haunt the present. In other words, ruins are '*lieux de mémoire*', in Nora's terms:

> "The ultimate embodiments of a memorial consciousness that has barely survived in a historical age that calls out for memory because it has abandoned it" (Nora, 1989: 12).

In Nora, *'lieux de mémoire'* are the former concentration camps and other genocide monuments that remind us of the Holocaust. In the case of goldsmiths, *'lieux de mémoire'* are first of all their former *'fabbriche'* and the benches at home. They are very well-known places that bring to mind experiences, memories, and actions of their previous activity: activities that had become impracticable due to the job loss. These places were described to me as prohibited and uncanny due to the suffering they caused. They evoked ambiguous, perturbing, disturbing emotions that artisans tended to avoid: where in their house, the artisans often removed their bench, taking it into their garage or cellar, or placing it in a closet where it was used as a bulky shelf, in the public space they preferred to avoid going to their firms or even passing in front of them. As Tatiana[10], explained:

> "It is woeful... So woeful to see my *'fabbrica'*... My former *'fabbrica'*. To see it reminds me what I was... A goldsmith... It reminds me of the dream of success I believed in and from which I have been excluded. In a city where every day, more and more goldsmiths are losing their jobs, I have to be realistic and not deceive myself by hoping tomorrow I will find a job as a bench - jeweller. But if I have to change, why do I have to suffer? Better not to remember... Every day I pass in front of the firm to go to the nursery school where my son stays. Every time I saw the *'fabbrica'* it was like a blade in my guts... Too many memories... Too many regrets... I forced myself to not pass in front of the firm... I invented a new route..."

In the same tone, Valerio admitted:

> "I removed the bench from the sitting room. In its place there is a red Ikea armchair. The bench is in a closet. I use it as a shelf for soaps... It is so as not to remember, you understand?"

While a firm and a bench are possibly closer to the original objects contemplated by Nora and Stoler, often goldsmiths presented a further ruin to the list: the work-social networks they had previously built, and mostly their friendships with their former colleagues.

As we have seen previously in the book, the jewellery industry represents a social and affective cosmos in which goldsmiths are embedded. In particular, *'fabbriche'*, especially small workshops, are closed systems where workers weave strong social relationships with their colleagues. In fact, as Valerio pointed out:

[10] When I met her in April 2010, Tatiana was thirty four. She grew up in central Italy but, following a suggestion from one of her relatives, moved to Valenza when she was fifteen to enrol at ISA Cellini. She graduated five years later and found a job as a goldsmith in an established firm where she worked for almost ten years. In 2006, she moved to another firm, for a better contract. Unfortunately the new firm closed in December 2009, leaving Tatiana unemployed.

> "You work for years with five, ten other guys for eight, ten, twelve hours every day. You play jokes on them. You socialise with them. At the end of the day they are a sort of second family if you are lucky... Or I should say cursed... Because when you lose your job you also see these bonds slowly loosen. And when you are at home you feel even lonelier."[11]

With the dismissal, the social ties loosen, because the reason for the prolonged everyday relationship ceases. However, the bond still persists, as Valerio highlighted:

> "They are still friends. You can meet them after they finished their day in the firm...In the empty days after the dismissal, you would like to meet them. However, it is too hard..."

Although the affective bond may be strong, goldsmiths indicated their difficulty in meeting former colleagues: such meetings are often perceived as painful experiences because they remind them of the loss and the expectations unemployed persons had for their job. Thus, the colleagues turn into ruins to be removed, for the reasons Tatiana explained:

> "At home, when my boys [her husband and son] were out, I was alone, and this means solitude most of the time. In all my free time I would have liked to meet my former colleagues. However, I could not bear to stay with them. I love them, but I could not stay with them. It was painful. They still had their job. They are happy... And I? I? I... What? I was just empty...I just preferred to stop meeting them. One day, when this 'Limbo' is over, I will call them and say 'Hello! Would you like a coffee?' but not now..."

In the place of these ruins, and the intangible ruins of the free, empty time left by the loss a job, a new landscape is built and established. Goldsmiths can choose a new route into the city to avoid passing in front of their old *'fabbrica'*, or can remove the bench from their houses. Alternatively they can decide to fill their free hours by attending a gym and turning this place into a new 'home': an apparently innocuous decision that hides a more profound suffering, as in the case of Marcello.

Marcello, a thirty-year-old (former) goldsmith, lost his job in summer 2010, after six months of *'cassa integrazione'*. His family lives about fifty kilometres away from Valenza, in a small town in Lombardy. He left home to attend ISA Cellini high school and since then he has lived

---

[11] A goldsmith in his late fifties, talking about his experience of unemployment during the mid-1990s, interviewed in June 2010.

exclusively in Valenza. He had worked for almost twelve years when he lost his position, after the firm closed down.

> "After highschool, I threw myself into the job. I was working and working. My family was away and I have not many friends [in Valenza]. Actually my friends were my colleagues. When the firm closed, many of them left the city. I don't want to leave Valenza... I put [emotionally] too much in this city... Thus... I felt almost alone and without a job... A few weeks after I had been fired, I decided to get a membership at a gym and enter some of its courses. I bought all the stuff I needed. It is not just for my body. It is a place where I meet people. I made some new friends over there. Even though the membership is expensive I continue to go. I do not want to also lose these new contacts... This new home..."

Although the flat where he was living when I met him, in April 2011, was his own, he was living off benefits, and to pay for his lifestyle, he was slowly eroding his savings:

> "Logically I should quit the gym, but I don't want to... There I can find people where I can stay with... Friends... I don't know... I don't know what to do..."

The stories of Valerio, Tatiana and Marcello show how the removal of the ruins and the creation of a new map appears first of all, as Deleuze suggests, as a process of evaluating the displacement, that is understanding the borders of the absence of goldsmithing work (Deleuze, 1997: 61). Moreover, it also shows the dramatic nature of this drawing in and the territorialisation of this new map, the embedding of the individual into a new regime of signs (Deleuze and Guattari, 1987: 322). The slow removal of the links, the creation of a new map, while they may mitigate suffering, but do not remove questions about the future. Removing the possibility of further imitations (Deleuze and Guattari, 1987: 219) of previous models of being a goldsmith, these processes instead bring the individual to reconsider their life, their former work. Thus, they open the individual to their becoming.

The Fall

In the description of the job loss and the strategies employed to cope with this void, previous testimonies have also shown the pragmatic dimension of jewellery-making in goldsmiths' everyday lives. However, they have also allowed the symbolic meaning of their former work to gleam through. Goldsmiths associate to jewellery-making expectations, dreams, and a particular form of sociality (Garofoli, 2004, Gaggio, 2007, Fontefrancesco, 2011). In this respect I argue that a job is an identity and symbolic cosmos that seems to be underpinned by an opposite 'global hierarchy of value' (cf. Herzfeld, 2004) – the broad ideology that underlies the national and local social stratification. Herzfeld introduced this concept studying artisanship in Crete. There, artisanship is seen as a badge of 'backwardness' within the local community and the broader context of the nation (Herzfeld, 2004: 1-37). In Valenza, instead, jewellery production is perceived as an elite occupation and a stairway to success (Chapter 4). In this sense, it can be argued that jewellery production was located at the top of Valenza's hierarchy of value.

In this context, the loss of jobs in a general context of insecurity for the entire jewellery sector has been equivalent to not only the frustration of the workers' economic expectations, but also the undermining of their perception of their position within the city. Echoing the Parisian informants of Bourdieu and his team, who spoke of a "fall" (Champagne, 1999 [1990]) or "the way down" (Pinto, 1999 [1990]), my informants also defined unemployment as '*una caduta*', a fall. So was it termed, for example, by Valerio:

> "[The job loss] was a fall... A fall from grace... I have seen all my expectations thwarted... I came here thirty years ago following a dream of success and now what am I? I cannot find an answer to this question, still."

The sense of defeat that emerges from these words is the same one expressed by other goldsmiths, of diverse ages, origins and gender, and who occupied different positions within the industry. For all of them, the loss of their jobs was a defeat that materialised through the reduction of economic gains, and that self-recognition of having changed position in the society: from being its centre to be cast almost outside it, in the 'Limbo' of being a goldsmith without work.

Herzfeld's model of the 'hierarchy of value' is underpinned by a stratified understanding of society in which social groups defined on the basis of their profession overlap with each other, describing in this way a hierarchy of prestige and power. A similar way of understanding society emerged during my interviews: when speaking about their city and country, goldsmiths described themselves at the top of society, in a position that was superior to professionals, civil servants, and all the other workers employed in other trades, such as commerce, or agriculture. Such an understanding, however, relies on the clear professional distinction between different social groups and a sense of belonging to society based on the active participation of an individual in a particular group/ trade. In this frame, the role of the dismissed person appears paradoxical: on the one hand, they are still a member of a group since they embody its distinguishing practices; on the other, however, they have no longer been active participants in the trade, since they lost their jobs. Thus, their status appears 'between and betwixt' (cf. Turner, 1967) legitimation and delegitimation, prestige and notoriety. In other words, they are stuck in 'Limbo'.

While the previous section portrayed the social suffering linked to a job loss, this symbolic consideration adds a further interpretative layer to understand and picture 'Limbo'. 'Limbo' is not just a physical and pragmatic transformation of everyday life: it is also a symbolic move, which drives the individual from the core of social legitimation to a peripheral, delegitimised condition within society, suspended between being and not being (a goldsmith).

This position is suffered as a 'stigma'. However, rather than being the result of a judgment of society, as theorised by Goffman (1963), this is perceived and explained by goldsmiths as a self-judgment, a self-stigmatisation, deeply rooted in the frustration of expectations and the problem of redefining themselves socially and professionally. This can be expressed with quiet or vibrantly dramatic tones, as Valerio did, following the previous quotation:

> "When I lost my job I felt... Lost... I was still a goldsmith, that is what I know how to do... But I was not a goldsmith any longer, because I no longer had a job. I was nothing. An invisible presence that had no place in this 'city of goldsmiths'. I felt like I was nothing. I tried to find a job as a goldsmith but all the doors were closed. So I am saying to myself that it may be time I started to be a non-goldsmith..."

The juxtaposition of antitheses paints a good portrait of the inner conflict that a goldsmith undergoes after dismissal: the contradiction of being a goldsmith, that is to still know and embody the practices and way of understanding production of a legitimised practitioner, and at the same time not being a goldsmith anymore, as a result of being cast away from that production. This contradiction turns into a peculiar self-stigmatisation since the condition of unemployment becomes an object through which the individual reconsiders their place in society and acknowledges their new, worse, status. However, while generally the concept of stigma is associated with the definition of a determined inferior status, in this case, the sense of inferiority arises from the indetermination of the condition of 'Limbo'.

To cut this Gordian knot of being and not-being, sacked goldsmiths put in place different strategies. Marcello and Matteo and most of the practitioners I met initially attempted to find a new occupation in the jewellery sector. Hence, they tried to escape the 'Limbo' by returning to *being* a goldsmith. However, experiencing the impossibility of this return, they then began a slow process of the complete departure from being. They removed the ruins of their past being and searched for a new, different job: a process that is not only explainable as an attempt at mitigating social suffering by removing those elements that remind them of their goldsmithing past, but can also be framed as a broader struggle that passes through the cessation of a previous being, and the opening of the self to becoming, in order to describe a new being and, hence, a new place in the hierarchy of value that characterises their community.

Conclusion

As Perelman (2008) argued, the ethnographic analysis of unemployment has shed light on different aspects of work, and by exploring the ruins left after job loss, it is possible to understand the ways in which it becomes part of the individual's life: that is through places, such as the workshop and the workbench, time, the time dedicated to jewellery production, and social relationships, with the colleagues. Thus, this analysis and exploration offer elements to appreciate the actual role that work plays in the everyday life of an individual and a community, both on a pragmatic and ideal level.

At the same time, this exploration has brought to the foreground the characteristics of an existential dimension that goldsmiths have to face once they lose their job and are unable to return to the trade due to the general economic situation of the local industry. This is described as a 'Limbo', a suspended condition where the individual is stuck between being and not being (a goldsmith). During this period, individuals live a profound, ontological transition through which they are forced to reinvent their time, space, and sociality. Unable to be reintegrated into the jewellery industry, (ex) goldsmiths have to 'unbecome' to open themselves to new possibilities.

In Chapter 4, I noticed that, even from the point of view of my informants, the jewellery industry can be considered a 'community of practice' as theorised by Lave and Wenger (1991). While these scholars focused their attention on the process of becoming part of the community, which is how the community expands, the strategies employed by goldsmiths to cease their suspension of being provide elements to understand how a 'community of practice' shrinks and the individual un-becomes part of the community. The removal of the ruins and the creation of a new map are the ways through which this transformation is actualised. While the process of becoming part of the community passes through the acquisition of traits, practices and objects that define the 'identity' and the individual's belonging to a community (Wenger, 1998: 173-87), this operation works by actually eliminating, weakening, and suspending these identity practices and objects. Matteo described this process with an effective metaphor:

> "A profession is like a garment you sew on to yourself. It is a garment that keeps you warm and dry. However, once you stop wearing it, it is very difficult to just unbutton it... [...] But you can always do it and then decide which new garment you want to put on."

Thus, through this unbuttoning, one excludes oneself from the 'community of practice' (cf. Lave and Wenger, 1991), and at the same time, one sets the basis for a new participation in (another) community.

Finally, while the case of unemployment has shown how (former) goldsmiths started a process of distancing themselves from the jewellery industry, and how the goldsmithing community has progressively shrunk, in the next chapter I will analyse the effect of this shrinking on the structure of the jewellery industry and the ways in which it is experienced by goldsmiths.

Fig. 12: 'Fabbrica' for rent

CHAPTER SEVEN

THE RUINATION OF THE NETWORK

September 2010. Luca was still smiling under his thick beard, although one could read the tiredness from a long day of work under that smile. That day had led him, a jewellery merchant in his fifties, to travel a thousand kilometres to visit clients, mainly jewellery shops, in the Emilia Romagna and Marche regions. A long journey that started at 4 am and that was finally ending. A journey that brought in some profit, but above all, preoccupation for an uncertain future. At about 9 pm, we met upon his arrival in Valenza in front of his house. We started chatting, while I helped him to unload the car and, later, upstairs in his flat. He told me that the trip was not completely useless – considering his normal tendency for understatement, it might have meant he got some good orders. However, he was frowning. I asked what happened, and he answered in a soft voice:

> "After this crisis, after these years, we've arrived at an endpoint. *'La Crisi'* cut the legs off this city... Our legs. It has been almost three years since this mess began and, now, maybe I would say, it is time we draw some conclusions about what has happened and what has changed. In the last year, above all, it has changed this city... Its jewellery industry...The dream of gold now appears to have ended..."

Luca stopped for a few seconds. He was watching outside, standing close to the window of the dining room, while I sat on the sofa, behind him. Then he continued:

> "Almost four thousand positions has been lost or endangered, more than three hundred firms have closed since the end of 2009. They are too many to pretend nothing happened; not to see the change that occurred in these years...Now we have to deal with this change... That's the only way to find a new future... Or the machine will go forth on the same road, as it has done in the past, losing other pieces until its full collapse."

***

Those may have been casual words offered at the end of a long day of work, words that I might have not taken seriously if they had not been echoing the voices of other goldsmiths, entrepreneurs and workers whom I met over the course of my fieldwork: voices that agreed that *'la Crisi'* had ended their dream –the expectations of success that, since the 1950s, generations of goldsmiths have associated with jewellery-making (Chapter 3).

The dream to which the goldsmiths refer is far from being a nocturnal effect of one's psyche (cf. Freud and Wilson, 1997). It is an interpretative grid for individual and collective lives that also conveys a particular interpretation of the economy and its sociality. In Miyazaki and Riles's terms, it is an 'orientation of knowledge' (cf. Miyazaki and Riles, 2005): an interpretation and an idealisation of the economy rooted in the materiality of the economic and social conditions of jewellery-making, which also expresses a goal and a way to reach it through a precise career, involving manual skills and creative knowledge (Chapter 4).

This system of certainties was undermined and uprooted by the changes occurred since 2008. In the previous chapter, I showed that *'la Crisi'* was perceived as an endpoint by the goldsmiths who lost their jobs during this period, in an economic context of almost completely impossible reintegration into the trade. However, it is not just to them that the economic crisis appeared as the endpoint of the dream. As it also emerges from the words of Luca, there was a change in perception of the dream for those who remained in the business shared it. Workers, owners of big and small firms, as well as those entrepreneurs who liquidated their enterprises but still thought of continuing somehow in the profession of goldsmithing, often repeated over the course of the two years that "the dream [was] over."

In this chapter, I am going to explore the causes and the processes that led this part of the goldsmith community to perceive the endpoint. While in Chapter 3 I showed how the industry is structured and how this structure is perceived and narrated by goldsmiths, here I am going to explore the transformations that occurred in the network economy after 2008 and how this change has been perceived by jewellery makers. In so doing, I will show that the worsening of economic conditions and the shrinking of the industry resulted in the ruination of the jewellery environment. Thus, the goldsmiths reconsidered their dream by facing the ruins left by *'la Crisi'* within the walls of the workshops and in the urban space of the city. I will show that, following the end of the dream, the process of reorientation of individuals' knowledge mostly coincided with a perception of the self as a subject deprived of her agency; a victim of the change. At the end of the fieldwork, the data collected show a process of redefinition still in progress. Thus, although it is not possible to be sure of which directions this change will lead to, the experience of Valenza goldsmiths can be taken as a basis for a broader reflection on the role of the individual and community in orienting knowledge.

'*La Crisi*' and the network economy

Since 2008, the Valenza jewellery industry has endured profound transformations of which the most noticeable effects were job cuts. Almost 300 firms closed, and 3,600 jobs were lost or endangered by the downturn (Chapters 5 and 6). As Luca noticed, these changes occurred alongside a worsening of both work conditions and of the quality of economic cooperation within the area. The testimony of Claudio elucidates this transformation.

Until December 2009, he was the owner of a workshop located near the Coinor area, in the western periphery of the city. The liquidation of the firm was, as he explained, the result of *'la Crisi'*:

> "You could not have believed what we went through. It was horrible. Over a few months orders literally disappeared. I am not saying they shrunk. No! I am saying that they disappeared. The problem was that there was no more work. I was used to working for big firms, but mainly for firms that worked for the big companies. You'd knock on their doors and they'd tell you that there was no work. That has kept happening since January; since Christmas [period] ended and we delivered the last pieces. 'There are no jobs'... It was a sort of refrain. Thanks to the *'cassa integrazione'*, I was able not to fire my people... At least not immediately. They stayed at home for weeks. And in that period we came to accept any kind of price... The clients fixed prices and time of delivery. And we had to say 'yes' because... Because there were no more jobs. The big firms as well were putting their people on *'cassa integrazione'*.
>
> We continued for some months with this story, for almost six months... Nothing was changing and I was not in a condition to reinvent my firm... To invent something we didn't have... I did not have the resources 'to explore the market', as you, erudite people, say. I tried to knock at the doors of other big companies to ask for some work. I explained I had already worked for them.... They gave me something. Yes... Crumbs... Crumbs that were not enough to pay the salaries of twelve people... That was not enough to balance the budget. Every month it was getting more and more in the red. Day after day I saw the dream of this business vanishing. I said 'enough'. I decided to close the firm. I closed on the 31st December. I did not want to squander everything I still had. I

> closed. I issued redundancies to the remaining workers and paid off my last debt.
>
> Now I am out. Finished. Now I will see what I will do. I am lucky because I am single, have no children and my parents are both retired. I will invent something... At the end of the day those crumbs [that the big firms give out] may be enough for a person or two to struggle along... Let's see… Maybe I will open a tiny studio with a partner... Maybe I will leave Valenza and open a drink stall on a paradise beach in the Caribbean...Who knows?"

This 'tale of the field' (cf. Van Maneen, 1988) highlights the double change that occurred during the period of 2009-2010. First of all, the worsening of work conditions that passed through the cycles of *'cassa integrazione'*, dismissals and formal or informal renegotiations of contracts. In his tale, Claudio appeared to have been particularly reluctant in employing these solutions to sustain his firm. I did not have the chance to verify his account, by interviewing his former employees. Regardless of whether it was true, his experience was embedded in a more general city-wide context in which the public economic debate hinged on the theme of 'competitiveness' of local products and entrepreneurship. Although this topic can be tackled through different perspectives (see also Fontefrancesco, 2009c), entrepreneurs and goldsmiths' professional associations tended to ascribe the 'lack of competitiveness' of Valenza firms only to the cost of the local work force. As the president of one of the largest goldsmith associations argued, during the inauguration of the *Valenza Gioielli 2010* fair:

> "The too high cost of work, and too heavy taxation. You cannot be obliged to pay ten, twenty Euros per hour to a worker when a Chinese one costs two or three. How can we be competitive against them? We need to cut costs..."

The reasoning of the president echoed a more general understanding in the city. An understanding that involved strategies of progressively cutting jobs, together with a reduction of wages, and cutting benefits as well as overtime pay. The results of these strategies were a) the loss of several hundred jobs; b) a general precariousness of work conditions; c) a consistent reduction of income for individuals[1] (Chapter 6).

---

[1] CGIL trade union calculated that, in the two years the standard net wage of a fully-fledged goldsmith decreased from 1,600 to 1,200 euros per month (CGIL, 2011)

These cuts occurred in a general context of increased precariousness of work between firms. As explained by Claudio, *'la Crisi'* manifested in Valenza as a chain reaction that, having originated from the market, reverberated through the city's big firms and out to the network of their suppliers. To understand this transformation, the work by Gereffi (2007) is illuminating. Studying Valenza's network structure before 2007, the scholar noted that this system was based on an asymmetric economic power relationship between a minority of 'free' firms that had a direct access to the market, with a direct outlet for their products on the market; and a majority of 'prisoners' that, instead, based their production on the orders from other enterprises and had their access to the market mediated by other enterprises (Gereffi, 2007: 35). This model predicted that, in case of a downturn, the latter group would be the most exposed and would mostly suffer the economic effects, since it would pay the entire social and economic cost of the change. This is, in fact, what happened.

In order to cope with the plunge in market demand, outsourcing firms re-internalised their production. Reduced outsourcing followed a logic that was clearly explained by a business consultant for one of the largest enterprises of Valenza:

> "In the face of such a difficulty in the markets, the most logical answer is to cut expenses in order to allow the maximum possible exploitation of the workforce that one already has on the payroll. If an enterprise discovers not to have some crucial, particular skills considered strategic for its production, it can decide to hire personnel or reconsider, in a careful and targeted way, the possibility of outsourcing. At the end of the day, in a context of crisis some (economically) new, interesting perspectives may also open that would make externalisation more profitable than what was in the past."

This reasoning echoes an approach to outsourcing often proposed by manuals of management and business planning (e.g. Walther and Skousen, 2010: 10-15). What manuals do not report are the actual social costs that such a strategy implies. In fact, it results in externalizing the loss to the firm's suppliers. In Valenza, with the reduction, sometimes the halt, of outsourcing, the larger enterprises redirected the social and economic costs that the downturn would have caused them, to their suppliers, leading them to endure more of the effects of the downturn, such as the scarcity of work and a reduction of their bargaining power with the outsourcers.

This strategy did not result in the end of the network economy (Chapter 3), but led to a twofold diminution of the network. First of all, the amount of networked orders reduced, resulting in a smaller number of economic relationships between firms. Moreover, the growing lack of jobs led to the closure of supplying firms, in a general diminution of the extent of the network. Furthermore, the conditions of paucity of work meant that those firms that still remained open had to endure a growing competition for the allocation of work, so that the power of outsourcers ended up being strengthened by the downturn. While a knowledge fostered in mutual trust between firms and firm-owners has often affected the allocation criteria of large firms preferring to distribute jobs among trusted partners rather than unknown but apparently more economically convenient suppliers, this trust built over time and through 'wooing' (Chapter 3) did not restrain large firms from exercising their power. They were able to impose their conditions on any collaboration: conditions that often were uneconomical for the suppliers. Claudio explained:

> "One of the most difficult things in our job is to calculate the exact costs of your work. I mean it is not only how much you are worth. You have to think of the rent, electricity, tools, taxes, *et cetera*, *et cetera*. However, when you have a more or less clear picture and understand that you must ask €10 for an hour of your work to bring home three, four Euros... That is roughly one thousand per month... You cannot accept to work for three, four Euros. Some of my colleagues have done it, but it is suicide... That's the reason I closed. It is better to stay at home than accept that game. At least I can say I liquidated my firm, others are going bankrupt."

Although the figures proposed by Claudio were just examples that are not representative of the prices during the 2009-10 period, they portray quite well the difficult economic scenario that faced supplying firms after 2008, and outline the embitterment of economic power relations between outsourcers and suppliers. The "new, interesting perspectives", which the accountant pointed out, consisted of a reduction in the price of the suppliers' work, the acceptance of longer payment terms, and, not unusually, the acceptance of informal linking contracts where the suppliers committed themselves to passing on part of their profits to the outsourcers. Although since summer 2009 rumours about these "new conditions" and the new, informal development occurring in the trade have abounded, most of the artisans I met were unwilling to talk about these rumours and preferred not to speak, quickly dismissing my questions. Only a few of them were actually open on this subject and willing to tell me about their experiences. One of these, Luigi, was actually a 'victim' of *'la Crisi'*. At the end of 2009, he closed his workshop where he had worked together with a partner for almost thirty years. On the verge of the pensionable age, faced with the recent changes they decided to just close the firm:

> "We decided to close the studio after a meeting. We had worked mainly for [an international company that is set up in the city]. A few months ago, one of their managers organised a meeting with quite a large number of its suppliers. We might be twenty or thirty firms, let's say. It was a very short meeting. He greeted us and quickly explained the new conditions for working for his enterprise. It was a diktat: 'Either you do what I tell you now, or you are out.' He then told us that he was going to pay 30% less for manufactured pieces and, and, we would be given those orders only if we accepted to pay them a deposit of 30% of the overall value of the order – 'Just in case' he said – while we would be paid 90-120 days after the delivery. After he said it, he left. What to do? There was no work and we did not want to spoil the only few chances we had to work by speaking out... Better to stay put and work, than reveal the change and starve... We refused the conditions and closed. Others did like us, but I think the majority remained."

Although the outsourcer later neglected to apply any linking contract to its suppliers, Luigi's narration matched the stories I was told by other entrepreneurs. Regardless of the factuality of the scenario described, these stories tell us of a worsening of inter-firm relations, and an imbalance of bargaining power between firms that became evident after 2008 and that still characterised the milieu when I left in 2011.

In Claudio's and Luigi's testimonies we see an outline of the city's economic transformation. It unfolds in a tangle of changes that betray the expectations associated with jewellery production and undermine some of the constitutive pillars of the dream, such as the large gains for the workers, and the possibility of 'easy' entrepreneurial success. Goldsmiths (both employees and employers) experienced the effects of this embitterment and witnessed the rapid change in the industry in a direction that was perceived and narrated not just as a worsening of their economic condition, but as a betrayal of the dream. They rarely mentioned the actual change in their wages and economic possibilities. Rather, they voiced their understanding and feelings through the narration of change in the places where they lived and worked. In this respect they talked about two distinct phenomena: *'desertificazione'* [desertification] of the workplaces and *'moria'* [pestilence] of firms. Two topoi (rhetorical themes) that portray the effects of two distinct but interconnected phenomena: the loss of jobs within firms and the closing down of firms in the city.

'Desertificazione'

'*Desertificazione*' [desertification] vocalises the job losses. As mentioned in the previous chapter, the period of 2009-2010 resulted in

1,500 positions being lost and over 2,000 others being rendered precarious. This change affected the lives of those who lost their job, but also had a side effect: the emptying of the shop-floors, their '*desertificazione*'.

In the two year period most of the firms shrank in size. This contraction left 'ruins' (cf. Stoler, 2008) in the workspaces: empty benches and vacant seats. The tools became dusty due to lack of use. The silence grew on the shop-floors that a few months earlier had been used by a dozen people, and then were occupied by three, maybe four artisans.

These are small but meaningful signs to the eyes of those goldsmiths who still work in the workshops, mirroring a more general transformation that, from the inside of the *'fabbrica',* was transforming the outside of the city too. These ruins become features on which goldsmiths based a general image of the being and unbecoming of the local jewellery industry. An example of these narrations is taken from the second interview with Santuzzo, a goldsmith whose story I presented in the last chapter, which took place in late December 2010:

> "Every day you go to the *'fabbrica'*; you sit at your bench and think: a few months ago, there was Giulio, there was Anselmo, there Marco, and so on... Then I look at the faces around, and count them. They are just a few... So few. The workshop has turned into a desert. Seeing the empty benches in front of me I cannot but understand that something went wrong in this trade, in this city... Our security, our dream appears to be gone... Faded away like the presence of Giulio, Anselmo, Marco, Paolo and all the others..."

He whispered these few words through his teeth, while, with bowed head, he was explaining to me that, since the last months of 2009, the firm had started shifts of *'cassa integrazione'* for all its personnel. After one year, however, since September 2010, they had laid off half their workers. The firm contracted down from twelve to six people, two of which were the firm's owners. Santuzzo was the last experienced goldsmith to remain. He did not experience particular cuts or reduction of wages but all the other people with whom he worked for decades were dismissed, because too expensive for the firm's budget. Instead the owners preferred to keep three goldsmiths, in their late twenties – early thirties, with only a few years of experience, because they were "much cheaper labour than experienced artisans."

In telling me his story, Santuzzo attached a sense of loss and defeat to the absence of his friends: an absence that ended up also involving the private life of the goldsmiths, since his friends had slowly grown distant from him:

> "They withdrew into their lives, cutting contact with most of their former friends and colleagues. Yes, we meet occasionally, but it is clearly not like it was in the past, and I see that they are uncomfortable with us. I guess it's due to the loss of jobs, but this makes me wonder about what happened to the jewellery industry we believed in... Its dream... Its success... All gone, I say to myself..."

In the previous chapter I offered a possible explanation for this disappearance, as a detachment necessary for the unemployed person to stop being a goldsmith. However, Santuzzo's words echo those of other goldsmiths who, in the course of the two years, did not lose their job (although they may have endured periods of *'cassa integrazione'*), and they narrated *'la Crisi'* by describing the emptying of their *'fabbrica'* and the social network that depended on that space. The changing environment of the *'fabbrica'* became a 'metonymous sign' (Mortara Garavelli, 2003: 148-51) of the general transformation of the business in the city, while the workspace itself turned into a ruined place haunted by a past inhabited by faces, sounds, actions that, over the span of two years, the informants saw fade away. Thus, the '*desertificazione*' became the subject of a reflection about undergoing business change, and appeared as clear evidence of the end of the dream in which goldsmiths believed.

'Moria'

While *'desertificazione'* portrays the loss of jobs, '*moria*' expresses the disappearing of firms from the city. This is a further element of the change that has been highlighted by most of the informants and in particular by entrepreneurs. In two years (31/12/2008 – 31/12/2010), about 300 firms, 25%[2] of the entire industrial milieu closed (Maggiora, 2010: 529). Goldsmiths and the media (e.g. Bottiroli, 2011) often referred to this wave of closures as a *'moria'*: a deadly pestilence that was affecting the entire city and decimating the milieu. This comparison arose from my informants' direct experience and the progressive reduction of the industrial fabric. This was pointed out spontaneously by workers and employers. However, the persons who based their work on an active interaction with various firms of the network were able to provide the most detailed and vibrant descriptions. An example was given by Anna, a

[2] This figure can be estimated from data collected by the City Council, by comparing the population of firms that own a registered hallmark over time. At the beginning of the crisis there were 903 (Bellini, 2008). At the end of 2009, their number had decreased to 839, (Bellini, 2010) to suffer a further reduction of 42 firms in 2009.

freelance designer and modeller in her forties, whom I interviewed in early January 2011, after she had completed a new work for Gianmario's firm (Chapter 3):

> "What has changed in the past years? Since this crisis started, almost two years have passed... Twenty months that have changed the structure of Valenza's jewellery trade. It is a *'moria'*... Every day we were able to feel its advance, in every knocked-on door that is not going to be opened. We watched Valenza disappearing, firm after firm. While the work is becoming tougher and tougher, many of my suppliers are closing, and even some of my most reliable customers have closed down. What they leave behind are empty places and large placards with 'Workshop for Rent or Sale' written on them. Valenza has been turned into a desert where very few survive. With every firm that closes down, I feel a part of the dream of this city no longer shines."

What Anna described as a *'moria'* is a rapid process of erosion of the city's productive fabric. What remains after this process is a desert, a wasteland punctuated with the debris of the past. The empty buildings and the placards appear as ruins of the past. To Anna they recalled the dream; at the same time they rendered visible a rift between the golden age of the past and the wasteland of the present.

The imagery of the wasteland often recurred. Goldsmiths as well as people not involved in the business added to the list of ruins other elements of the city landscape. An example is offered by Lucia, an active woman in her seventies. Until 2001, when she retired, she had worked as an accountant and saleswoman for the firm that she owned together with her husband. Since the 1980s, they have lived in a flat in one of the modernist condominiums half a kilometre from Piazza Duomo, where their firm was located. They liquidated the firm in 2001, when they both retired. However, as commonly happens, theirs had not been the only enterprise in the building:

> "In this building, downstairs, there had been four workshops until a few months ago. One big one, with a few dozen workers; the other three, smaller, with three or four people working there. You know what remains of them? Nothing. Just the bars at the windows. In the buildings around this condominium there were other firms. What remains of them? Some awkward cameras that were their security systems. Those cameras are now the blind eyes of corpses. I never imagined experiencing anything like that. The jewellery industry gave a lot to me, but now, what remains of it? I think of my son... I think of all of you. I am very concerned for you, young people. It seems that everything is ending... But I hope I am wrong..."

The list of ruins encompassed the bars on the windows and security cameras. These became the sources of a broader sense of insecurity that also affected the goldsmiths' ability to interpret Valenza's landscape. Bars and security cameras were, in fact, still small signs that indicated the presence of invisible firms in the urban fabric of Valenza (Chapter 2). However the process of becoming ruins made them into 'uncanny signs' (cf. Freud, 1919) whose meaning has become uncertain. As clearly expressed by Anna:

> "Once, when I saw a security camera, I was sure there was a jewellery firm in that building. Now I don't know whether there is a *'fabbrica'* anymore."

These objects appear suspended between the clear indexicality of signs of presence (of an active, that is, living, firm, as explained in Chapter 2), and absence (of a firm that once existed there). Because of this semiotic tension these features of the urban landscape turned into 'evocative objects' (cf. Turkle, 2007) with a haunting sense of suspension between the remembrance of the past and an uncertain future.

The end of the dream

'Desertificazione' and *'moria'* intertwined in describing a ruined environment; a wasteland that involved workspaces as well as the entire city, objects and human relationships. By listing and describing these ruins, goldsmiths completed a representation of present Valenza and the jewellery industry permeated by a sense of insecurity and uncertainty for the future, while the past of the city appears to be romanticised into a landscape of certitude where the insecurity and anxieties for the future that goldsmiths experienced at the time, as emerges from the pages of old newspapers, are silenced and forgotten (e.g. Rubino, 1992; Castellaro, 1994; Bottino, 1984; Bottino, 1983). This image became the mirror in which goldsmiths reflected and compared the expectations they had for the business. Moreover, in describing the ruins, they acknowledged the 'end of the dream': a radical rift between a rosy past and a gloomy present.

In the second interview I had with him, Santuzzo's last remark offered a vibrant description of this rupture:

> "What I see now, it is just the end of that dream... The end of that era... We were the masters of the world. For years, by the time we produced something, it was already sold. Here, though you had arrived with naught, you could build your fortune... Open your firm. With a few files and your skills you were able to become well-off. Instead... Instead now...Do you

> know that painting by Friederich? That one with a man who stares at the mountain peaks, the clouds and the cliffs? Sometimes I feel as if I were that person. I see the change in this city. A big and terrifying thing like the depth of a gorge. Like that man, I cannot do anything, facing the spectacle in front of me. We are witnessing the failure of a dream... Maybe it was all a dream... But, now, we must wake up..."

So he concluded, frowning. His blue eyes darkened. He was no longer looking at me, but gazing at the square behind me, that square that was almost devoid of cars on that winter evening. Maybe not even the square but, in an ideal way, the entire city, passing over the borders created by the dark condominiums. Gazing at that city in which he had arrived thirty-five years before and made his home. Gazing at that industry that had allowed him to achieve wealth, buy a large flat for his family in Valenza and a house at the seaside close to his native village. That jewellery production for which he was still working, realizing that dream was gone and would never come back. His words sounded like a confession that was revealing a malaise caused by *'la Crisi'*: a sense of disempowerment that stemmed from the perception that a model of economy and a dream of life had been irremediably compromised by the recent changes.

Like in this interview, when goldsmiths revealed their memories of the past and observed the departure of present times from the reality of the dream, a combination of sadness, concern and anger swiftly emerged and, eventually, broke the mask of self-imposed quiet detachment that many of them adopted when they talked with me. The recognition of the end of the dream entailed the expression of a sense of betrayal that they seemed to feel towards a trade and a world of institutions and people that led them to the loss of their past 'state of grace'. They recounted a vast array of events, decisions, and agents that supposedly caused this fall, multiplying *'la Crisi'* in a tangle of changes (Chapter 5). They blamed different groups and institutions for the seriousness of the current situation. A vast array that encompassed the national government that led Italy to pursue the dream of global markets, but which was economically unprepared to face such a challenge[3]. They blamed other Valenza producers who were not

---

[3] The opinions of my informants resemble those of Nesi (2010), a textile ex-entrepreneur from Prato and a nationally well-known writer. In his works, Nesi described the decline of another ID, Prato. It resembles Valenza in its entrepreneurial characteristics and economic history. Nesi pointed out that the decline of the Italian IDs, of which Valenza and Prato are examples, was caused first of all by the decision of the political elite that ruled in the 1990s to pursue the dream of the global market without realizing that the Italian economy was not ready to face such a scenario and the forces that acted there.

able to cooperate better and create stronger policies to protect their production, or just bad luck. In this multiplication of objects and events, only rarely the game of blame attribution included the speaking subject. In particular, company directors (of both outsourcing and supplying firms) did not recognise the role that their choices may have had in participating in the creation and propagation of *'la Crisi'*. Instead, employers and employees alike explained *'la Crisi'* as an external force, which the subjects endured and to which they reacted by adjusting themselves to it. Narrating their experiences, *'la Crisi'* and the end of the dream, goldsmiths spoke of themselves in terms of objects rather than subjects of the change. In so doing they tended to externalise agency and allocate it to a distant reality that temporally (*'la Crisi'* as a result of past actions), geographically (*'la Crisi'* as an effect of the change in international markets), fatalistically (*'la Crisi'* as a matter of chance) or socially (*'la Crisi'* was caused by the reckless actions of 'other' goldsmiths) is detached from the individual. This externalisation of agency, in the light of the clear distinction between a past golden age and an uncertain present and future, appears to be complementary to what Bauman describes as the transfer of '*Unsicherheit'* (insecurity and uncertainty) to the self (Bauman, 1999: 5). In other words, goldsmiths felt a growing insecurity due to the impossibility of relying on those networks and structures, and above all on their work, which previously had sustained them and given them security. In present times they were seen to be falling apart. They felt helpless in the face of a change that they perceived as uncontrollable and independent from their actions: in this sense, they presented themselves as passive bystanders and not agents of this transformation.

It is on the basis of this dynamic and the recognition of a substantial difference between past and present that goldsmiths reimagined their dream and considered *'la Crisi'* as its endpoint:

> "A moment at which a project is apprehended retrospectively as complete, closed, and in the past." (Miyazaki and Riles, 2005: 325)

As Miyazaki (2006) explained, the endpoint of a dream does not only correspond with a failure in a career or an economic loss. Narrating the vicissitudes of Tada, a Japanese businessman, Miyazaki showed that an endpoint represents the individual's a) acknowledgement of the impossibility of reaching a pre-fixed goal; b) recognition of the limit of knowledge or means previously employed in seeking that goal; c) a reconfiguration of the previous 'orientation of knowledge' (cf. Miyazaki & Riles, 2005), that is a past dream, so that they can proceed in a new direction, towards a new dream. However, before completing this reorientation, an individual has to pass through a moment when they are 'betwixt and between' a dream that is no more and another that is to come: a 'Limbo' (see previous chapter) in which they must find the resources to discover or invent a new dream.

Due to the intermittent contacts that Miyazaki had with Tada, the anthropologist did not provide an account of the 'Limbo' and only hinted at the difficulties involved in terms of insecurity and uncertainty. This reorientation appears, in his account, almost automatic and painless. However, ethnographies of communities that have experienced the effects of the end of an economic dream reveal stories of difficult transitions (e.g. Vargas-Cetina, 2000; Ferguson, 1999; Jancius, 2006) or even entrapment in the 'Limbo', a time when:

> "[The past] arises in the present. Grand causes and ultimate consequences gather themselves around the everyday in the trembling space/time where the question of 'meaning' finds itself caught in a signification that is at once contingent and receptive, overwhelming and inconclusive, tactile and uncertain. The past, like the future, comes and goes, drifting in an out of visions, but it haunts things until there's no telling what might happen and what people might do." (Stewart, 1996: 116)

These words, written by Stewart in her ethnography of a former mining community in West Virginia, well describe the feelings and the way of describing the world that goldsmiths expressed even when I left the field for the last time, almost two years and a half after *'la Crisi'* started. In the early months of 2011, goldsmiths were acknowledging the changes that the downturn brought along. They were acknowledging the end of their dream; they were still struggling to find a new one.

Conclusion

At the end of this chapter, the voice of Luca still resonates:

> "The dream of gold appears to be gone... Now we have to deal with this change... That's the only way to find a new future..."

For almost three decades, the jewellery trade conveyed this dream of opulence that made the city into a centre receiving people willing to join the industry. However, in the light of the recent changes this seems to have come to an endpoint.

The recent transformations, the worsening of work conditions in the workshop and among firms, ruined the environment in which goldsmiths lived; the environment that embodied the dream. In the two years of 2009-

10, a rift between past and present opened up in front of the goldsmiths, while the jewellery industry turned into a wasteland disfigured by the ruins of the recent past: absences and leftover objects that evoked the goldsmiths' dream, the world as it was. In referring to their work and work life, goldsmiths described a reality of remembrance and mourning of the past. In so doing, they affirmed the end of the past dream and showed that no new goal replaced it. In the early months of 2011, when I left, they appeared still in transition. However, their knowledge has been reoriented: not to define new goals, but to justify their current status of un-success. Past self-confidence and proactive attitudes towards the market turned into an insecure idea of the self as an object at the mercy of the change.

This reorientation may be the first phase of a broader phenomenon: a moment of separation that potentially could usher in a more profound reformulation of expectations. However, leaving the field, traces of this new dream were not distinct. Rather, the general conviction was that, paraphrasing Luca, the jewellery industry was still moving on, but losing pieces along the way to its full collapse.

This general conviction seems to suggest that the 'orientation of knowledge' (cf. Miyazaki & Riles, 2005) I noticed could be the final result of the post-*'crisi'* transformation. Thus, unlike Miyazaki, we may conclude that when a dream arrives at its endpoint, what comes after may not be another dream, but ruins, ashes and mourning for a past. In this regard, the experiences of anthropologists, such as Stewart, Ferguson and Jancius also suggest this conclusion.

In the case of Valenza, I cannot untie this knot on the basis of my sources. Differently from the cases described by those anthropologists, the industry, the subject of the dream, is still active at the moment I am writing and is not an experience irrecoverably segregated into the past. Thus, I am not going to proclaim the impossibility of a re-'orientation of knowledge' (cf. Miyazaki & Riles, 2005) that involves the creation of a new dream for jewellery production in Valenza. Paraphrasing Manzoni's poem, *5 Maggio*, I leave the future generations of researchers make this difficult judgment. Thus, leaving unsolved this teleological indeterminateness, this case opens out to questions about the subjective redirection of knowledge in a context of change, that is, "who creates the dream? And how?"

Since the 19th century, social and economic theories have addressed the problem of knowledge, work and change. These include Marshall's economic district, Marx's theory of class struggle, passing through structural functionalist anthropology, Bourdieu's '*habitus*', and Foucault's discourse, have pointed out in different ways the centrality of group dynamics. Reconsidering the experience of Valenza goldsmiths in this wide-angle perspective, the social body of goldsmiths appeared not to be engaged in a general debate on possible futures. Rather, it appeared involved in a process of fragmentation after the disappearance of the social glue that bound its members together, that is, the economic context described by the dream, and an emotional and inspirational distancing of goldsmiths from the jewellery industry. Retrospectively, these processes demonstrate the important function that expectations had as a social glue and a motor for the entire system. However, if they are the collective phenomenon that directs individuals, it would appear difficult to understand why some, maybe a minority, of goldsmiths participated in public discussions or initiatives about new strategies for the sector.

Miyazaki and Riles (2005) suggest that collective re-'orientation of knowledge' (cf. Miyazaki & Riles, 2005) is a process undertaken primarily on an individual level. In order to find a new goal after a failure, it is the individual, not the community, who reconsiders her skills and capacities on the basis of the environment in which she lives. In this regard, the individual would need to adjust to the environment to find new ways to success.

Following from Miyazaki and Riles' reasoning, the environment emerges not as a fixed, unmodifiable stage, but as social itself, made by other people who look (also) to the individual to reorient their own knowledge. Hence, by adjusting herself to her environment, the individual ends up modifying her environment, which is her community. Thus, I would argue that in the context of an economy, the link between the individual and the community is established in a way that is not reducible to a mere union of individuals' independent actions, nor to the individual's passive embodiment of a collective dynamic; rather to a dimension that goes beyond the distinction between individual and community's transformation. Dealing with the environment, the individual adjusts herself to it, as explained by Lave and Wenger (1991), but at the same time changes the environment, by giving feedback to other people by manipulating objects. In this respect, the individual is neither subject nor object, but a participant of the environment. Acknowledging this role, however, leads to the recognition of a complex tangle of social relations that links individuals together. Through these relationships, information flows, and is redirected, manipulated, and embodied.

Profound transformations such as the one endured by Valenza goldsmiths change the configuration of the network. However, they do not interrupt the very essence of the network, that is, the relational nature of the network. Although participants can disappear, and individuals can feel a growing sense of insecurity towards their future, the network remains social, made up by people who interact with each other. In this respect, it is this relational character that can offer a simple answer to the conundrum; a solution that passes through the recognition of individuals' experience as motors of a collective re-'orientation of knowledge' (cf. Miyazaki & Riles, 2005).

As Miyazaki showed, the re-'orientation of knowledge' (cf. Miyazaki & Riles, 2005) emerges by talking about new objectives, doing new or different things from those done in the past. Since the individual is not suspended in a vacuum, these changes can be seen by others, and can be judged, becoming sources of perplexity, annoyance or inspiration. In this way, the individual's actions can contribute to a more general, maybe slow, reconfiguration of knowledge. Moreover, single individuals with their decisions, charisma and possibilities can contribute to create a radical change. In the case of Valenza, Vincenzo Morosetti and Vincenzo Melchiorre, back in the 19th century (Chapter 3), with their personal enterprises, were able to transform the city, introducing a new understanding of production, such as with large factories and the networking among firms. Hegel talked about such persons as 'heroes' (Beiser, 2005: 269), Gramsci as 'vanguards' (Showstack Sasson, 2010: 248). Besides the single theorisations of how the appearance of such persons must be framed, single individuals, disregarding their original social and economic position, can be catalysts even for a rapid change in general 'orientation of knowledge' (cf. Miyazaki & Riles, 2005).

These premises can outline an answer to the question about the role of the individual and community in orienting knowledge, by pointing out the significant role of each individual in generating this transformation. However, to fully appreciate how individuals reorient their knowledge, we are missing a key element: to understand the very dimension where the reorientation takes place. In other words, how the economic transformations caused by *'la Crisi'* in Valenza, become a tool of knowledge to reconsider a business and the very idea of community: a topic I will explore in the next chapter.

CHAPTER EIGHT

A CRACK IN THE IDENTITY LINK

The 28th of September 2010. I had come to the workshop to interview its owner, Giovanni, and to ask him for information concerning his experience as a goldsmith in Valenza, as well as about the history of his workshop. Having a yearly turnover of more than two million Euros, the firm was well known and established. However, the office of its director and owner was small and unadorned. A little over ten square metres, the room had a black linoleum floor whose colour sharply contrasted against the plain white of the walls. Near the entrance, there were a couple of grey, metal lockers. Together with the plain metal writing desk and three chairs probably bought from Ikea, they were the only pieces of furniture in the room: no photos, no pictures on the wall. There was no computer either. Giovanni was in his seventies and never familiarised himself with what he called '*diavolerie moderne*', modern diabolical gadgetry. The computers were in another office and were used by a secretary and the CAD designer. Behind the desk, Giovanni was seated in one of the chairs. While answering my questions, he was reading some of the bills and receipts that crowded the desk. Small, anonymous packages wrapped up in white tissue paper emerged from among the papers. The only clue to understanding the precious contents of those small parcels were the few figures hastily written on each envelope. The numbers indicated the price of the pieces of jewellery that were enclosed, and the carats of the mounted stones.

His answers allowed me to reconstruct the history of his life and activity. Giovanni opened the firm with his brother in the 1970s, after twenty years spent working employed in various small and large Valenza jewellery workshops. In the 1990s, Giovanni's brother left the firm. After having interviewed Giovanni for an hour, my last question was about the last few years of history in Valenza, and this is what he replied:

> "It is *'la Crisi'*... It is the difficulty in finding new clients, and making them pay on time. *'La Crisi'* is in Valenza. It is rooted in the souls of Valenza people. You see it in the eyes of the people, in the eyes of the

> other goldsmiths. It lies in the growing lack of trust for the future of jewellery making, our trade. I saw *'la Crisi'* in the eyes of many of our apprentices and workers. [...] This is *'la Crisi'* of the jewellery trade: the young people go away and the old ones remain... I will continue to work so long as I have the strength to work. Then, I will sell the workshop. However, this is *'la Crisi'* of our economy. It's not just the economy... It's not just the market... It is in the city: it's the too many firms that have had to close, it's the too many empty workshops that are now on sale... But it's also in our heads: it is the fear, the insecurity, the sense of resignation and lack of future that Valenza people feel."

***

In the previous chapter, I have brought forward the analysis of the downturn. I explored the genealogy of the trope of '*la Crisi*' in the unfolding of a non-linear history of the downturn (Chapter 5). I moved to explore the impact of the downturn on the lives of goldsmiths –both those who lost their jobs (Chapter 6) and who maintained them (Chapter 7) – and the production milieu of the city (Chapter 7). The words of Giovanni, however, mark a further dimension of '*la Crisi*': the level of the city and its community.

In this chapter, I aim to explore this level by showing how the downturn affected Valenza and how the economic change has triggered a broad reconsideration of the overlapping of identity between the city and the jewellery industry. In highlighting this cultural tendency, I will point out how the perception of the downturn in the landscape has become the motive for actions that are shaping the future of the city, and how at the same time, '*la Crisi*' has turned into a 'keyword' (cf. Williams, 1983) of a broader discussion about the future of Valenza.

In order to do so, I begin by showing how the meaning of '*la Crisi*', since its first occurrence in the public debate of Valenza, has shifted from a problem that involved only the jewellery industry to an emergency for the entire city. I will, then, investigate the effects of the downturn on the city, and, finally I will move to explore how the downturn has resulted in a problematisation of the idea of *'città orafa'*.

The emergence of '*la Crisi*'

My fieldwork ended in January 2011, two years after the beginning of my research and about twenty-five months after the start of this latest downturn. Over the course of this period, I, alongside the population of the city, lived through the transformation of the urban environment, witnessed the closing down of firms, the increase in unemployment, and the erosion of the jewellery industry: what appeared to me to be the possible twilight of *'città orafa'*. The night before my last departure, a friend of mine, an apprentice archivist at that time, called me. He was a man more or less my age, born and raised in Valenza. He was calling to bid me goodbye. We chatted for a while. Then, concluding the call he asked me:

> "When do you think you'll come back to our *'città orafa'*?"

There was no irony in this appellation, or allusion to the downturn. It was just the normal way for him and other Valenzani to speak about their city. Despite the changes the city was undergoing, in two years, including fifteen months spent in the city, I continued to hear Valenza politicians, goldsmiths and non-goldsmiths, talk about their city as a 'city of gold,' 'a city of goldsmiths,' 'a goldsmithing city' (Chapter 1). The form of this rhetoric appeared untouched by the change and the decline of the jewellery industry. It continued to be woven according to a history that originated in the 1960s, when jewellery industry had become the centre of Valenza's economy. It was meaningfully carried on (Chapter 1), and goldsmiths and non-goldsmiths continued to describe their Valenza in terms of a large *'fabbrica' (*Chapter 2), marking an unchanged importance of the trade for the city as metre and metronome of its social life.

However, a new rhetoric emerged alongside this one in the last weeks of 2008. It was a broad narration that involved not just the goldsmithing community, but the entire city, and it hinged on the particular trope of *'la Crisi'*. In Chapter 5, I explored the origins of the discourse about '*la Crisi*'. I showed how, over the course of the last months of 2008, the ongoing recession of the jewellery market, initially perceived and described by goldsmiths, authorities, and journalists as a normal downturn within a cyclical dynamic of the market, a *'molla'* in the local dialect, came to be seen as an extraordinary change in the jewellery economy. This shift in the understanding of the downturn occurred with the spreading of a public recognition of '*la Crisi*' as an emergency for the entire city, rather than just for its goldsmiths.

As explained before (Chapter 5), the 19th of December 2008 marks the first occurrence of the trope in a public statement by one of the local authorities. In an interview, the mayor of Valenza addressed the downturn as '*la Crisi*'; however, he explained it as a limited event, involving only the jewellery trade. In spite of a negative prediction of a reprisal of the international market economy during the first semester of 2009, Raselli tried to reassure the reader, arguing that the quality of local productions and the capacity of goldsmiths to "*fare sacrifici*" [making sacrifices for the firms] would allow Valenza to surpass the "conjuncture". In this way, implicitly, Raselli tried to transform a *'crisi'* into a *'molla'*, by acknowledging the current difficulties but reducing them to a momentary and non-destabilizing event for the locale. Moreover, restricting *'la Crisi'* to the ambit of the jewellery industry, he was glossing over other social effects that the downturn was having on the city.

These changes were, however, already pointed out by Valenzani on an everyday basis. By listening to the conversations between Valenzani in the cafés, in the streets, or in the shops, it clearly emerged that there was a growing awareness that *'la Crisi'* of the jewellery sector was far more than just an economic problem limited to one section of the population. This was apparent even in small changes in the urban landscape. An example of this understanding is offered by this episode, a conversation between friends queuing in a supermarket.

***

The 24th of December 2008, about 6 pm, I was queuing in the largest supermarket of Valenza. During the year, the thirty or so checkouts are enough to make the wait quite quick. Not so on Christmas Eve, when hundreds of people throng the supermarket, buying the last, essential things for the dinner and Christmas lunch. I was able to reach the counter in about ten minutes. Around me, people with their carts, mostly half-empty; families with (often howling) kids, couples, groups of friends or just people on their own. In front of me in the queue, two women were chatting. The first, Giovanna, was in her late forties; the second, Patrizia, was in her mid-fifties. Both of them were born and raised in Valenza. Giovanna had worked for a year as a secretary in a goldsmithing firm. There she met her husband, the owner of the firm. They married in the mid-1990s. After they had their son, in the late 1990s, Giovanna left work, to look after the child and the house. Patrizia, instead, was a teacher in one of the city's high schools. She met her husband, an accountant who worked in Lombardy, during her university years. When she was appointed in Valenza in the late 1980s, they decided to move to live in her home town.

The friends were chatting quite loudly, so I had a chance to follow their conversation[1]. Giovanna was talking about her husband's business. She was visibly preoccupied. For her, and her family, the firm was not just

[1] Some of the background information that I intertwined in this narration were provided to me by the two women in interviews that followed this encounter.

a matter of pride, but the principal source of earnings. She was talking about "a bad condition of the market," the "disappearance of customers," the *'cassa integrazione'* that "my husband had to 'ask' for many of his employees."

Her friend was listening carefully. She wore a sad expression on her face. She and her family were not exposed to the effects of the jewellery industry's downturn, but seeing her friend in such anguish was something that "touched [her] deeply." To her friend, she answered:

> "I know, I know how this *'crisi'* is bad... Also I can see *'la Crisi'*... It is in the streets; it is in the many parking lots left empty; it is in people who throng the coffee shops without having a coffee... It is in the half-empty trolleys of this supermarket...I understand *'la Crisi'* is around us... I am asking what'll become of this *'città orafa'*."

Giovanna nodded. She appeared on the verge of tears. Patrizia, noticing her friend's expression, abruptly steered the conversation away from the topic. She started speaking about her Christmas roast beef, and the fact that she was never good at doing it in comparison with Giovanna's gastronomic bravura, and asked for any suggestions. Giovanna smiled – I do not know whether because she had understood the intention of her friend, or thinking of the 'proverbial' clumsiness of Patrizia in cooking –, and smiling, she answered her friend.

***

In the description Patrizia gave, *'la Crisi'* permeated the city. Superficial changes, variations in the normality of the urban landscape, wrinkles in aspects of everyday life in the city were described by her. In her narration, they were transformed into indices of a profound transformation that was altering Valenza. A transformation that had been generated in the jewellery industry but now was engulfing the entire city.

Already by December, in the streets of the city, goldsmiths and non-goldsmiths had started to equate 'la Crisi' of the jewellery industry to 'la Crisi' of the entire city, and spur a discourse on the possible future of the city: a future without gold. Until May 2009, this cultural dynamic remained unaccounted for by the local press, which continued describing the downturn as an event limited to the jewellery industry (e.g. Zemide, 2009a). In March 2009, the local news radio, *Radiogold*, was the first (and only) mass-media outlet that tried to portray and present this discussion in a broadcasting series: *Valenza: le persone, l'oro e la Crisi* [Valenza:

people, gold and *'la Crisi'*]. As indicated by its title[2], the broadcast aimed to offer an account of the downturn, highlighting how it was changing not just the jewellery industry, but the entire city's industry. The series ran weekly from the 12th March to the 7th May. During the series the commentators, myself among them (see Introduction), highlighted the effects that the downturn of the Valenza jewellery industry was having on other sectors of the city, such as commerce (e.g. Rossi, 2009b) or education (e.g. Fontefrancesco, 2009a), and on the perception of the city by Valenza people (e.g. Rossi, 2009a; 2009c). The programme was a success with the public. Numerous listeners called the radio or commented on-line on the different episodes, and local authorities (both on a city level and a provincial one), as well as representatives from goldsmith associations asked to participate. Most relevantly, it was not rare to find people, in the days after the broadcasting of an episode (on-air every Thursday morning from 8.30 to 9.00 am), commenting on its contents in cafés and in the workshops of Valenza.

The broadcast represented a turning point in the history of the discourse. In its nine episodes, it was able to attest and publicly legitimise a new narration (Chapter 5) of *'la Crisi'*: a holistic understanding of *'la Crisi'* as a collective problem and transformation of the entire city, rather than a transformation restricted to the borders of a niche (the jewellery industry and its market).

After a few weeks, other media, such as the local newspaper *Il Piccolo*, and the city's political debate, began approaching the topic of the downturn in this perspective (e.g. Zemide, 2009a; 2009b; Comune di Valenza, 2009a). During the long plunge of 2009 and the following precarious stabilisation[3], so the discourse grew, steady in equating the jewellery industry's downturn with the decline of Valenza and describing

---

[2] This title denotes a change in the rhetorical conception and representation of *'la Crisi'*. The title's syntactic structure portrays a disaggregation of an original object, Valenza, into three fundamental components: people, gold (both as symbol of the jewellery industry and centre of the identity rhetoric of the community), and *'la Crisi'*. These elements are juxtaposed, which suggests an objectification of the three. Thus, they appear as separate and distinct entities. Consequentially, *'la Crisi'* appeared *per se* to be distinct from the others and a co-participant in the description of the whole of Valenza. The title, thus, shows an understanding of *'la Crisi'* not just as an economic feature concerning the jewellery industry, or more broadly the local economy, but an independent object distinguishing the entire city.

[3] On a turnout level that was lower than the one of the first semester 2008 (Servizio Studi e Ricerche, 2010a: 18, Servizio Studi e Ricerche, 2011: 8).

a picture of growing insecurity for the future of the city and its community.

A change in the city

This narration, thus, brings to the foreground the relevance that the jewellery downturn had in the city. It voiced the change that Valenzani were experiencing and pointing out by listing details of their experiences of their place. These detailswere indices of the change of Valenza, in the same way that "swelling, pain, redness and heat are indices of inflammation" (Zeman, 1977: 38). However, if, as noted by Piece:

> "Indices furnish positive assurance of the reality and the nearness of their objects [, ...] With the assurance there goes no insight into the nature of those objects." (Hartshorne and Wiess, 1933: 531)

Thus, empty trolleys, and empty workshops provide assurance of the affective and material proximity and meaningfulness of '*la Crisi*'. However, to get a better insight into it, it is necessary to look to other elements that can complete the picture of the transformation: ethnographic data as well as newspaper articles and official reports produced by public and private institutions, all of which shed light on different aspects of the city, are the resources for this task.

To describe this transformation, I want to start from the signs proposed by Patrizia. In her words, '*la Crisi*' is first of all a material change of landmarks. To the eyes of a person who was detached, probably even emotionally, from the jewellery business, '*la Crisi*' appears through a landscape of absences: empty parking lots, half-full trolleys, people who crowd cafés without having even a coffee. They are anomalous aspects of a city that contradict how Valenza was experienced and perceived by Patrizia. In fact, in an interview in June 2009, she explained that Valenza before '*la Crisi*' appeared to her:

> "Usually crowded and busy [; ...] A place full of things and people, stuffed with the jewellery industry. [... However,] the present appeared to betray that past, as emerging from small signs"

In that situation, she listed the same elements she pointed out in the supermarket, adding a further landmark to her list:

> "The many venues left empty, vacant by the demise of some jewellery firm which in the past few months went bankrupt or was liquidated."

Patrizia, like other Valenzani I met and interviewed and the guests on *Valenza: le persone, l'oro, la Crisi* described post-October 2008 Valenza as an environment that was slowly being emptied. Instead of presences and fullness, meaningful empty spaces populated the landscape. These gaps, as seen in the previous chapter, are 'evocative objects' (cf. Turkle, 2007) that mark the distancing of the present from a past of the city that was perceived as an age of abundance and plenty including by non-goldsmiths. Past symbols of abundance –such as full trolleys, businesses and full parking lots– and of jewellery production –such as cameras, armoured shutters (see also previous chapter) and, later, "for rent" placards left up on empty workshops to bleach in the sun over the course of months– turned into ruins: *'lieux de mémorie'* (cf. Nora, 1989) of the change. While invisibility has been a meaningful sign of the presence and activity of the jewellery industry (Chapter 2), these new visible signs appear as indisputable symptoms of the emptying and depauperation of the urban landscape that undermine the meaningfulness of invisibility.

Besides these symptoms, other data, primarily those concerning the state of the real estate market, indicate an impoverishment of the urban fabric. By comparing the reports released by the local branch of FIAIP, the national association of professional estate agents, concerning 2009 and 2010, we can observe an accentuated negative trend in real estate prices in Valenza (FIAIP, 2008; 2009; 2010; 2011). In two years, residential and commercial places lost about 25% of their market value, while production venues, such as jewellery workshops, lost 40%. This trend is peculiar to the city and diverges from those of the rest of the provinces. In the other cities, in fact, after a plunge in 2009, the market value re-increased in 2010 and, in the first semester of 2011, reached or surpassed pre-Credit Crunch prices. Newspaper journalists explained this trend as an effect of the continuing difficulties of the jewellery industry (e.g. Scozzesi, 2010; Radiogold, 2010). I gathered similar comments from estate agents working in Valenza, who described an overall critical situation of the real estate market in the city: a surplus of offers of venues in of the face of a low demand, almost completely absent in the case of production workshops. The commentary offered by the manager of one of the largest estate agencies of the city serves as an illustration:

> "The number of venues for rent or sale has increased day after day since 2009. Valenzani are trying to sell their second or third houses to get some money to cope with the lack of work. Losing their job, many people who had been in Valenza just for work left and went back to their home towns. So if you need a place to rent, there are plenty of them. Many firms closed down and their workshops are on sale now. It is astonishing to see so

> many of those spaces to let. My agency is offering about thirty of them now, and I would guess more than two hundred spaces are available on the market nowadays. So many. Until 2008, I never expected to have to deal with so many offers and with no sign of any interest from the market. If someone needs a proof of the decline of the jewellery industry, please tell them to talk with me."

This testimony leads to another feature of the transformation of the city: its depopulation.

The official statistics on permanent population released by the City Council show a substantial stability of the population over the course of the two years.[4] Moreover, the demographic balance of the permanent resident population highlights a substantial continuity with past trends, with a substantial parity between immigration and emigration and a natural growth rate close to 0% (precisely -0.05%). However, these data do not include temporary residents, who are all the inhabitants of the city registered as permanent residents in other towns in the country. In this respect, the Valenza City Council as well as other public and private institutions did not produce official surveys. However there are informal statistics. As explained by one of the city directors, in a phone call on April 2011:

> "Some of the municipal taxes are sources for this kind of information. In particular, the waste disposal tax that is calculated for residences on the basis of the actual people living in the building. From that we estimate there were about 23-24,000 inhabitants in Valenza in the city in 2008, against the only 22,000 of 2010."

Other local agencies provided similar figures. Although imprecise, these data offer a measure to understand the actual decrease of the local population. Temporary residents were often apprentices or goldsmiths in the early years of their careers. A large number of those were not native to Valenza and arrived in the city for study and work; commonly they did not apply for a new permanent address when they stayed in Valenza. The decline of the non-resident population shows first of all the impact of the downturn in the jewellery community, but also the actual emptying of the city.

The downturn, however, also resulted in an impoverishment of the city, as a whole, and its inhabitants. In the previous chapter, I showed the effect of the downturn as a reduction of gains for goldsmiths. The job loss,

---

[4] The population of the city passed from 20,282 inhabitants in 2008 to 20,169 in 2010 (Comuni-Italiani.it, 2011a). See also: Morselli, 2012.

'cassa integrazione', and renegotiation of job contracts led to a notable reduction of goldsmiths' incomes. However, this represented a more general trend for the entire city. Tax declarations for Valenza compiled in 2009 (tax declarations for the 2008 fiscal year) and 2010 (tax declarations for the 2009 fiscal year), and more specifically, the data for the calculation of IRPEF, the regional duty on natural people's incomes, show an abrupt reduction in Valenzani earnings. While in 2008, the average net annual salary was €11,669, in 2009 this dropped to €10,981, in a general context of Valenza's economy having lost about 10% of its annual turnover[5] (Comuni-Italiani.it, 2011b). Although the available data do not help to distinguish between the losses of goldsmiths and non-goldsmiths, they offer a clear grasp of the general impoverishment of the city.

Such a transformation was often remarked upon by the professional associations of shopkeepers, Confesercenti and Ascom. Since April 2009 (Rossi, 2009b), representatives of the two associations have often foregrounded the reduction of Valenzani spending power, speaking of a 30% loss of income. In the two years, no official reports have been produced about this drop, so that figure appears as an empathic rather than an analytical portrayal of growing difficulties in a sector that is not directly connected with the jewellery industry but still at the centre of the life of the city. Over the course of the two years, in the in-depth interviews I had with shopkeepers, all of them emphasised a reduction in the expenses of Valenzani. In the words of a bookseller, a woman in her late forties and employed in the trade since the 1990s, whom I interviewed in December 2010:

> "These two years were particularly difficult for this city. For the goldsmiths, but also for us. The cuts in the jewellery industry cut the legs of many families who relied on that industry. Before *'la Crisi'* they bought without much thought of the price, today they are very strict in buying just what they need, not a penny more. I understand what they are doing and why they do it, and I am not complaining against them. Not at all. What I am saying is that their actions, the cuts in the jewellery industry are not just touching goldsmiths but are affecting the entire city. Because, if a goldsmith has no money, they will not spend, and if they do not spend, we will see our income reduce, and if we have our gain reduced, we are not going to buy. [...] So the entire economy will just slump and then I do not know what we will do with the debris of this city..."

[5] Unfortunately, the 2011 and 2012 tax declaration data are not available at the moment of writing, so it is not possible to estimate the current figures.

The words of the bookseller conclude an outline, which emerges in this paragraph, of a social and economic system that was profoundly affected by the downturn of the jewellery industry. In this respect, we can see the social repercussions of the jewellery industry downturn affect the entire city.

A rational decision: choosing a future career during '*la Crisi*'

This account brings to the fore Valenza's overall impoverishment and emptying. Indeed, although official statistics tend to generalise this point, the downturn affected those individuals and families involved in the business more directly than people, like Patrizia, who were employed in public administration and whose incomes did not depend on the jewellery business. Although they might have been economically untouched by the downturn, this group of people, as well as goldsmiths, perceived the change of the city. In this respect the downturn represented a collective experience for the entire community.

In this context, many informants spoke about '*la Crisi*' as the end of the jewellery industry and the decline of the '*città orafa*'. However, alongside these words, some particular patterns of decisions point to a change in the trust that linked Valenza's population at large to the industry (see Chapters 3 and 4). Some of these decisions, such as to leave the city or de-invest in the jewellery trade, have emerged in these pages and in the previous chapters (see Chapters 6 and 7). Another important decision concerns the introduction of new generations to the jewellery trade.

In the past thirty years, school education and training in workshops played the main role in introducing new generations to jewellery making (Chapter 4). Still in the mid-2000s, parents encouraged their children to follow an education in jewellery-making and then a goldsmithing career, in particular if their children were endowed with artistic talent and showed no clear propensity to study. This attitude, together with the arrival of students from outside Valenza, had permitted the rapid growth of the business and vitality of the network between the 1980s and 1990s. For two decades, about 300 students came every year to study in the city. In the 2000s, this figure decreased to 200 before 2008, then abruptly falling to about 100 in 2009 and 50 in 2010 (Comune di Valenza, 2011). In the same years, non-goldsmith schools, such as Liceo Alberti, increased in the number of students, reaching about 350 students per year.[6] While until the late 1990s, the ISA Cellini was the primary choice for the teenagers of Valenza and neighbouring cities, because it offered a course of studies perceived as guaranteeing a remunerative job at the end of the five years, with the increasing difficulties of the jewellery market, and in particular the abrupt plunge of 2008, the same families preferred to send their children to a 'non-goldsmithing school', in Valenza or outside the city.

This is the case of Benvenuto, who enrolled his son in a professional school in Alessandria.

Benvenuto came to Valenza in the early 1980s from one of the surrounding villages, after finishing high school. He worked as an accountant for most of his life, being employed by goldsmithing and non-goldsmithing firms. In the late 1990s, when the goldsmithing firm for which he worked closed down, he found a new job as a bookkeeper in Alessandria, and since then he commuted every day from Monday to Friday from Valenza to Alessandria. His wife, born and raised in Valenza and a few years younger than Benvenuto, was working as a clerk in a public institution of her home city.

The couple had one son: Gianpaolo. He was fifteen years old, and at that time had just finished the first year of high school. After unimpressive results in middle school, his parents opted to enrol him in a technical school. Despite the artistic vein of their child, who appeared to be talented in painting and drawing, they opted to enrol him in a technical school in Alessandria.

I was talking about high school and higher education with Benvenuto over a cup of coffee in June 2010. Explaining the difference between the Italian and British systems, we came to talk about Gianpaolo and the decision to enrol him in that school. Benvenuto explained it in these terms:

> "So that [Gianpaolo] can learn a job in these years. A good electrician or mechanic have been always welcome in the market. And then he can even continue with a degree in engineering."

I asked why they did not consider ISA Cellini. This technical school placed in Valenza, still in the early 2000s, was the primary choice for teenagers (Valenza and the neighbouring cities) who wanted to 'learn a job'. The courses of the school were organised into five-year curriculums,

---

[6] In particular, between 2008 and 2009, the goldsmithing school ISA Cellini, which ten years earlier was the largest school in Valenza with over 600 students, shrank to only 100, while the non-goldsmithing Liceo Alberti, in the early 2000s a school of 250 students, surpassed the 350 mark.

specialised in different areas of goldsmithing production, such as gem appraisal and cutting, metal-crafting, and restoration. Upon completion of the degree, the student would have full access to university, even though most of the graduating students opted for architecture, design, history of arts, or fine arts. Benvenuto looked puzzled at my question.

> "I would have thought about it a few years ago, but have you heard of *'la Crisi'*? Everyone in this city is saying that everything is getting worse and worse, that the market sucks; should I have sent my son to face the risk of unemployment after five years? Ours was clearly a rational choice. If you look around, all you can see are firms that are closing down. I do not know if it will worsen. However, who knows what is going to happen in five years? Better to choose something more secure for my son."

***

The answer of Benvenuto denoted the incisiveness of *'la Crisi'*, which emerged as the principal reason for the choice of school for his son. This motivation was common among the families and students I interviewed. In April 2009, for example, I distributed a questionnaire to six classes of Liceo Alberti (one 1st year, one 2nd year, two 3rd year, two 4th year), contacting 122 students. Among the students who lived in Valenza (97), 82 had at least one parent employed in jewellery-making. When asked the reason of their choice of school, 43 of them answered as addressing problems in the jewellery industry: 34 of those were enrolled in the first year.

'La Crisi' and the growing insecurity of the jewellery business appear to have been a determining factor in a choice that is not made on economic grounds. In fact, in a country where high school education in a state school, such as ISA Cellini, Foral or Liceo Alberti, is almost completely free (the annual fees are about one hundred Euros per year plus books and stationery), the choice is mainly made on the basis of anticipating a future. A difficult prevision that imposes on families to imagine a future in five (end of highschool certificate), eight (end of a bachelor degree), or ten (end of master degree) years: 'remote' futures that go beyond the limit of the few months that most market specialists currently use to plan their activities (Prediction Markets, 2009). In this respect, what is presented by Valenzani as an economic 'rational choice', emerges as a choice that is heavily conditioned by contingencies. "Today, the jewellery industry does not give opportunities, thus it will not give them in the future" appeared to be the general principle with which parents justified their decision. Rather than to appear driven by logical reasoning, this assumption, which can also find in the words of Benvenuto, appears to be motivated by a lack of trust

in the jewellery trade: an emotional response in the face of an unfathomable future.

This pessimism and the decisions that follow bring to the foreground profound repercussions of the downturn in the city. Pessimism shows a rupture in the relationship of trust between Valenzani and the jewellery industry: that relationship that relied on a dream and was substantiated by the idea that the jewellery industry was a stairway to success, which everyone could climb (Chapter 4). The resolution to not enrol one's children in a goldsmithing school, as well as the decision to leave the city or to not invest in the jewellery industry, all appear to be examples of what Miyazaki and Riles (2005) would term attempts at reorienting knowledge after an old dream appears to have reached its endpoint, and acting according to a new dream that arises from the problematisation of the role of jewellery making in the future of Valenza.

Futures

The dimension of the problematisation emerged in the everyday discourses interwoven throughout the city. As mentioned before, in 2009-2010 the identity rhetoric of *'città orafa'* did not fade away but, instead, continued to be employed by the media, politicians, and Valenzani in their everyday chats and discussions (Chapter 1). However, '*la Crisi*' appeared to have triggered the reconsideration of the identity paradigm that the trope underpins (Chapter 1) and led to the imagination of new futures for Valenza.

***

In the early days of October 2010, just after the opening of the *Valenza Gioielli* fair, I met a couple of friends for coffee. One of them was Marco (Chapter 4); the other, Giampiero, was also a goldsmith, in his fifties. He worked for a large international company and, besides a few weeks of *'cassa integrazione'* he did not endure any particular effects of the downturn: he kept his job as a bench-jeweller, and was paid regularly at the end of each month, although the opportunities for overtime work had reduced.

On that occasion, we started chatting, and Marco related to us what he claimed the president of a prominent goldsmiths' association had said to a group of journalists at the end of the opening ceremony:

> "He said that, I repeat exactly what I heard, that he thinks that there is no future for the city without the jewellery industry!"

All of us appeared quite surprised at that exclamation. Giampiero was the one to comment:

> "Well... Maybe there is no present without the jewellery industry, but after these years, still enduring *'la Crisi'*, I guess it is time for us goldsmiths to start thinking something different for our future..."

Marco agreed. I took note of these words.

The conversation continued for a few minutes, and exposed the problem of a future for Valenza that appeared uncertain and not entirely guaranteed by the jewellery industry. Neither Marco nor Giampiero, however, were able to suggest an alternative or describe a future without jewellery production.

***

In the late months of 2009 and in 2010, as goldsmiths' associations and local government bodies argued in the media for the centrality and irreplaceable nature of the jewellery industry for the future of Valenza, conversations like the one between Marco and Gianpaolo became a recurrent feature of the landscape of the city. At work, as well as in more domestic situations, Valenzani began discussing the future of their city. Since *'la Crisi'* urged them to rethink the jewellery industry, this imagination took different forms, but some common features distinguished goldsmiths' from non-goldsmiths' futures.

In the meetings with jewellery makers, I often had repeated to me the necessity of a more plural model of economy, in which jewellery production nonetheless had to have a role as protagonist. In this sense, *'la Crisi'* resulted in a critique rather than an abandonment of that industry and its primacy (Chapter 7).

Non-goldsmiths, instead, presented a more radical distancing from the jewellery industry. Phrases such as "the future does not belong to jewellery", "*'la Crisi'* taught us that Valenza must look in other directions", and "we need alternatives to build our future" occurred often in the interviews. '*Alternative*' [alternatives] was a fundamental 'keyword' (cf. Williams, 1983) of their discourse: a word the use of which was underpinned by the often non-implicit idea of the necessity of reducing the role played by the jewellery industry through developing other features of the city. The barkeeper of one of the coffee shops in the historic city centre, in January 2010, explained:

> "Valenza is not only jewellery. There are shops. There are offices. There are other firms that produce stuff such as bricks and roof tiles. We must

> not forget it. *'la Crisi'* touches all of us, but it does not mean there are no other alternatives. History teaches us that this city experienced another terrible crisis some decades ago, that of the shoe industry. However, the city found an alternative. [...] I am sure this city will find an alternative to stem the effects of this '*crisi*'. We have to look to our land and the opportunity it offers. Why not tourism?"

This statement is extracted from an interview in which the barkeeper, a man in his late thirties with more than ten years of experience of working in the city, mainly discussed the effects that the rise in unemployment was having on the rest of Valenza's economy, which included the restaurant industry. This account echoed other ideas and expectations I collected during the months of fieldwork. Tourism and commerce were two of the most frequent 'alternatives' listed by informants, while other forms of manufacturing already existing in Valenza, such as tile- and brick-making, were perceived as opportunities for employment that could complete a broader and more diversified model of the city. At the root of this idea of the city, it was always the experience of *'la Crisi'*, interpreted as the experience that made the weakness of 'the city of goldsmiths' emerge, which created a break between the past and the desired future.

'*La Crisi*' as object of Knowledge

The problematisation of the ideal of the goldsmithing city as well as the decisions taken by Valenzani in light of '*la Crisi*' shows, first of all, how the downturn destabilised the 'sense of place' (cf. Field and Basso, 1996) of Valenza. On the other hand, however, they indicate that *'la Crisi'* has assumed a precise instrumental function for the individuals. It appears as an object of performative knowledge: an attitude towards the change of the city and an active interpretative category used to make decisions, to formulate judgments of the present of Valenza, and imagine its future.

Reconsidering the words and actions of Benvenuto and the other informants, we can see their affinity with what Giovanni said in the opening of the chapter: '*la Crisi*' appears to be "in the head" of Valenzani insomuch as it is the concept that triggers their imagination and is used to justify their actions; the knowledge that the object conveys drives them. '*La Crisi*', in this respect, can be considered an object of knowledge. However, it is not a universal, implicit template that distinguishes a culture and a society, such as the cultural categories theorised by Benedict (1989 [1935]), Lévi-Strauss (1962), Douglas (1966) and other anthropologists. Nor is it the unspoken set of socially learned understanding, behaviours and predispositions that is a '*habitus*' in Bourdieu's (1977) terms, or a subject-less discursive formation as described by Foucault (1994 [1969]). Rather, it is a gnoseological object rooted in the individual's life, emotiveness and ways of living in the world; an object whose profile is outlined in the discourse of the change of the city and moulded by the very actions that the individual undertakes, as well as by the transformation of the world outside them. Echoing the symbolic interactionist reflection of Blumer (1969), *'la Crisi'* appears to be the result of a continuous creative game of combination of meanings, symbols and events through which the individual defines and makes sense of her world. From the explanation of what '*la Crisi*' is given to me by the informants, it appears that this object is assembled in an implicitly deductive process, by drawing from the experience of life and elements of the discourse that surrounds the individuals. In this process, individuals answer the stimuli they receive from the environment and the social context in which they live, by selecting particular elements; establishing correlations within this selected information, they create an image of the reality in which they live through a process that is substantially personal and subjective, even though not altogether free from the dynamics that characterise the sociality in which they are embedded.

However, through this object, individuals not only qualify the social reality in which they live, but, on the basis of the interpretation of the world that it conveys, as we have seen in the case of Benvenuto, Marco and other informants, they also base their prediction of the future and determine their actions and strategies. Thus, the transformation of a city, of its economy and society, is objectified into an object of knowledge: a tool that changes as the world changes, and through which individuals engage with the world, imagine and lay the basis of its future.

Recalling, thus, the words of Giovanni and in so doing, echoing the idea of Foucault's embodiment of the categories of the discourse (Foucault, 1978 [1976]), '*la Crisi*' can be seen as not just an abstract object, external to the individuals, but part of them, their way of thinking and seeing the world, thus, metaphorically in 'their heads'.

Conclusion

In this chapter I intended to show the symptomatic transformations that occurred in Valenza with the downturn of its jewellery industry. These involved material changes that can be read as the impoverishment and emptying of Valenza. At the same time, the transformations also encompass broad cultural change that can be considered a category of a problematisation of the idea of the '*città orafa*': a rhetoric that, however, did not cease to be propagated by Valenzani. This process passes through the reconsideration of the centrality of the jewellery industry in the life and economy of Valenza, which is expressed in the everyday discourses about the future of the city as well as the decisions taken in planning the future of individuals' lives. This process thus indicates the rupture of a bond that had identified a particular form of Valenza with an ideal city.

The trope of '*la Crisi*' is a key element in the problematisation. While it expressed the change that occurred after 2008, this trope became something more than a simple metonymic expression of a broader shifting human landscape or the acknowledgement of a change in an abstract market. As Giovanni noticed during our encounter, '*la Crisi*' did not only pertain to the economic sphere of business and production. It was an object of knowledge, rooted in the very conception of Valenza, on the basis of which Valenzani were planning their lives and formulating ideas of the future.

In this chapter, moreover, the exploration of the material changes of the city and the ways in which they become part of the discourse of Valenza show an important link between economy and society. While, since Polanyi's (2001 [1944]; 1971; Polanyi et al., 1957) works, anthropologists have argued that economic practices are embedded in the wider fabric of societal institutions, such as religion and politics (Beckert, 2009), the case of Valenza shows how an economic change, with its repercussions on the locale, can become an object of knowledge, a gnoseological tool employed by individuals in shaping, conceptualising their world. Hence, '*la Crisi*' was embedded in the very way of thinking of Valenzani. In this respect, it appears as a critique of the locale that leads individuals to rethink their city, that is, to reorient their knowledge of the place.

Thus, to conclude, if we consider the city as a whole, an economic change appears not just as a factual transformation of the landscape and its features. It is also an object of knowledge that people uses to express and makes sense of the change. This object of knoweldege, thus, appears a fundamental element for opening a community to a new becoming.

CONCLUSIONS

EXPLORING AN ECONOMIC CRISIS

In these conclusions, I want to reconsider the main findings of the previous chapters in order to respond to questions raised in the introduction that revolved around the meaning of an economic crisis.

The arguments of this book can be read on three levels. Firstly, it shows that the downturn in Valenza represented a phenomenon of erosion of the social body of the industry that propelled a collective process of re-'orientation of knowledge' (cf. Miyazaki & Riles, 2005). This has led individuals to reconsider the jewellery industry, their participation in it, and the bond that linked the industry to the city.

More broadly, this account doubles up as an analysis of the development of an ID in a context of economic recession. I point out the transformation within the network of firms, in particular the reduction of firms, involved an increasing power-role played by large companies, and a marginalisation of small enterprises. This transformation has fundamental social repercussions for the district. In fact, the downturn marks the demise of the entrepreneurial model of small artisan workshops, prefiguring the end of a fundamental element of the social mobility and cohesion of the social body of Valenza's goldsmiths. Moreover, the profound erosion of the goldsmiths' social body, caused by layoffs and the shutting down of firms, has further undermined this fundamental resource for the district's competitiveness. These dynamics, which dip into the very elements that sustain the district's performativity, can be seen in other Italian districts as well. In this respect, they foreshadow the future of the IDs and indicate an uncertain future for Italian industry.

Finally, this book is a contribution to the understanding of economic downturns from an anthropological perspective. The study of Valenza shows the entanglement of the material and symbolic nature of the transformation of the place and the community's 'sense of place' (cf. Field and Basso, 1996) . It follows that an economic crisis can be read as a traumatic renegotiation of symbols, landmarks, memories, and worldviews that individuals have to face when their principal form of economy declines.

The downturn in Valenza

This book aimed to explore Valenza's economic downturn and its effect on the city's goldsmiths and more broadly on the entire community, their way of engaging with the business of jewellery production, and considering the city and its industry.

To goldsmiths, the downturn represented the crisis of a system of expectations and a particular way of conceptualising production that revolved around the idea of *'artigianalità'* (Chapter 4). After the 1950s, the need for trained hands on which the goldsmithing industry and crafts were based, the high incomes offered by the profession, and the availability of outsourced work that allowed for the proliferation of small supplier workshops, led generations of youngsters to embrace jewellery production, since they saw in it a way to an otherwise unreachable economic success (Chapter 4). The industry became the subject of a dream, which the effects of the downturn shattered. As the hope for a rapid recovery had been frustrated by the slump of 2009 and stagnation of 2010, the dream appeared to have reached an endpoint. During the two years, the job-cuts and the shutdown of firms eroded the social body of practitioners, the fundamental resource on which the efficiency and competitiveness of Valenza's industry is based, foreshadowing the future of this economy.

This disaggregation, moreover, triggered fundamental transformations in the goldsmithing community. Since 2009, goldsmiths have attempted to readjust their conception of themselves and of production, in order to find new goals for their future. Employed and unemployed goldsmiths were involved in this redefinition, although the process took different forms for these artisans. Goldsmiths who maintained their positions post-2008 did not reconsider their status as goldsmiths, though they began questioning the structure and future of the city's industry once the district, as well as the work itself, appeared to slowly become devoid of meaning and promises, while the very network of firms was disrupted (Chapter 7). In contrast, those who suffered the traumatic experience of job loss responded to the change by departing from what it meant to them to be goldsmiths. They un-became goldsmiths by ceasing daily practices and routines anchored to their participation in the production, and by attempting to embed their everyday existence into a new regime of non-goldsmith signs (Chapter 6).

Considering more broadly the transformation that occurred in the city, over the course of the chapters, I pointed out, on the one hand, the precarisation of jewellery work, the rise in unemployment, and the reduction of per capita income, and showed how these changes forced individuals to reconsider jewellery production and change their daily routine to cope with the decline of the industry, particularly in the case of goldsmiths who lost their jobs in the course of the 2008-2010 period (Chapter 6). On the other hand, I showed the physical transformation of the domestic and urban space that took placfe during my fieldwork. Small and large changes in the familiar landscape of the '*grande fabbrica*' of Valenza (Chapter 2), such as home workbenches becoming unused due to the unavailability of overtime work commonly carried out within the domestic space, empty and unused premises left behind after firms had closed, and the silencing of the shop-floors after massive layoffs turned into elements of ruination of the landscape of the 'city of gold'.

To portray this transformation, from the early chapters, I explained the profound link between the city, its community and the jewellery industry. As the jewellery industry is the main object around which the identity rhetoric of this city revolves – a rhetoric that underpins recurring appellatives such as 'the city of goldsmiths' and 'the city of gold' (Chapter 1) – similarly, jewellery production is at the very basis of the articulation of space and time in the city: an activity that penetrates deeply into the urban fabric, becoming part of the public and domestic lives of Valenzani (Chapter 2). In this respect, while the jewellery industry can be seen as the icon, the meter and metronome of Valenza, in the course of about fifty years, it had become the very pillar of Valenzani's sense of their place, their way of understanding, describing and feeling the city (Basso, 1996: 54).

The transformations that occurred after 2008 appeared to have destabilised this awareness of the place and the worldview that it underpinned. The experience of uncertainty and hardship that the downturn brought along connected with the changing of the landscape. Those objects and places, such as workbenches, CCTV cameras or units formerly occupied by workshops, that had represented the symbols of the centrality of the jewellery industry in the city until a recent past, turned into a haunting debris that recalled memories of a lost age when the industry had provided a way for goldsmiths to become affluent and made Valenza one of the richest cities in North-Western Italy (Gaggio, 2007; Garofoli, 2004). Thus, the city became a space made up of 'evocative objects' (cf. Turkle, 2007) that pointed out a troublesome present, and prefigured an uncertain future.

In the months of fieldwork, uncertainty and lack of confidence towards the industry that, only a few years before, Valenzani had considered an everlasting pillar of their city were feelings shared by goldsmiths and non-goldsmiths alike. Facing the ruination of the landscape and experiencing the growing insecurity of the trade, Valenzani began questioning the identity equation 'Valenza=Jewellery industry' and its indisputability. In other words, the downturn had ushered in a general re-'orientation of knowledge' (cf. Miyazaki & Riles, 2005) for the entire community, which started to challenge the necessity and possibility of a monocultural industry and began to look for a new model of economy to embrace (Chapter 8).

'La Crisi'

2009-2010 was, moreover, the temporal setting for a particular dynamic in the city's discourse (Chapters 5 and 8). Valenzani, while experiencing the ruination of the city, discussed this change; *'la Crisi'* emerges as a key feature of this discourse. *'La Crisi'* is a locution that objectifies the on-going transformations and frames them in economic terms – *'crisi'* is the common expression used in Italian to refer to an economic crisis – in order to describe and explain them. By employing economic jargon, Valenzani provided an initial genealogy of the transformation of their city, as an event propagated from a market trend that reverberated through to other aspects of urban life. However, despite the clarity with which this trajectory of change was described, the social and historical causes of the transformation were a matter of discussion (Chapter 5). Alongside an interpretation embraced by the scholarship that sees the present downturn as a direct consequence of the Credit Crunch, goldsmiths highlighted other concatenations of events, other histories, such as long-term trends in the market and particularities in Valenza entrepreneurship, which could have helped create the conditions for the local downturn. This tangle of narrations, thus, outlined a profile of *'the downturn* that resists any simple historical linearisation (De Landa, 1997). *'La Crisi'* emerges as an object that underpins a non-linear history through which Valenzani describe themselves as ambiguous actors in the global economy: local producers that are not just victims of the global process, as suggested by Gudeman (2010), but actors suspended between pure agency and patiency in shaping and being shaped by the global economy.

'La Crisi' has a further role in the description of Valenza's history. It is used as an expression to represent present times in contrast with a lost, golden age. Thus, *'la Crisi'* represents a threshold between a past rooted in the jewellery monoculture and the memories of the wealth generated from the business, and a present and future of uncertainty and ruins in which the jewellery industry seems not to be able to fulfil the expectations once placed in it. Consequentially, *'la Crisi'* appears underpinned by the urgency

for a change in the way of understanding the jewellery industry and its link to the city. In this re-'orientation of knowledge' (cf. Miyazaki & Riles, 2005), *'la Crisi'* played a fundamental role. It has emerged not just as a conceptual framework through which the world has been objectified, but an object of knowledge through which they see, understand and imagine their city, and, consequently, reorient their knowledge and change their practices (Chapter 8). This dynamic, however, shows a divorce in temporalities and meanings between the economic aspects of the downturn and its cultural experience. In a context of economic decline or stagnation, the enactment of *'la Crisi'* based on a foreshadowing of a future without the jewellery industry anticipates economic difficulties and forces people to find alternatives to cope with that future. In this respect, it can be seen as an adaptive cultural dynamic to manage the economic downturn. However, following the jeopardisation of the bond between the community and the jewellery industry in the last few years, if the international market booms again in the near future, it is uncertain whether and how the signs of the revival will be read by the Valenza community and, thus, which role the jewellery industry will again play in its way of conceptualising the industry and the city.

Industry in perspective

The downturn of Valenza also offers elements for a broader reflection of the transformation of Italian industry, and in particular of its IDs.

After the mid-2000s, scholars, mostly economists, have focused on this ongoing transformation and identified a reorganisation in the structure of IDs (e.g. Rabellotti et al., 2009; Crestanello, 2009; Bianchi Renzo, 2009; Ramazzotti, 2008). Some transformations of national and international markets, such as the disappearance of the competitive advantage secured by the protectionist measures and devaluation policies adopted by the Italian government from the 1950s to the late 1990s, and the intensifying of competition in national and international markets, have led to a progressive marginalisation of those (generally small) firms not provided with the managerial tools (such as recognizable brands and direct access to market) and financial resources for competing in the global market. The scholarship has indicated the decline of small enterprises, and outlined a future made up of a larger–scale, less interdependent agglomerations of firms than found in present districts.

The transformations that Valenza underwent seem to lead to such a future. When the city's industry was mostly made up of small workshops that lacked a developed interface with the national and international market, merchants and large firms provided them with orders and, in so doing, mediated the access of the small ‘’*fabbriche*’ to the market. While work flowed within the district and connected large and small firms through subcontracting practices and social relations between the different actors of the districts, the difference in market access created an implicit subordination of small firms to the needs of their market intermediaries (Chapter 3). Between the 1970s and 1990s, while international demand was expanding, this potential disparity of bargaining power did not prevent a generalised redistribution of wealth among the different actors of the districts. In that context, small workshops that based their trade exclusively on the outsourcing from other firms proliferated: it is this model of entrepreneurship that most Valenzani considered to typify Valenza and embody its goldsmithing ethos (Chapter 4). However, after 2008, the slump in demand, the reduction of orders, and the boom in raw material prices resulted in a shock for the entire system. The effects of these changes were the progressive drying up of outsourcing and the overall reduction of profit margins in manufacturing. Moreover, the disparity of bargaining power between the actors of the district became evident: after outsourcers had reduced the outsourced production, suppliers started to accept less advantageous contracts and agreements in order to remain in business (Chapter 7). This contraction of profitability of the trade also led to large-scale redundancies in both small and large firms. Thus, this dynamic has resulted, for most of the city’s firms, in an inevitable reduction of incomes, and a progressive worsening of economic conditions for workers and entrepreneurs. Facing these transformations, firms reacted by attempting a thorough reorganisation of production lines and personnel. Some small enterprises, moreover, had tried to compensate for this downturn by starting commercial strategies to gain access to the market. However, in spite of these strategies, the general trend has been a slow but steady marginalisation and expulsion from the market of small enterprises: a trend that mirrors the more general phenomenon highlighted by the scholarship (Rabellotti et al., 2009; Ramazzotti, 2008; Bianchi Renzo, 2009). However, at the end of 2010, the jewellery industry encompassed over 800 workshops, most of them (over 600) employing less than 15 people (Bellini, 2011; CCAl, 2011a). Despite the worst scenarios outlined by the scholarship, it appears that the overall structure of the network industry has withstood the change, although the density of this economic fabric has been reduced.

The massive wave of firms’ closures and job losses, however, brings to the foreground another alarming datum that foreshadows the future growth for IDs. Marshall’s theories (Loasby, 2009) and the past studies on Italian

IDs (Sforzi, 2009; Bianchi Patrizio, 2009) highlighted the centrality of production knowledge and skills owned by the industry's practitioners, as well as the unity and dynamism of this social body. The recent changes indicate, however, the erosion of the social body (Chapter 6 and 7) and in particular a halt in its dynamism and social mobility.

Considering specifically the case of Valenza, the failure of the entrepreneurial model of the small workshops appears to have destroyed one of the fundamental elements that allowed this mobility and a bridging between the roles of the worker and the entrepreneur. While until the 1990s, goldsmithing entrepreneurs were often jewellery-makers who, after a few years of training, decided to invest their gains in opening a business of their own, in the 2010s, entrepreneurship appears to revolve more around the entrepreneur's technical knowledge in bookkeeping and marketing rather than his or her artistic skills. Thus, while in the past there was no big difference in knowledge and education between an entrepreneur and a worker, and the availability of abundant outsourced work made large amounts of capital not necessary to open a firm, the future seems to preclude a jewellery worker, with often at best a high school education and not the capital to finance a business able to interface with an international market and launch its own recognised brand, being able to emerge and turn into a successful entrepreneur. This seems to prefigure a crack in the social body of goldsmiths that may mean that goldsmiths shift from being artisan workers into factory workers prevented from a complete access to the means of production.

From a broad point of view, the phenomena that are occurring in Valenza can be read against ID theory. In fact, it is hard not to recognise that the precarisation of work conditions, layoffs, and the decline of the model of small firms represent forms of disaggregation of the social body and damping of social mobility: the key elements that sustain the vitality of an ID's economy. This dynamic, thus, opens an interrogation on the survival and competitiveness of a form of production based on the cooperation between firms and sustained by a united and dynamic social body of practitioners.

Social security cushions may have slowed down the disaggregation of the social body, delaying layoffs and giving unemployed people, after their dismissals, the security of a minimum social wage that preserved individuals from the compelling necessity of finding a job and abandoning the city, and gave them the possibility to wait for some months in Valenza, hoping or maybe just deceiving themselves that they could resume their original trade. However, after months of inactivity, the artisans may find themselves in a condition of not being able to fit in a stagnant and highly competitive job market in any case, being ultimately unable to be fully reintegrated into the industry. Thus, the social security cushions should not be an excuse to not recognise the on-going erosion of the district's 'community of practice' (cf. Lave and Wenger, 1991). However, when the general performativity of an industry is so fundamentally based on the extension and vitality of the community of its practitioners, the expulsion of individuals not only raises a social problem for a city, but results in a depletion of the very fundamental resources (knowledge, skills, and experience) that sustain the industry: the erosion of the very pillars of the district. Such erosion is furthered by another dynamic that Valenza shows well. An economic crisis can break the link of trust that binds the district's population to the industry, which is seen as no longer providing security for the future. This reverberates in the decrease in youths starting a career within the local industry. This decrease means that the business is not taken over and continued by a new generation. All these dynamics highlight major problems for the continuation of a district industry in the medium and long run. Thus, in the current economic crisis, what is at stake is not just the question of the future shape of Italian industry, but who will be the protagonists of this future and what knowledge and sociality will sustain this new form of economy.

Therefore, to question the future of Italian industry is also to question the role of the State. The State is one of the key actors of the industrial sector (Narotzky and Smith, 2006; Narotzky, 2009) because it sets the legal framework in which the industry develops – in so doing, shaping the possibilities of development by regulating employment, the use of resources, forms of entrepreneurship and economic transactions – and intervenes on the trends of the industry, by supporting it with stimuli, imposing customs and taxes, and instituting social security cushions. Since 2008, the principal intervention of the state, through its local bodies, had been to ensure social security cushions for those workers in artisan firms who would normally have been excluded from these welfare measures due to national regulations (Chapter 6). However, since the beginning of the economic crisis in 2008, the national government has not put in place any measures to support entrepreneurship through stimuli or tax reliefs, did not launch any measures of production promotion or protection, and did not it answer the appeals of professional associations, trade unions and local governments from the districts. On the contrary, the increasing austerity measures have furthered the effects of the downturn. As a result of this lack of response, the sense of separation between citizens and the central government, and with it, the lack of confidence in national politics, increased. Six years after the beginning of '*la Crisi*'. The question about which role national politics will play in the future in supporting national industry and that form of industry it will support is still to be made clear.

From this short excursus, many questions are raised: what future is in store for Italian districts? What will happen to the community of practitioners that live in the districts? What role will politics play in supporting national industry?

These questions are still to be addressed, and together define a field of research in which anthropologists can play a fundamental key role in exploring the local and the comparative side of these issues, and along with other social scientists, formulate answers to these important questions.

Anthropology and economic crisis

Moreover, this ethnography of Valenza offers elements to reconsider anthropologically the cultural and social meaning of an economic crisis. From this analysis it emerges that an economic crisis is not (just) an adjustment in market relations. It is an individual's redefinition of the way of seeing the market and their role within this context; it is an alteration in work conditions and the way of understanding work; it is a change in the materiality of the landscape and the way of sensing the place; it is a change in a community and the way of understanding it. This book showed and explored this complexity (Law and Mol, 2002: 1).

In particular, the ethnography explored the material and cultural transformations that a society undergoes after the decline of its main economy. It also investigated the way these changes are experienced, felt by individuals and the way in which they emerged in the community's discourse, through particular objects, such as *'la Crisi'*. Thus, it pointed out that a downturn affects society by undermining the basic material conditions of life and sociality, as pointed out by Gudeman (2010), and destabilizing the 'sense of place' (cf. Field and Basso, 1996) and belonging that are the pillars on which a community stands.

The ethnography portrayed the phenomenology of the ruination of the city. Ruination is a material and symbolic process that turns a familiar, welcoming landscape into an expanse of ruins that constantly remind the individuals of their past wealth and the precariousness of the present. At the same time, it is connected to a weakening of a system of meanings associated with the work and that revolves around the expectations of success associated with this form of economy. The industrial decline results in a fall in the 'global hierarchy of value' (cf. Herzfeld, 2004) for those people who embraced that model of economy and believed it to be a potential way to attain economic wealth and social prestige. Unlike the downturn of the mining industry in Zambia described by Ferguson (1999), Valenza's fall and the dissolution of the material and symbolic value of its economy did not become the starting point for reconsidering and regaining possession of previously abandoned models of sociality and economy. Instead, in the city, the community had to face the uncertainty of seeking and experimenting with new models that the city's past did not provide.

From this analysis, the participation in a particular form of economy and the cultural consequences of its downfall shed light on the adjustment that follows a market crisis in the social body that, in economic terms, can be called the 'offer'. While economic theory mostly explains this change as an automatic transformation that follows a principle of rational calculation, Valenza shows that non-rational elements, such as expectations, hopes, fears, and beliefs play a major role in shaping the body, so that the adjustment appears to pertain to a collective 'economy of dreams' (cf. Miyazaki, 2006), rather than to a rational and mechanical process.

These transformations, moreover, offer elements to reconsider the role of local (economic) actors within the global capitalist economy. In a context of global insecurity, anthropologists (e.g. Gudeman, 2010; Hart et al., 2010; Wilson, 2009) have described these actors as victims of global capitalism. However, this interpretation, by implying a victimisation of the local community under the weight of global capitalism, does not recognise the agency of the local community in being able to operate in and impact on the global market. Tsing (2005) had previously pointed out that the relationship between local and global actors is a friction, a two-way relationship of mutual adjustments. The case of Valenza shows that, first of all, beyond a downturn there are multiple concatenations of events that resist both a linear history and a simplistic description of the effects of the global on the local economy. Secondly, this non-linearity shows a more complex condition for the local actors, individuals and enterprises, always suspended between agency and passivity in their economic practices, as it emerges from goldsmiths' narrations of the reasons for the downturn and its effects. While this tension shows the fragility and, at the same time, the robustness of these actors, this ambiguity points out an anthropology of economic actors that goes beyond the paradigm of pure activeness and agency, supported by the classical economic idea of *homo oeconomicus*, or passiveness, portrayed by certain parts of the scholarship. This ambiguous status refers the researcher to the study of the very way in which an individual and a community make sense of the (global) economy and act within it.

Finally, from an urbanological perspective, in this work, the transformations of the city have been investigated by relating them to the emergence and the employment of a particular object of the local discourse: *'la Crisi'*. This exploration and the analysis of this object required the acceptance of 'economic crisis' as an emic category. However, this heuristic move, which takes example from the anthropology of finance (Maurer, 2005; Callon et al., 2007; Callon, 1998; MacKenzie, 2009), requires a fundamental methodological shift in the position and task of researchers. The researcher, in fact, must not attempt to compare the local reality to a theoretical model, as in the theorisation of an economic crisis as framed in economic and social theory, so as to detect the particularities of a local experience, and from them eventually challenge the theory. Rather, they will attempt to collect the different ways in which a category is used, to elucidate its meanings, uses, and from them gain insight into the substance that underpins the category. To apply this methodology to the category of 'economic crisis' means to explore its social and cultural meaning in the community and its employment to describe the changes in the world. Of particular interest is how the transformation of the city is seen, felt and narrated, and how it is associated with other elements, such as symbols, landmarks, memories, leading to a better insight of the worldview and the way of understanding the economy, the global and the local of the community studied. While in the case of Valenza, this heuristic move resulted in a positive tool to fathom the becoming of that community, the extension of this method to other communities may result in a rich avenue of research to better understand what an economic downturn is in the everyday life of individuals and to produce a theory of a human economy (Hart et al., 2010) with the individuals as its centre, and that moves from their understanding to consider and imagine the global economy.

Conclusion

In conclusion, this book has been an exploration of a community and the becoming of their relationship with an industry. I enquired into the concept of 'economic crisis' in order to investigate this bond and its transformation. I have shown how an industry has declined, and with it, how an idea of pride that a community embraced has faded away. "Valenza may not shine anymore", as I was often told by my informants, but history has not come to an end, instead continuing its becoming. Thus, the question about tomorrow remains unsolved and is, itself, becoming.

BIBLIOGRAPHIC REFERENCES

Adamson, Glenn. 2007. *Thinking through Craft*. Oxford: Berghahn.

—. (ed). 2010. *The Craft Reader*. Oxford: Berghahn.

—. 2013. *The Invention of Craft*. London: Bloomsbury.

Amatori Franco, Duccio Bigazzi, Renato Giannetti, and Luciano Segreto, eds. 1999. *L'industria*. Turin: Einaudi.

Amin, Ash. 2002. "Industrial Districts." In *A Companion to Economic Geography*, edited by Eric Sheppard and Trevor J. Barnes. Oxford: Blackwell.

Amin, Ash, and Nigel Thrift. 2002. *Cities: Reimagining the Urban*. Cambridge: Polity.

Anderson, Benedict 1991. *Imagined Communities: Reflections on the Origin and Spread of Nationalism. Revised Edition*. London: Verso.

AOV. 1972. *Valenza nel mondo: l'oreficeria valenzana attraverso le sue mostre in Italia e all'estero*. Valenza: Associazione Orafa Valenzana.

—. 2006. *Aov Notizie no. 4*. Valenza: Associazione Orafa Valenzana.

Appadurai, Arjun. 1986. "Introduction: Commodities and the Politics of Value." In *The Social Life of Things: Commodities in Cultural Perspective*, edited by Arjun Appadurai. Cambridge: Cambridge University Press.

—. 1996. *Modernity at Large: Cultural Dimensions of Globalization*. Minneapolis: University of Minnesota Press.

Appay, Beatrice. 2010. "'Precarization' and Flexibility in the Labour Process: A question of Legitimacy and a Major Challange for Democracy." In *Globalization and Precarious Forms of Production and Employment*, edited by Carole Thornley, Steve Jefferys and Beatrice Appay. Cheltenham: Edward Elgar Publishing Limited.

Applebaum, Herbert. 1986a. "The Antropology of Work in Industrial Society: Part I." *Anthropology of Work Review* 7, no. 3: 25-32.

—. 1986b. "The Antropology of Work in Industrial Society: Part II." *Anthropology of Work Review* 7, no. 4: 41-51.

Attali, Jacques. 2009 [2008]. *La crisi e poi?* Rome: Fazi Editore.

Baba, Marietta L. 1998. "Then Anthropology of Work in the Fortune 1000: A Critical Retrospective." *Anthropology of Work Review* 18, no. 4: 17-28.

—. 2006. "Anthropology and Business." In *Encyclopedia of Anthropology*, edited by H. James Birx. London: Sage.

Bachelard, Gaston. 1994. *The Poetics of Space*. Boston: Beacon Press.

Bagnasco, Amaldo. 1977. *Tre Italie: la problematica territoriale dello sviluppo italiano*. Bologna: Il Mulino.

—. 2009. "The Governance of Industrial Districts." In *A Handbook of Industrial Districts*, edited by Giacomo Becattini, Marco Bellandi and Lisa De Propris. Cheltenham: Edward Elgar.

Baldursson, Stefan. 2002. "The Nature of at-Homeness." www.phenomenologyonline.com. Last access: 27/04/13.

Barghini, Andrea, Vera Comoli, and Anna Marotta. 1993. *Valenza e le sue fortificazioni*. Alessandria: Cassa di Risparmio di Alessandria.

Barozzi, Piero. 1976. *L'artigianato orafo di Valenza*. Genova: Istituto di Scienze Geografiche.

Bassano, Clara. 2008. *I distretti orafi italiani*. Foggia: Edizioni Scientifiche Italiane.

Basso, Keith. 1996. "Wisdom Sits in Places: Notes on a Western Apache Landscape." In *Senses of Place*, edited by Steven Feld and Keith Basso. Santa Fe, NM: School of American Research Press.

Bauman, Zygmunt. 1998. *Globalization: The Human Consequences*. New York: Columbia University Press.

—. 1999. *In Search of Politics*. Oxford: Polity.

Baumann, Gerd. 1996. *Contesting Culture: Discourses of Identity in Multi-Ethnic London*. Cambridge: Cambridge University Press.

Becattini, Giacomo. 1978. "The Development of Light Industry in Tuscany: An Interpretation." *Economic Notes* 7, no. 2-3: 107-23.

—. 1979. "Dal Settore Industriale Al Distretto Industriale. Alla Ricerca Dell'Unita D'analisi Dell'economia Industriale." *Rivista di Economia e Politica Industriale* 1, no. 1: 7- 21.

—. 1989. "Riflessioni sul distretto industriale marshalliano come concetto socio-economico." *Stato e Mercato* 25: 11-28.

—. 2006. "Industrial District." In *International Encyclopedia of Economic Sociology*, edited by Jens Beckert and Milan Zafirovski. London: Routledge.

Becattini, Giacomo, Marco Bellandi, and Lisa De Propris. 2009. "Critical Nodes and Contemporary Reflections on Industrial Districts." In *A Handbook of Industrial Districts*, edited by Giacomo Becattini, Marco Bellandi and Lisa De Propris. Cheltenham: Edward Elgar.

Beck, Ulrich, and Elisabeth Beck-Gernsheim. 2001. *Individualization: Institutionalized Individualism and Its Social and Political Consequences*. London: Sage.

Beckert, Jens. 2009. "The Great Transformation of Embeddedness: Karl Polanyi and the New Economic Sociology " In *Market and Society: The Great Transformation Today*, edited by Chris Hann and Keith Hart. Cambridge: Cambridge University Press.

Beiser, Frederick. 2005. *Hegel*. London: Routledge.

Bellassai, Alessandro. 2004. *La mascolinità contemporanea*. Rome: Carocci.

Bellini, Liviano, ed. 2008. *Valenza nei marchi 2008*. Valenza: Studio AF.

—. 2009. *Valenza nei marchi 2009*. Valenza: Studio AF.

—. 2010. *Valenza nei marchi 2010*. Valenza: Studio AF.

—. 2011. *Valenza nei marchi 2011*. Valenza: Studio AF.

Benedict, Ruth. 1989 [1935]. *Patterns of Culture*. Boston: Houghton Mifflin.

Benini, Romano. 2010. *Saper fare. Il modello artigiano e le radici dello stile italiano*. Rome: Donzelli.

Benton, Lauren A. 1989. *Invisible Factories: The Informal Economy and Industrial Development*. New York: State University of New York Press.

Benzi, Cesare. 2004a. "L'attività Produttiva e l'organizzazione della produzione." In *Il distretto orafo di Valenza*, edited by Gioacchino Garofoli. Milan: Franco Angeli.

—. 2004b. "Punti di forza e criticità del modello di sviluppo locale." In *Il distretto orafo di Valenza*, edited by Gioacchino Garofoli. Milan: Franco Angeli.

Benzi, Cesare, and Paola Fugagnoli. 2004a. "Mercato del lavoro: problemi di reclutamento e strategie formative." In *Il distretto orafo di Valenza*, edited by Gioacchino Garofoli. Milan: Franco Angeli.

—. 2004b. "Struttura e dinamica del sistema orafo Valenza." In *Il distretto orafo di Valenza*, edited by Gioacchino Garofoli. Milan: Franco Angeli.

Bianchi, Patrizio. 2009. "Crisi economica e politica industriale." *Quaderni DEIT* 21: 1-75.

Bianchi, Renzo. 2009. "The Italian Revival of Industrial Districts and the Foundations of Political Economy." In *A Handbook of Industrial Districts*, edited by Giacomo Becattini, Marco Bellandi and Lisa De Propris. Cheltenham: Edward Elgar.

Bini, Piero. 2005. "Teoria, cultura e politica economica negli anni del miracolo italiano: 1953-1968." *Storia del Pensiero Economico* 2, no. 1: 5-34.

Blim, Michael. 1990. *Made in Italy: Small-Scale Industrialization and Its Consequences*. New York: Praeger.

Blumer, Herbert. 1969. *Symbolic Interactionism: Perspective and Method.* Englewood Cliffs: Prentice-Hall.

Bohannan, Paul. 1955. "Some Principles of Exchange and Investment among the Tiv." *American Anthropologist* 57, no. 1: 60-70.

Boholm, Åsa. 2001. "The Cultural Nature of Risk: Can There Be an Anthropology of Uncertainty?" *Ethnos: Journal of Anthropology* 68, no. 2: 159-78.

Boni, Federico. 2008. *Il Superleader. fenomenologia mediatica di Silvio Berlusconi*. Rome: Meltemi.

Bosco, Fabio. 2004. 2004. *Oroscuro*. Alessandria: Falsopiano.

Bottino, Piero. 1984. "Valenza sfida la crisi." *La Stampa Sera (ed. Alessandria)*, 27/04.

Bottiroli, Angelo. 2011. "Valenza e Tortona, Tira solo l'export: diminuisce il numero delle imprese, la ripresa non si vede all'orizzonte." *La Provincia Pavese*, 8/05

Bourdieu, Pierre. 1977. *Outline of a Theory of Practice*. Cambridge: Cambridge University Press.

—. 1984. *Distinction: A Social Critique of the Judgement of Taste*. London: Routledge & Kegan Paul.

—. 1985. "Forms of Capital." In *Handbook of Theory and Research in the Sociology of Education*, edited by H. John Richardson. New York: Greenwood.

—. 2005. *The Social Structures of the Economy*. Oxford: Polity Press.

Bovero, Stefano, ed. 1992. *Vivere a Valenza: mondo orafo e disagio urbano*. Valenza: Unità Socio-Sanitaria Locale N.71.

Bowker, Geoffrey C., and Susan Leigh Star. 1999. *Sorting Things Out: Classification and Its Consequences*. Cambridge, MA: MIT Press.

Boyer, Dominic. 2005. *Spirit and System: Media, Intellectuals, and the Dialectic in Modern German Culture*. Chicago: The University of Chicago Press.

Bravo, Gian Luigi. 2001. *Italiani. Racconto etnografico*. Rome: Meltemi.

—. 2005. *La complessità della tradizione: festa, museo e ricerca antropologica*. Milan: Franco Angeli.

Brettel, Caroline B. 2000. "Theorizing Migration in Anthropology: Thesocial Construction of Netyworks, Identies, Communities, and Global Scapes." In *Migration Theory; Talking across Disciplines*, edited by Caroline B. Brettel and James F. Hollifield. London: Routledge.

Briziarelli, Marco. 2011. "Neoliberalism as a State-Centric Class Project: The Italian Case." *Continuum: Journal of Media & Cultural Studies* 25, no. 1: 5-17.

Brolis, Renzo. 1991. *Sicurezza e salute negli ambienti di lavoro.* Milan: Giunti-Marzocco.

Brunetti, Giorgio, Mario Marelli, and Federico Visconti. 2000. *Euro e distretti industriali: una ricerca nella realtà lombarda.* Milan: Franco Angeli.

Bruni, Attila, Silvia Gherardi, and Barbara Poggio. 2004. "Doing Gender, Doing Entrepreneurship: An Ethnographic Account of Intertwined Practices." *Gender, Work & Organization* 11, no. 4: 406-29.

Buckley, Frank M. 1971. "An Approach to a Phenomenology of at-Homeness." *Duquesne Studies in Phenomenological Psychology* 1: 198-211.

Bulgari Group. 2006. *Consolidated Half-Year Report.* Rome: Bulgari Group.

Burawoy, Michael. 1979. "The Anthropology of Industrial Work." *Annual Review Anthropology* 8: 231-66.

Burman, Patrick. 1988. *Killing Time, Losing Ground: Experiences of Unemployment.* Toronto: Wall and Thompson.

Callon, Michel, ed. 1998. *The Laws of the Markets.* Oxford: Blackwell.

Callon, Michel, Yuval Millo, and Fabian Muniesa. 2007. "An Introduction to Market Devices." In *Market Devices*, edited by Michel Callon, Yuval Millo and Fabian Muniesa. Oxford: Blackwell.

Calvino, Italo. 1993. *Le città invisibili.* Milan: Mondadori.

Campbell, Ben. 2010. "Rhetorical Routes for Development: A Road Project in Nepal." *Contemporary South Asia* 18, no. 3: 267-79.

Candea, Matei. 2007. "Arbitrary Locations: In Defence of the Bounded Field-Site." *Journal of the Royal Anthropological Institute* 13, no. 1: 167-84.

—. 2010. *Corsican Fragments: Difference, Knowledge, and Fieldwork.* Bloomington, IN: Indiana University Press.

—. 2011. "'Our Division of the Universe': Making a Space for the Non-Political in the Anthropology of Politics." *Current Anthropology* 52, no. 3: 309-34.

Cappellieri, Alba. 2008. "Il gioiello Del Novecento tra arte, moda e design." *Patrimonio di oreficeria adriatica* 2, no. 2.

Carcano, Luana. 2007a. "I rapporti tra industria e distribuzione nei mercati maturi." In *Miti da sfatare nel gioiello. Le relazioni industria distribuzione in Italia e nel mondo*, edited by Luana Carcano, Antonio Catalani and Paola Vaccara Capello. Milan: Egea.

—. 2007b. "Le dimensioni economiche della gioielleria internazionale." In *Miti da sfatare nel gioiello. Le relazioni industria distribuzione in*

Italia e nel mondo, edited by Luana Carcano, Antonio Catalani and Paola Vaccara Capello. Milan: Egea.

Carrier, James. 1992a. "Emerging Alienation in Production: A Maussian History." *Man* 27, no. 539-58.

—. 1992b. "Occidentalism: The World Turned Upside-Down." *American ethnologist* 19, no. 2: 195-212.

—. 1995. *Occidentalism: Images of the West.* Oxford: Clarendon Press: Oxford University Press.

Carrithers, Michael. 2005. "Why Anthropologist Should Study Rhetoric." *Journal of the Royal Anthropological Institute* 11, no. 3: 577-583.

—. 2007. "Story Seeds and the Inchoate." *Durham Anthropology Journal* 14, no. 1: 1-20.

—. 2008. "From Inchoate Pronouns to Proper Nouns: A Theory Fragment with 9/11, Gertrude Stein, and an East German Ethnography." *History and Anthropology* 19, no. 2: 161-86.

—. 2009. *Culture, Rhetoric, and the Vicissitudes of Life*. Oxford: Berghahn.

Casas-Cortés, Maria Isabel. 2009. *Social Movements as Sites of Knowledge Production: Precarious Work, the Fate of Care and Activist Research in a Globalizing Spain.* Doctoral Thesis, Univerisity of North Carolina.

Castellaro, Rodolfo. 1994. "Mocef, solo segnali di crisi per l'oreficeria valenzana." *La Stampa (ed. Alessandria),* 08/09: 32.

Castells, Manuel. 1996. *The Rise of the Network Society.* Oxford: Blackwell.

CPI. 2009. *The Jewellery Market in the EU*. Amsterdam: Centre for the Promotion of Imports from developing countries.

CCAl. 2011a. *Saldo imprese orafe a Valenza 1970-2010.* Alessandria: Camera di Commercio di Alessandria.

—. 2011b. *Saldo imprese orafe a Valenza 2007-Primo Semestre 2011*. Alessandria: Camera di Commercio di Alessandria.

Cento Bull, Anna, and Paul Corner. 1993. *From Peasant to Entrepreneur: The Survival of the Family Economy in Italy*. Oxford: Berghahn.

CGIL. 2011. *Mutamenti Salariali Del Settore Orafo 2008-2010.* Alessandria: Confederazione Generale Italiana del Lavoro.

Champagne, Patrick. 1999 [1990]. "The Fall." In *The Weight of the World*, edited by Pierre Bourdieu. Cambridge: Polity Press.

Chan, Selina Ching 2006. "Love and Jewelry: Patriarchal Control, Conjugal Ties, and Changing Identies." In *Modern Loves; the Anthropology of Romantic Courtship and Companiate Marriage*, edited by Jennifer S. Hirsch and Holly Wardlow. Ann Arbor, MI: University of Michigan Press.

Chibnik, Micheal. 2011. *Anthropology, Economics, and Choice.* Austin: University of Texas Press.

Clark, Andy, and David J. Chalmers. 1998. "The Extended Mind." *Analysis* 58: 10-23.

Clarke, Simon. 2006. "Economic Crisis." In *International Encyclopedia of Economic Sociology*, edited by Jens Beckert and Milan Zafirovski. London: Routledge.

Clemente, Pietro. 1997. "Paese/Paesi." In *I luoghi della memoria: stutture ed eventi dell'Italia unita,* edited by Mario Isnenghi. Bari-Rome: Laterza.

Cohen, Jon S., Giovanni Federico, and Economic History Society. 2001. *The Growth of the Italian Economy, 1820-1960.* Cambridge: Cambridge University Press.

Coleman, James Samuel. 1988. "Social Capital in the Creation of Human Capital." *American Journal of Sociology*, no. 94/ Supplement: 95-129.

—. 1990. *Foundations of Social Theory*. Cambridge, MA: Harvard University Press.

Colli, Andrea. 2010. "Dwarf Giants, Giant Dwarfs. Reflections About the Italian 'Industrial Demography' at the Beginning of the New Millennium." *Journal of Modern Italian Studies* 15, no. 1: 43-60.

Comaroff, John L., and Jean Comaroff. 2009. *Ethnicity, Inc.* Chicago: The University of Chicago Press.

Comune di Valenza. 2009a. *Crisi economica: è urgente per Valenza il sostegno al sistema economico locale.* Valenza: Comune di Valenza.

—. 2009b. *Per la Gente di Valenza.* Valenza: Comune di Valenza.

—. 2011. *Report sintetico su tasso di iscrizioni a scuole superiori valenzane 1975-2011*. Valenza: Comune di Valenza.

Comuni-Italiani.it. 2009. "Principali città della regione Piemonte." www.comuni-italiani.it. Last access 26/04/2013.

—. 2011a. "Popolazione: Valenza 2001-2011.". http://www.comuni-italiani.it. Last access 26/04/2013.

—. 2011b. "Valenza: Redditi Irpef." http://www.comuni-italiani.it. Last access 26/04/2013.

Connerton, Paul. 2009. *How Modernity Forgets.* Cambridge: Cambridge University Press.

Cook, Karen S. 2001. *Trust in Society*. London: Sage.

Cook, Karen S., and Alexandra Gerbasi. 2006. "Trust." In *International Encyclopedia of Economic Sociology*, edited by Jens Beckert and Milan Zafirovski. London: Routledge.

Corsín Jiménez, Alberto. 2011. "Trust in Anthropology." *Anthropological Theory* 11, no. 2: 177–96.

Cospito, Giuseppe. 2004. "Egemonia." In *Le parole di Gramsci: per un lessico dei quaderni del carcere*, edited by Fabio Frosini and Guido Liguori. Rome: Carrocci.

Crainz, Guido. 1996. *Storia del Miracolo italiano: culture, identità, trasformazioni fra anni Cinquanta E Sessanta.* Rome: Donzelli.

—. 2003. *Il Paese mancato: dal Miracolo economico agli anni Ottanta.* Rome: Donzelli.

Crestanello, Paolo. 2009. *L'industria orafa italiana. Problemi e sfide competitive.* Rome: Carrocci.

Cristofaro, Angela. 2011. *Made in Italy. Alla conquista del Mondo: come le buone idee possono trasformarsi in grandi imprese.* Rome: Gremese.

Daniell, Mark Haynes. 2000. *World of Risk: Next Generation Strategy for a Volatile Era*. New York: John Wiley & Sons.

De Blasio, Guido, Massimo Omiccioli, and Luigi Federico Signorini. 2009. "Measuring the District Effect." In *A Handbook of Industrial Districts*, edited by Giacomo Becattini, Marco Bellandi and Lisa De Propris. Cheltenham: Edward Elgar.

De Certeau, Michel 1984. *The Practice of Everyday Life.* Berkeley, CA: University of California Press.

De Landa, Manuel. 1997. *A Thousand Years of Nonlinear History.* New York: Zone Books.

—. 2006. *A New Philosophy of Society: Assemblage Theory and Social Complexity.* New York: Continuum.

De Martino, Ernesto. 2003 [1948]. *Il mondo magico.* Torino: Bollati Boringhieri.

Deleuze, Gilles. 1989. "Qu'est-Ce Qu'un Dispositif?" In *Michel Foucault Philosophie: Rencontre International Paris 9, 10, 11 Janvier 1988*, edited by Georges Canguilhem. Paris: Seuil.

—. 1997. *Essays Critical and Clinical.* Minneapolis: University of Minnesota Press.

Deleuze, Gilles, and Fe lix Guattari. 1987. *A Thousand Plateaus: Capitalism and Schizophrenia.* London: Athlone.

Di Quirico, Roberto. 2010. "Italy and the Global Economic Crisis." *Bulletin of Italian Politics* 2, no. 2: 3-19.

Diedrich, Richar-Michel. 2004. "Passages to No-Man's Lands: Connecting Work, Community, and Masculinity in the South Wales Coalfield." In *Workers and Narratives of Survival in Europe: The Management of*

Precariousness at the End of the Twentieth Century, edited by Angela Procoli. New York: State University of New York.

Donati, Pierpaolo. 2000. "Il dono in famiglia e nell altre sfere sociali." *Studi Interdisciplinari sulla Famiglia* 18: 55-102.

Doney, Patricia M., and Joseph P. Cannon. 1997. "An Examination of the Nature of Trust in Buyer-Seller Relationships." *The Journal of Marketing* 61, no. 2: 35-51.

Douglas, Mary. 1966. *Purity and Danger: An Analysis of Concepts of Pollution and Taboo*. London: Routledge & Kegan Paul.

Douglas, Mary, and Baron C. Isherwood. 1979. *The World of Goods: Towards an Anthropology of Consumption.* London: Allen Lane.

Dunford, Micheal. 2006. "Industrial District, Magic Circles, and the Restructuring of the Italian Textiles and Clothing Chain." *Economic Geography* 82, no. 1: 27-59.

Durant, Alan. 2006. "Raymond Williams's Keywords: Investigating Meanings 'Offered, Felt for, Tested, Confirmed, Asserted, Qualified, Changed'." *Critical Quarterly* 48, no. 4: 1-26.

Durkheim, Mile. 1976 [1912]. *The Elementary Forms of the Religious Life.* London: Allen and Unwin.

Eliade, Mircea. 1987 [1957]. *The Sacred and the Profane: The Nature of Religion.* San Diego: Harcourt Brace Jovanoich Publishers.

Emery, Steve. 2010. *In Better Fettle: Improvement, Work and Rhetoric in the Transition to Environmental Farming in the North York Moors.* Doctoral thesis, Durham University

Engels, Friedrich. 1972 [1884]. *The Origin of the Family, Private Property and the State.* London: Lawrence and Wishart.

—. 2010 [1880]. *Socialism: Utopian and Scientific*. www.marxist.org. Last access 27/04/13.

Fabian, Johannes. 1983. *Time and the Other: How Anthropology Makes Its Object.* New York: Columbia University Press.

FDI. 2011. *Sezione anagrafica: distretto industriale di oreficeria di Valenza.* Venice: Federazione dei Distetti Italiani.

Feld, Steven, and Keith H. Basso. 1996. *Senses of Place.* Santa Fe, NM: School of American Research Press.

Ferber, Michael. 2007. *A Dictionary of Literary Symbols.* Cambridge: Cambridge University Press.

Ferguson, James. 1999. *Expectations of Modernity: Myths and Meanings of Urban Life on the Zambian Copperbelt.* Berkeley, CA.: University of California Press.

—. 2002. "Global Disconnect: Abjection and the Aftermath of Modernism." In *The Anthropology of Globalization: A Reader*, edited by Jonathan Xavier and Renato Prosaldo. Oxford: Blackwell.

Festa, Lodovico, and Giulio Sapelli. 2009. *Capitalismi: crisi globale ed economia italiana, 1929-2009.* Milan: Boroli.

FIAIP. 2008. *Osservatorio immobiliare urbano Alessandria: II semestre.* Alessandria: Federazione Italiana Agenti Immobiliari Professionisti.

—. 2009. *Osservatorio immobiliare urbano Alessandria: II semestre.* Alessandria: Federazione Italiana Agenti Immobiliari Professionisti.

—. 2010. *Osservatorio immobiliare urbano Alessandria: II semestre.* Alessandria: Federazione Italiana Agenti Immobiliari Professionisti.

—. 2011. *Osservatorio immobiliare urbano Alessandria: I semestre.* Alessandria: Federazione Italiana Agenti Immobiliari Professionisti.

Field, John. 2003. *Social Capital.* London: Routledge.

Fine, Ben. 2001. *Social Capital Versus Social Theory: Political Economy and Social Science at the Turn of the Millennium.* London: Routledge.

—. 2010. *Theories of Social Capital: Researchers Behaving Badly.* London: Pluto Press.

Fondazione Cassa di Risparmio di Alessandria, and The European House Ambrosetti. 2010. *Forum: la valorizzazione del monferrato per lo sviluppo della provincia di Alessandria.* Alessandria Fondazione Cassa di Risparmio di Alessandria.

Fondazione Gianfranco Pittatore, and The European House Ambrosetti. 2011. 2° *Forum: la valorizzazione del monferrato per lo sviluppo della provincia di Alessandria.* Alessandria Fondazione Cassa di Risparmio di Alessandria.

Fontefrancesco, Michele Filippo. 2006a. *I fiori dell'inverno.* Turin: Omega.

—. 2006b. *Un'impresa sociale. Ciss 1996-2006.* Valenza: Consorzio Intercomunale Servizi Sociali.

—. 2009a. "E le nuove speranze?" www.radiogold.it. Last access 15/02/12.

—. 2009b. "Gioiello Valenza: cambio di consumi, valore immateriale e possibili nuove prospettive del mercato orafo." Unpublished paper presented at the conference "Val^{2}". Valenza: May..

—. 2009c. "La città che cambia," www.radiogold.it. Last access 15/02/12.

—. 2009d. "Valenza: le persone, l'oro, la Crisi...e la Letteratura," www.radiogold.it Last access 15/02/12.

—. 2009e. "Verso un nuovo disegno di città," www.radiogold.it Last access 15/02/12.

—. 2011. "City of Goldsmiths: Economy, Local Identity and Rhetoric in Valenza." *Anthropological Notebooks* 17, no. 1: 21-59.

—. 2012. "Crafting the Local: Gis, Jewelry and Transformations in Valenza, Italy." *Social Analysis* 56, no. 3: 89-107.

Fortis, Marco. 1998. *Il Made in Italy*. Bologna: Il Mulino.

Foucault, Michel. 1973. *The Birth of the Clinic: An Archaeology of Medical Perception*. London: Routledge.

—. 1978 [1976]. *The History of Sexuality*. New York: Pantheon Books.

—. 1991. "What is an author?" in *Foucault Reader* edited by Paul Rabinow. New York: Pantheon.

—. 1994 [1969]. *L'archeologia Del Sapere: Una Metodologia Per La Sotria Della Cultura*. Milan: Rizzoli.

—. 2001 [1966]. *The Order of Things: An Archaeology of the Human Sciences*. London: Routledge.

—. 2003. "28 January 1976." In *Society Must Be Defended: Lectures at the Collège De France 1975-76*, edited by Mauro Bertani and Alessandro Fontana. New York: Picador.

Fox, Christopher. 2009. *Luxury Market Update 2012 Outlook*. New York: Bain & Company.

Franchi, Claudio. 2009. "Craftsmanship and the Value of the Unique in Jewellery Craft." *Il Giornale AGCN* 3: 40-43.

Freud, Sigmund. 1919. "Das Unheimliche." *Imago* 5, no. 5-6: 297-324.

Freud, Sigmund, and Steven Wilson. 1997. *The Interpretation of Dreams*. Hertfordshire: Wordsworth Editions Ltd.

Fukuyama, Francis. 1995. *Trust: The Social Virtues and the Creation of Prosperity*. London: Hamish Hamilton.

Gaggio, Dario. 2006. "Pyramids of Trust: Embeddedness and Economic Change in Two Italian Gold Jewelry Districts." *Enterprise and Society* 7, no. 1: 19-58.

—. 2007. *In Gold We Trust: Social Capital and Economic Change in the Italian Jewelry Towns*. Princeton, NJ: Princeton University Press.

Gaibisso, Anna Maria. 1995. *L'industria orafa italiana: struttura e strategie di settore*. Milan: Franco Angeli.

Garofoli, Gioacchino. 1981. "Lo sviluppo delle aree periferiche nell'economia italiana degli anni Settanta." *L'Industria* 2, no. 3: 37-39.

—. ed. 2004. *Il distretto orafo di Valenza: tendenze evolutive e prospettive*.Milan: Franco Angeli.

Gereffi, Gary. 2007. "La catena del valore dell'oro e del gioiello nel distretto di Valenza." *Newsletter dell'Osservatorio Internazionale del Distretto di Valenza* 1: 21-44.

Gereffi, Gary, Joonkoo Lee and Valentina De Marchi. 2010. "Gli effetti della recessione economica sulle catene del valore del gioiello in oro: le tendenze in atto nei mercati globali e nei distretti orafi italiani." *Newsletter dell'Osservatorio Internazionale del Distretto di Valenza* 3: 2-9.

Ghezzi, Simone. 2007. *etnografia storica dell'imprenditorialità in Brianza. Antropologia di un'economia regionale*. Milan: Franco Angeli.

Gladwell, Malcom. 2000. *The Tipping Point*. London: Abacus.

Goddard, Victoria. 1978 "Domestic Industry in Naples." *Critique of Anthropology* 3: 139-50.

—. 1996. *Gender, Family and Work in Naples*. Oxford: Berghahn.

Goffman, Erving. 1963. *Stigma: Notes on the Management of Spoiled Identity*. Englewood Cliffs: Prentice-Hall.

Governa, Francesca, Cristiana Rossignolo, and Silvia Saccomani. 2009. "Turin: Urban Regeneration in a Post-Industrial City." *Journal of Urban Regeneration and Renewal* 3, no. 1: 20-30.

Graeber, David. 2001. *Toward an Anthropological Theory of Value: The False Coin of Our Own Dreams*. New York: Palgrave.

Granovetter, Mark. 1985. "Economic Action and Social Structure: The Problem of Embeddedness." *American Journal of Sociology* 91: 481-510.

Grasseni, Cristina. 2003. "Packing Skills: Calibrating Cheese to the Global Market." In *Commodifying Everything: Relationships of the Market*, edited by Susan Strasser. London: Routledge.

—. 2004. "Skilled Vision. An Apprenticeship in Breeding Aesthetics." *Social Anthropology* 12, no. 1: 41-55.

—. 2007. "Conservation, Development and Self-Commodification: Doing Ethnography in the Italian Alps." *Journal of Modern Italian Studies* 12, no. 4: 440-49.

Greenhalgh, Paul. 1997. "The History of Craft." In *The Culture of Crafts*, edited by Paul Dormer. Mancherster: Mancherster University Press.

Grimaldi, Piercarlo. 1993. *Il calendario rituale contadino: il tempo della festa e del lavoro fra tradizione e complessità sociale*. Milano: Franco Angeli.

—. 2012. *Cibo e rito. Il gesto e la parola nell'alimentazione tradizionale*. Palermo: Sellerio.

Gros, Daniel, and Cinzia Alcidi. 2010. *The Impact of the Crisis on the Real Economy*. Brussels: CEPS Policy Brief 201.

Gudeman, Stephen. 2001. *The Anthropology of Economy: Community, Market, and Culture*. Oxford: Blackwell.

—. 2005. "Community and Economy: Economy's Base." In *A Handbook of Economic Anthropology*, edited by James Carrier. Cheltenham: Edward Eldar.

—. 2008. *Economy's Tension: The Dialectics of Community and Market.* Oxford: Berghahn.

—. ed. 2009. *Economic Persuasions.* Oxford: Berghahn.

—. 2010. "Creative Destruction. Efficiency, Equity or Collapse." *Anthropology Today* 26, no. 1: 3-7.

Gudeman, Stephen, and Alberto Rivera. 1990. *Conversations in Columbia: The Domestic Economy in Life and Text.* Cambridge: Cambridge University Press.

Guelpa, Fabrizio. 2010. *Monitor dei distretti: ottobre.* Turin: Banca Intesa-Sanpaolo.

Gupta, Akhil. 1995. "Blurred Boundaries: The Discourse of Corruption, the Culture of Politics, and the Imagined State." *American Ethnologist* 22, no. 2: 375-402.

GWC. 2011. *Gold: A Commodity Like No Other.* London: Gold World Council.

Halford-Strevens, Leofranc. 2005. *The History of Time.* Oxford: Oxford University press.

Hann, Chris, and Keith Hart. 2011. *Economic Anthropology: History, Ethnography, Critique.* London: Polity.

Hart, Keith. 1973. "Informal Income Opportunities and Urban Opportunities in Ghana." *Journal of Modern African Studies* 11, no. 61-89.

—. 2008. "Human Economy." *ASAonline* 1, no. 1.

—. 2010. "Informal Economy." In *The Human Economy*, edited by Keith Hart, Jean-Louis Laville and Antonio David Cattani. Cambridge: Polity.

Hart, Keith, Jean-Louis Laville, and Antonio David Cattani. 2010. "Building the Human Economy Together." In *The Human Economy*, edited by Keith Hart, Jean-Louis Laville and Antonio David Cattani. Cambridge: Polity.

Hart, Keith, and Horacio Ortiz. 2008. "Anthropology in the Finantial Crisis." *Anthropology Today* 26, no. 6: 1-3.

Hart, Neil. 2009. "External and Internal Economies." In *A Handbook of Industrial Districts*, edited by Giacomo Becattini, Marco Bellandi and Lisa De Propris. Cheltenham: Edward Elgar.

Hartshorne, Charles, and Paul Wiess, eds. 1933. *Collected Papers of Charle Sander Charles.* Cambridge MA, USA: Harvard University Press.

Herman, Edward S., and Noam Chomsky. 1994. *Manufacturing Consent: The Political Economy of the Mass Media.* London: Vintage.

Hertz, Ellen. 1998. *The Trading Crowd: An Ethnography of the Shanghai Stock Market*. Cambridge: Cambridge University Press.

Herzfeld, Michael. 1997. "Social Poetics in Theory and Practice: Regular Guys and Irregular Practices." In *Cultural Intimacy: Social Poetics in the Nation-State*, edited by Michael Herzfeld. New York: Routledge.

—. 2004. *The Body Impolitic: Artisans and Artifice in the Global Hierarchy of Value.* Chicago: University of Chicago Press.

—. 2010. "Essentialism." In *Encyclopedia of Social and Cultural Anthropology. Second Edition*, edited by Alan Barnard and Jonathan Spencer. London: Routledge.

—. 2011. "Crisis Attack: Impromptu Ethnography in the Greek Maelstrom." *Anthropology Today* 27, no. 5: 22-26.

Hesmondhalgh, David, and Sarah Baker. 2008. "Creative Work and Emotional Labour in the Television Industry." *Theory, Culture, Society* 25, no. 97.

Hilton, Mattew. 2004. "The Legacy of Luxury: Moralities of Consumption since the 18th Century." *Journal of Consumer Culture* 4: 101-23.

Holmes, Douglas R. 1989. *Cultural Disenchantments: Worker Peasantries in Northeast Italy.* Princeton, NJ: Princeton University Press.

Howe, Lea. 1990. *Becoming Unemployed in Northern Ireland: An Ethnographic Study.* Cambridge: Cambridge University Press.

Hunter Bradley, Betsy. 1999. *The Works: The Industrial Architecture of the United States.* New York: Oxford University Press.

Huysseune, Michel. 2000. "Masculinity and Secessionism in Italy: An Assessment." *Nations and Nationalism* 6, no. 4: 591-610.

Il Piccolo. 2010. "Expopiemonte fra Cavallera e Borioli." *Il Piccolo*, 26/05.

IMF. 2011. *World Economic Outlook Database.* Washington, DC: International Monetary Fund.

Inda, Jonathan Xavier, and Renato Prosaldo. 2002. "Tacking Global Flows." In *The Anthropology of Globalization: A Reader*, edited by Jonathan Xavier Inda and Renato Prosaldo. Oxford: Blackwell.

Ingold, Tim. 2000. *The Perception of the Environment: Essays on Livelihood, Dwelling and Skill.* London: Routledge.

Isnenghi, Mario. 1997. "La Piazza." In *i luoghi della memoria: strutture ed eventi dellIitalia unita*, edited by Mario Isnenghi. Bari-Rome: Laterza.

ISTAT. 2001. *Censimento generale per l'industria e i servizi.* Rome: Istituto Nazionale di Statistica.

James, Duncan. 2007. *Antique Jewellery. Its Manufacture, Materials and Design.* Princes Risborough: Shire Publications.

Jancius, Angela. 2006. "Unemployment, Deindustrialization, and 'Community Economy' in Eastern Germany." *Ethnos: Journal of Anthropology* 71, no. 2: 213-32.

Jones, Sian, and Thomas Yarrow. 2012. "Craft as Detached Engagement: An Ethnography of Stone Masonry." Unpublished paper presented at the Department of Anthropology of University College of London, February 29.

Kahan, Richiard. 2005. "Intimacy." In *Encyclopedia of Social Theory*, edited by George Ritzer. London: Sage.

Keller, Charles M., and Janet Dixon Keller. 1996. *Cognition and Tool Use: The Blacksmith at Work.* Cambridge: Cambridge University Press.

Kemp, Simon. 1998. "Perceving Luxury and Necessity." *Journal of Economic Psychology* 19: 591-606.

Kemper, Robert V., and Jack R. Rollwagen. 1996. "Urban Anthropology." In *Encyclopedia of Cultural Anthropology*, edited by Melvin Ember David Levinson. New York: Henry Holt and Co.

Kessler, Ronald C., J. Blake Turner, and House James S. 1989. "Unemployment, Reemployment, and Emotional Functioning in a Community Sample." *American Sociological Review* 54, no. 4: 648-57.

Knight, Daniel Martyn. 2011. *Crisis and Prosperity: Status, Accountability and Time in Central Greece.* Doctoral Thesis, Durham University.

Kontradiev, Nikolaj Dmitrievic. 1981 [1925]. *I cicli economici maggiori.* Bologna: Cappelli.

Kuper, Adam. 1994. "Culture, Identity, and the Project of a Cosmopolitan." *Man* 29: 537-54.

Langley, Paul. 2008. *The Everyday Life of Global Finance: Saving and Borrowing in Anglo-America.* Oxford: Oxford University Press.

Latour, Bruno. 1987. *Science in Action: How to Follow Scientists and Engineers through Society.* Cambridge, MA: Harvard University Press.

—. 2005. *Reassembling the Social: An Introduction to Actor-Network-Theory.* Oxford: Clarendon.

Lave, Jean. 1993. "The Practice of Learning." In *Understanding Practice. Perspectives on Activity and Context*, edited by Seth Chaiklin and Jean Lave. Cambridge: Cambridge University Press.

Lave, Jean, and Etienne Wenger. 1991. *Situated Learning: Legitimate Peripheral Participation.* Cambridge: Cambridge University Press.

Law, John, and Annemarie Mol. 2002. "Complexities: An Introduction." In *Complexities: Social Studies of Knowldege Practices*, edited by John Law and Annemarie Mol. Durham NC: Duke University Press.
Lazzarato, Maurizio. 2004. *The Political Form of Coordination.* Vienna: EIPCP.
Leana, Carrie R., and Daniel C. Feldmann. 1988. "Individual Responses to Job Loss: Perceptions, Reactions, and Coping Behaviors." *Journal of Management* 14, no. 3: 375-89.
—. 1992. *Coping with Job Loss: How Individuals, Organizations, and Communities Repond to Layoffs.* New York: Lexington Books.
Lee, Jaewoo, Rau Rabanal, and Damiano Sandri. 2010. *U.S. Consumption after the 2008 Crisis.* Washington, DC: International Monetary Fund.
Lee, Raymond M. 1985. "Redundancy, Labour Markets and Informal Relations." *Sociological Review* 33, no. 2: 469-95.
Lee, Sherman E. 1963. "Janus in Limbo." *The Bulletin of the Cleveland Museum of Art* 50, no. 1: 3-6.
Leins, Stefan. 2011. "Pricing the Revolution: Financial Analysts Respond to the Egyptian Uprising." *Anthropology Today* 27, no. 4: 11-14.
Lenti, Lia. 1994. *Gioielli e gioiellieri di Valenza. Arte e storia orafa: 1825-1975.* Turin: U.Allemandi.
—. 2008. *Melchiorre&C. Dal 1873 al 1933.* Valenza: For.Al.
—. 2010. *Valenza ou la joaullerie italienne*. Sardigliano: Nuvole.
Lenti, Lia, and Maria Cristina Bergesio. 2005. *Dizionario del gioiello italiano del XIX e XX secolo* Torino: Allemandi.
Lenti, Libero, and Gino Pugnetti. 1974. *Arte orafa valenzana*. Alessandria: Cassa di Risparmio di Alessandria.
Lerner, Gad. 1991. *Profondo Nord I.T. P91316/001*. Rome:RAI.
Lévi-Strauss, Claude. 1971. *Tristes Tropiques.* Paris: Plon.
—. 1962. *La Pensée Sauvage.* Paris: Plon.
Lewis, Oscar. 1961. *The Children of Sanchez*. New York: Random House.
—. 1963. *The Culture of Poverty.* New Brunswick, NJ: Transaction Publishers.
—. 1966. La Vida: A Puerto Rican Family in the Culture of Poverty -San Juan and New York. New York: Random House.
Limes. 2011. *L'Italia dopo l'Italia.* Rome: L'Espresso.
Little, Craig B. 1976. "Technical-Professional Unemployment: Middle-Cass Adaptability to Personal Crisis." *The Sociological Quarterly* 17: 262-74.
Loasby, Brian J. 2009. "Industrial Districts in Marshall's Economics." In *A Handbook of Industrial Districts*, edited by Giacomo Becattini, Marco Bellandi and Lisa De Propris. Cheltenham: Edward Elgar.

Loftsdóttir, Kristín. 2010. "The Loss of Innocence: The Icelandic Financial Crisis and Colonial Past." *Anthropology Today* 26, no. 6: 9-13.

Lovell, Nadia. 1998. "Introduction: Belonging in Need of Emplacement?" In *Locality and Belonging,* edited by Nadia Lovell. London: Routledge.

Lucie-Smith, Edward. 1981. *The Story of Craft: The Craftsman's Role in Society*. Oxford: Phaidon.

MacKenzie, Donald A. 2009. *Material Markets: How Economic Agents Are Constructed.* Oxford: Oxford University Press.

Maggiora, Pier Giorgio. 2010. *Il Novecento a Valenza*. Valenza: Giordano.

Magni, Carlo. 1999. *Modelli di sviluppo a macchia d'olio: ipotesi di lettura dell'evoluzione di sistemi locali.* Milan: Franco Angeli.

Maher, Vanessa. 2007. *Sarte, sartine e cambiamento sociale 1860-1960.* Turin: Rosenberg & Sellier Editori.

Malanima, Paolo, and Vera Zamagni. 2010. "150 Years of the Italian Economy, 1861–2010." *Journal of Modern Italian Studies* 15, no. 1: 1-20.

Malinowski, Bronislaw. 1932 [1922]. *Argonauts of the Western Pacific: An Account of Native Enterprise and Adventure in the Archipelagoes of Melanesian New Guinea.* London: Routledge.

Mandel, Ernest. 1968. *Marxist Economic Theory*. London: Merlin.

Marchand, Trevor H. J. 2001. *Minaret Building and Apprenticeship in Yemen*. Richmond: Curzon.

—. 2009. The Masons of Djenné. Bloomington, IN: Indiana University Press.

—. 2010a. "Embodied Cognition and Communication: Studies with British Fine Woodworkers." Journal of the Royal Anthropological Institute 16: S100-S20.

—. 2010b. "Making Knowledge: Explorations of the Indissoluble Relation between Minds, Bodies, and Environment." *Journal of the Royal Anthropological Institute* 16: S1-S21.

Markowitz, Fran. 1996. "Living in Limbo: Bosnian Muslim Refugees in Istrael." *Human Organization* 55, no. 2: 127-32.

Markusen, Ann. 1996. "Sticky Places in Slippery Space: A Typology of Industrial Districts." *Economic Geography* 72, no. 3: 293-313.

Marshall, Alfred. 1920. *Principles of Economics: An Introductory Volume*. London: Macmillan.

Marshall, Alfred, and Mary Paley Marshall. 1879. *The Economics of Industry.* London: Macmillan.

Marx, Karl. 1959 [1844]. "Enstranged Labour." In *Economic and Philosophic Manuscripts of 1844*, edited by Karl Marx. Moscow: Progress Publishers.

—. 2010 [1867]. *Capital: A Critique of Political Economy. Vol. I.* www.marxists.org. Last access 23/04/13.

Marx, Karl, and Friedrich Engels. 2000 [1848]. *Manifesto of the Communist Party.* www.marxists.org. Last access 23/04/13.

Maurer, Bill. 2005. "Finance." In *A Handbook of Economic Anthropology*, edited by James Carrier. Cheltenham: Edward Eldar.

Mauss, Marcel. 1967 [1925]. *The Gift: Forms and Functions of Exchange in Archaic Societies.* London: W.W. Norton.

Mazzocchi, Antonio. 2006. *Le mani nel tempo. Storia della cultura artigianale italiana.* Rome: Edigraf.

Micelli, Stefano. 2011. *Futuro artigiano: l'innovazione nelle mani degli italiani*. Venice: Marsilio.

Miller, Daniel. 2010. *Stuff*. Cambridge: Polity

—. 2012. *Consumption and its consequences*. Cambridge: Polity.

Miron, Jeffrey A. 1986. "Seasonal Fluctuations and the Life Cycle-Permanent Income Model of Consumption." *Journal of Political Economy* 94, no. 6: 1258-79.

—. 1996. *The Economics of Seasonal Cycles.* Cambridge, MA: MIT Press.

Misztal, Barbara A. 1996. *Trust in Modern Societies: The Search for the Bases of Social Order*. Cambridge: Polity.

Mitchell, Tymothy. 1991. "The Limits of the State: Beyond Statist Approaches and Their Critics." *The American Political Science Review* 85, no. 1: 77-96.

Miyazaki, Hirokazu. 2006. "Economy of Dreams: Hope in Global Capitalism and Its Critiques." Cultural Anthropology 21, no. 2: 147-72.

Miyazaki, Hirokazu, and Annelise Riles. 2005. "Failure as an Endpoint." In *Global Assemblages: Technology, Politics, and Ethics as Anthropological Problems,* edited by Aihwa Ong and Stephen J. Collier. Oxford: Blackwell.

Molé, Noelle J. 2012. *Labor Disorders in Neoliberal Italy.* Bloomington: Indiana University Press.

Molina, Maria Grazia, and Maria Carla Manenti. 1994. *Oro e lavoro: cento anni oreficeria in Valenza 1840-1940.* Turin: Lindau.

Mollona, Massimiliano. 2009. *Made in Sheffield: An Ethnography of Industrial Work and Politics*. Oxford: Berghahn.

Morandi, Corinna. 2006. "Milano e Torino." *Territorio* 39: 69-72.

Morselli, Danilo. 2012. "La provincia di Alessandria in cifre: 2012". *Rassegna Economica della Camera di Commercio di Alessandria.* No. 3: 24-33.

Morris, William. 1888. "The Revival of Handicraft." *Forthnightly Review*, November.

Mortara Garavelli, Bice. 2003. *Manuale di Retorica.* Milan: Bompiani.

Mosco, Marilena. 2003. "Eros et Voluptas: il piacere del gioiello sulla pelle." In *Gioielli in Italia: donne e ori. storia, arte, passione*, edited by Lia Lenti. Venice: Marsilio Editore.

Narotzky, Susana. 1997. *New Directions in Economic Anthropology.* London: Pluto.

—. 2009. "Regulation and Production in a Globalized World; What Ethnography Brings to Comparison." *Ethnology* 48, no. 3: 175-93.

Narotzky, Susana, and Gavin A. Smith. 2006. *Immediate Struggles: People, Power, and Place in Rural Spain.* Berkeley, CA: University of California Press.

Nas, Peter J. M. 2002. "Masterpieces of oral and intangible culture: Reflections on the UNESCO world heritage list." *Current Anthropology*, 43, no. 1: 139-48

Navaro-Yashin, Yael. 2002. *Faces of the State.* Princeton, NJ: Princeton University Press.

Neilson, Brett, and Ned Rossiter. 2005. "From Precarity to Precariousness and Back Again: Labour, Life and Unstable Networks." *The Fibreculture Journal* 5.

—. 2008. "Precarity as a Political Concept, or, Fordism as Exception." *Theory, Culture & Society* 25, no. 7-8: 51-72.

Nesi, Edoardo. 2010. *Storia della mia gente.* Milan: Bompiani.

New York Times. 2011. "Credit Crisis - the Essential." www.nytimes.com. Last access 15/02/12.

Newman, Harold. 1981. *An Illustrated Dictionary of Jewelry.* London Thames and Hudson.

Newman, Katherine S. 1989. *Falling from Grace: The Experience of Downward Mobility in the American Middle Class.* New York: St. Martin's Press.

Nora, Pierre. 1989. "Between Memory and History: Les Lieux De Mémoire." *Representations* 26, no. 7-25.

O'Brien, Robert T. 2006. "Unemployment and Disposable Workers in Philadelphia: Just How Far Have the Bastards Gone?." *Ethnos*: *Journal of Anthropology* 71, no. 2: 165-90.

Oliva, Federico 1988. "Milano, Torino e Genova." *Urbanistica* 93: 104-121.

OPML. 2011. *Indicatori occupazionali a Valenza tra Il 2009 Ed Il 2010.* Alessandria: Osservatorio Provinciale Mercato del Lavoro.
Orengo, Vladi, Gianfranco Isoardi, and Carlo Tarchi. 1964. *02501: Gli eredi di Benvenuto Cellini.* Italy: INCOM.
Ortiz, Sutti. 2005. "Decisions and Choises: The Rationality of Economic Actors." In *A Handbook of Economic Anthropology*, edited by James Carrier. Cheltenham,: Edward Eldar.
Ouroussoff, Alexandra. 2010. *Wall Street at War: The Secret Struggle for the Global Economy.* Cambridge: Polity.
Paetcher, Carrier. 2003. "Learning Masculinities and Femininities: Power/Knowldege and Legitimate Peripheral Partecipation." *Women's studies international forum* 26, no. 6: 541-52.
Paradiso, Rocco. 2007. "Commercio internazionale: un segnale positivo " *Newsletter dell'Osservatorio Internazionale del Distretto di Valenza* no. 0: 8-11.
—. 2008a. "All'interno delle imprese per rilanciare il distretto: lo study tour." *Newsletter dell'Osservatorio Internazionale del Distretto di Valenza* 1, no. 1: 12-20.
—. 2008b. "L'industria alessandrina della gioielleria: i principali indicatori." *Newsletter dell'Osservatorio Internazionale del Distretto di Valenza* 1, no. 2: 32-33.
—. 2008c. "L'industria alessandrina della gioielleria: il commercio internazionale." *Newsletter dell'Osservatorio Internazionale del Distretto di Valenza* 1, no. 1: 1-11.
—. 2008d. *Valorizzare Valenza nella catena globale del valore.* Unpublished paper presented at the conference "Osservatorio Internazione del Distretto Valenza". Valenza, October.
—. 2009. *Progetto Val^2 E Analisi Del Commercio Internazionale Orafo.* Unpublished paper presented at the conference "Val^2". Valenza, May.
Pardo, Italo. 1996. *Managing Existence in Naples: Morality, Action, and Structure.* Cambridge: Cambridge University Press.
Parry, Jonathan P. 2005. "Industrial Work." In *A Handbook of Economic Anthropology*, edited by James Carrier. Cheltenham: Edward Eldar.
Parry, Jonathan P., and Maurice Bloch. 1989. "Introduction: Money and the Morality of Exchange." In *Money and the Morality of Exchange*, edited by Jonathan P. Parry and Maurice Bloch. Cambridge: Cambridge University Press.
Penna Ivaldi, Grazia. 2008. *La Camera del Lavoro di Valenza: 1945/1955.* Alessandria: Camera del Lavoro di Alessandria.

Perelman, Mariano D. 2008. "Theorizing Unemployment: Toward an Argentine Anthropology of Work." *Anthropology of Work Review* 28, no. 1.

Petsimeris, Petros. 1998. "Urban Decline and the New Social and Ethnic Divisions in the Core Cities of the Italian Industrial Triangle." *Urban Studies* 35, no. 3: 449-66.

Pietrasanta, Massimo. 1991. *Mondo orafo e disagio.* Valenza: Unità Socio-Sanitaria Locale 71.

Pinto, Luis. 1999 [1990]. "Broken Careers." In *The Weight of the World*, edited by Pierre Bourdieu. Cambridge: Polity Press.

Piore, Micheal, and Charles F. Sabel. 1984. *The Second Industrial Devide.* New York: Basic Books.

Pipyrou, Stravroula. 2011. *Power, Governance and Representation: An Anthropological Analysis of Kinship, the Ndrangheta and Dance within the Greek Linguistic Minority of Reggio Calabria, South Italy.* Doctoral Thesis, Durham University.

Poggio, Eleonora. 2011. " Distretto orafo, emergenza occupazione." *La Provincia Pavese*, 13/12.

Polanyi, Karl. 2001 [1944]. *The Great Transformation: The Political and Economic Origins of Our Time.* Boston, MA: Beacon Press.

—. 1971. *Primitive, Archaic, and Modern Economies: Essays of Karl Polanyi*. Boston: Beacon Press.

Polanyi, Karl, Conrad Maynadier Arensberg, and Harry W. Pearson, eds. 1957. *Trade and Market in the Early Empires: Economies in History and Theory*. Glencoe: Free Press & Falcon's Wing Press.

Porporato, Davide, ed. 2010. *Nuove pratiche di comunità. I patrimoni culturali etnoantropologici fra tradizione e complessità sociale*. Turin: Omega.

Portelli, Alessandro, Bruno Bonomo, Alice Sotgia, and Ulrike Viccaro. 2006. *Città di parole. Storia orale da una periferia romana*. Rome: Donzelli.

Porter, M. 1990. *The Competitive Advantage of Nations.* New York: Free Press.

Prandi, G. 2000. *A summa 'd Valensa : canzoni in dialetto valenzano e rime in lingua*. Valenza: Battezzati.

Prediction Markets. 2009. "An Uncertain Future." *The Economist,* 26/2.

Putnam, Robert David. 2000. *Blowing Alone: The Collapse and Revival of American Community.* New York: Simon & Schuster.

Putnam, Robert David, Leonardi Robert, and Raffaella Y. Nanetti. 1993. *Making Democracy Work. Civic Tradition in Modern Italy.* Princeton, NJ: Princeton University Press.

Quaroni, Ferruccio, and Silvio Zeppa. 2005. *Valenza in...fatti. 2000/2005: bilancio di una città che è cambiata*. Valenza: Comune di Valenza.

Rabellotti, Roberta, Anna Carabelli, and Giovanni Hirsh. 2009. "Italian Industrial Districts on the Move: Where Are They Going." *European Planning Studies* 17, no. 1: 19-41.

Radiogold. 2010. "Mercato Immobilire: Ovada Vola, Valenza Precipita." www.radiogold.it. Last access 15/02/12.

Ramazzotti, Paolo. 2008. "Industrial District and Economic Decline in Italy." *Quaderni del Dipartimento di Istituzioni Economiche e Finanziarie* 45: 2-32.

Rankin, Katharine N. 2004. *The Cultural Politics of Markets: Economic Liberalization and Social Change in Nepal*. London: Pluto.

Raselli, Gianni, and Massimo Mensi. 2007. "La Newsletter come collegamento da e per il territorio." *Newsletter dell'Osservatorio Internazionale del Distretto di Valenza* 1, no. 0: 3.

Reed, Adam. 2002. "City of Details: Interpreting the Personality of London." *Journal of the Royal Anthropological Institute* 8, no. 1: 127-41.

Regione Piemonte, Associazione Orafa Valenzana, and Expopiemonte. 2010. *Valenza Gioielli. Catalogo 2010*. Valenza: Associazione Orafa Valenzana

Richardson, Frederick L. W. 1979. "Social Interaction and Industrial Productivity." In *The Uses of Anthropology*, edited by Walter Goldschmidt. Washington D.C.: American Anthropological Association.

Ricoeur, Paul. 2000. *La memoire, l'histoire, l'oubli.* Paris: Seuil.

Robbins, Richard. 2009. "Anthropologizing Economics: Lessons from the Latest Crisis." *Anthropology News* 50, no. 7: 11-12.

Rogers, Yvonne, Jenny Preece, and Helen Sharp. 2011. *Interaction Design: Beyond Human-Computer Interaction*. Oxford: Blackwell

Romano, Fulvio. 2009. "Il protocarnevale di San Martino, tra calendario lunare e meteorologia popolare." In *Il teatro della vita: le feste tradizionali in Piemonte*, edited by Piercarlo Grimaldi and Luciano Nattino. Torino Omega.

Romeo, Rosario. 1988. *Breve storia della grande industria in italia 1861-1961*. Milan: Il Saggiatore.

Rossi, Elena. 2009a. "Crisi." *Radiogold*, 29/3.

—. 2009b. "Il Commercio a Valenza." *Radiogold*, 23/4.

—. 2009c. "Vita e lavoro nella Valenza che (non) cambia." *Radiogold*, 30/4.

Røyrvik, Email A. 2011. The Allure of Capitalism. An Ethnography of Managment and the Global Economy Crisis. Oxford: Berghahn.

RP-Ricerche e Progetti. 1979. *Il ciclo orafo: il caso dell'area attrezzata di Valenza Po*. Milan: Franco Angeli.

Rubino, Margherita. 1992. "La crisi tocca l'oreficeria." *La Stampa* (ed. Alessandria), 05/02.

Ruido, Maria, and Jaron Rowan. 2007. "In the Mood for Work." In *Producta 50*, edited by YProductions. Barcelona: Generalitat de Catalunya.

Ruskin, John. 1851. *The Stones of Venice. London*: Smith, Elder, and co.

Sabel, Charles F. 2004. "District on the Move; Note on the Tedis Survey of the Internationalization of District Firms" in *La governance dell'internazionalizzazione produttiva: L'osservatorio* edited by Antonia Rossi and Andrea Cenderello. Rome: Formez.

Sanjek, Roger. 2010. "Household." In *Encyclopedia of Social and Cultural Anthropology. Second Edition*, edited by Alan Barnard and Jonathan Spencer. London: Routledge.

Sartori, Giovanni. 1999. *Homo Videns*. Roma-Bari: Laterza.

Schneider, Jane, ed. 1998. *Italy's "Southern Question". Orientalism in One Country*. Oxford: Berghahn.

Schneider, Jane, and Peter Schneider. 1976. *Culture and Political Economy in Western Sicily*. London: Academic Press.

Schumpeter, Joseph Alois. 1994 [1943]. *Capitalism, Socialism and Democracy*. London: Routledge.

—. 2008 [1939]. *Business Cycles: A Theoretical, Historical and Statistical Analysis of the Capitalist Process*. Saguenay: Lagrange.

Schwegler, Tara A. 2009. "The Global Crisis of Economic Meaning." *Anthropology News* 50, no. 7: 9, 12.

Schwittay, Anke. 2009. "Anthropologists Take on the Financial Crisis: Interviews on Money and Finance." *Anthropology News* 50, no. 7: 26-26.

Scozzesi, Enzo. 2010. "Il mattone torna conveniente." *Il Piccolo*, 9/07.

Searce. 2009. *The Jewellery Market in the EU.* Rotterdam: Centre for the promotion of imports from developing countries.

Seeger, Matthew Wayne, Timothy Lester Sellnow, and Robert R. Ulmer. 1998. "Communication, Organization, and Crisis." *Communication Yearbook* 21: 231–75.

Seligman, Adam B. 1997. *The Problem of Trust*. Princeton, N.J.: Princeton University Press.

Sennett, Richard. 2008. *The Craftman*. London: Pinguin Books.

Servizio Studi e Ricerche. 2010a. *Economia e finanza dei distretti industriali III*. Milan: Intesa Sanpaolo, Serivizio Studi e Ricerche.
—. 2010b. *Monitor dei distretti II*. Turin: Banca Intesa-Sanpaolo.
—. 2011. *Monitor dei distretti I*. Turin: Banca Intesa-Sanpaolo.
Sforzi, Fabio. 2009. "The Empirical Evidence of Industrial Districts in Italy." In *A Handbook of Industrial Districts*, edited by Giacomo Becattini, Marco Bellandi and Lisa De Propris. Cheltenham: Edward Elgar.
Sg Valenza. 2005. "Sciopero!" *Sinistramente* 1, no. 4: 8.
Sharma, Pramodita. 2004. "An Overview of the Field of Family Business Studies: Current Status and Directions for the Future." *Family Business Review* 17, no. 1: 1-36.
Showstack Sasson, Anne 2010. "Gramsci's Subversion of the Language of Politics." In *Gramsci, Language, and Translation*, edited by Peter Ives and Rocco Lacorte. Lanham, MD: Lexiton Books.
Solinas, Giovanni. 2006. "Integrazione dei mercati e raggiustamento nei distretti industriali." *Sinergie* 69.
Soprani, Pierguido, ed. 2006. *Codice della sicurezza: disciplina della prevenzione e dell'igiene sui luoghi di lavoro*. Milan: Il Sole 24 Ore.
Sorba, Carlotta. 1998. "Identità locali." *Contemporanea* 1, no. 1: 157-70.
Spooner, Brian. 1986. "Weaver and Dealers: The Autenticity of an Oriental Carpet." In *The Social Life of Things: Commodities in Cultural Perspective*, edited by Arjun Appadurai. Cambridge: Cambridge University Press.
Stacul, Jaro. 2003. *The Bounded Field: Localism and Local Identity in an Italian Alpine Valley*. Oxford: Berghahn.
—. 2007. "Understanding Neoliberalism: Reflections on the 'End of Politics' in Northern Italy." *Journal of Modern Italian Studies* 12, no. 4: 450-59.
Stacul, Jaro, Christina Moutsou, and Helen Kopnina. 2006. *Crossing European Boundaries: Beyond Conventional Geographical Categories*. Oxford: Berghahn.
Standing, Guy. 2011. *The Precariat: The New Dangerous Class*. London: Bloomsbury.
Star, Susan Leigh, and James R. Griesemer. 1989. "Institutional Ecology, 'Translations' and Boundary Objects: Amateurs and Professionals in Berkeley's Museum of Vertebrate Zoology, 1907-39 " *Social Studies of Science* 19, no. 3: 387-420.
Stewart, Kathleen. 1996. *A Space on the Side of the Road: Cultural Poetics in an "Other" America*. Princeton, NJ: Princeton University Press.

—. 2007. *Ordinary Affects*. Durham, N.C.: Duke University Press.

Stoler, Ann Laura. 2008. "Imperial Debris: Reflections on Ruins and Ruination." *Cultural Anthropology* 23, no. 2: 191-219.

Strathern, Marilyn. 1996. "Cutting the Network." *Journal of the Royal Anthropological Institute* 2, no. 3: 517-35.

Stuart Mills, John. 2009 [1848]. *Principles of Political Economy*. Salt Lake City, UT: Project Gutenberg Literary Archive Foundation.

Swedberg, Richard. 2003. *Principles of Economic Sociology*. Princeton, NJ: Princeton University Press.

Sztompka, Piotr. 1999. *Trust: A Sociological Theory*. Cambridge: Cambridge University Press.

Tak, Herman. 1990. "Longing for Local Identity: Intervillage Relations in an Italian Mountain Area." *Anthropological Quarterly* 63, no. 2: 90-100.

Taleb, Nassim Nicholas. 2007. *The Black Swan: The Impact of the Highly Improbable*. London: Penguin Books.

Taylor, Frederick Winslow 2004 [1911]. "The Principles of Scientific Management." In *Essays on Some Unsettled Questions of Political Economy*, edited by John Stuart Mill. Salt Lake City, UT: Project Gutemberg.

Tett, Gillian. 2009a. *Fool's Gold: How Unrestrained Greed Corrupted a Dream, Shattered Global Market and Unleashed a Catastrophe.* London: Little Brown Books.

—. 2009b. "Icebergs and Ideologies: How Information Flows Fuelled the Financial Crisis." *Anthropology News* 50, no. 7: 6-7.

Thrift, Nigel. 2004. "Intensities of Feeling: Towards a Spatial Politics of Affect." *Geografiska Annaler: Series B*, Human Geography 86, no. 1: 57-78.

Tiffany, Donald W., James R. Cowan, and Phyllis M. Tiffany. 1970. *The Unemployed: A Social-Psychological Portrait*. Englewood Cliffs, NJ: Prentice-Hall.

Tinelli, C., MC. Oppezzo, A. Bulgheroni, G. Sassi, and A. Marinoni. 1990. "Health Status of Goldsmiths of the Ussl 71 in Valenza." *Giornale Italiano Medicina del Lavoro* 12, no. 1: 9-14.

Triglia, Carlo. 2009. "A Meeting Ground for the Social Sciences." In *A Handbook of Industrial Districts*, edited by Giacomo Becattini, Marco Bellandi and Lisa De Propris. Cheltenham: Edward Elgar.

Troin, Jean-François. 1997. *Le metropolis del mediterraneo.* Milan: Jaka Book.

Tsing, Anna Lowenhaupt. 2005. *Friction: An Ethnography of Global Connection*. Princeton, NJ: Princeton University Press.

Turkle, Sherry. 2007. "Introduction: The Things That Matter." In *Evocative Objects: Things We Think With,* edited by Sherry Turkle. Cambridge, MA: MIT.

Turner, Victor Witter. 1967. *The Forest of Symbols: Aspects of Ndembu Ritual.* Ithaca: Cornell University Press.

—. 1977. "Variations on a Theme of Liminality." In *Secular Ritual*, edited by Sally F. Moore and Barbara G Myerhoff. Assen: Van Gorkum.

UP. 2010. *Occupazione in Piemonte*. Turin: Unioncamere Piemonte.

Valentine, Charles A. 1968. *Culture and Poverty: Critique and Counter-Proposals*. Chicago: University of Chicago Press.

Van Gennep, Arnold. 1960. *The Rites of Passage.* London: Routeledge and Kegan Paul.

Van Maanen, John. 1988. *Tales of the Field: On Writing Ethnography.* Chicago: University of Chicago Press.

Vargas-Cetina, Gabriela. 2000. "From Handicraft to Monocrop: The Production of Pecorino Cheese in Highland Sardinia." *Commodities and Globalization: Anthropological Perspectives*, edited by Angelique Haugerud, M. Priscilla Stone and Peter D. Little. Lanham, MD: Rowman and Littlefield Publishers.

Venkatesan, Soumhya. 2009. "Rethinking Agency: Persons and Things in the Heterotopia of 'Traditional Indian Craft'." *Journal of the Royal Anthropological Institute* 15, no. 1: 78-95.

Villemez, Wayne J. 2000. "Povery." In *Encyclopedia of Sociology Second Edition*, edited by Edgar F. Borgatta and Rhonda J.V. Montgomery. New York: MacMillan Reference USA.

Wadel, Cato. 1973. *Now Whose Fault Is That? The Struggle for Self-Esteem in the Face of Chronic Unemployment.* San Francisco, CA: Bolerium Books.

Walther, Larry M., and Christopher J. Skousen.2010. *Analytics for Managerial Decision Making: Budgeting and Decision Making.* www.booksboon.com. Last access 15/04/13.

Wenger, Etienne. 1998. *Communities of Practice. Learning, Meaning, and Identity*. Cambridge: Cambridge University Press.

Wilensky, Harold. 1959. "The Skidder: Ideological Adjustments of the Downardly Mobile Worker." *American Sociological Review* 24: 215-31.

Williams, Raymond. 1983. *Keywords: A Vocabulary of Culture and Society*. London: Fontana.

Wilson, Tamar Diana. 2009. "Economic Crisis and the Decline of Remittances to Mexico." *Anthropological Quarterly* 82, no. 2: 587-97.

Yanagisako, Sylvia Junko. 1991. "Capital and Gendered Interest in Italian Family Firms." In *The Family in Italy*, edited by David I. Kertzer and Richard P. Saller. New Haven: Yale University Press.

—. 2002. *Producing Culture and Capital: Family Firms in Italy*. Princeton, NJ: Princeton University Press.

Zamagni, Vera. 1993. *The Economic History of Italy, 1860-1990.* Oxford: Clarendon Press.

Zeman, Jay. 1977. "Peirce's Theory of Signs." In *A Perfusion of Signs*, edited by Thomas A. Sebeok. Bloomington: Indiana University Press.

Zemide, Roberta. 2002. "Mostra orafa scaccia crisi?" *Il Piccolo*, 4/10.

—. 2005. "Polo espositivo: il progetto." *Il Piccolo*, 23/11.

—. 2008. "Sacrifici contro la Crisi." *Il Piccolo*, 19/12.

—. 2009a. "Crisi del distretto: dati allarmanti." *Il Piccolo*, 27/02.

—. 2009b. "Iniziative comuni anticrisi." *Il Piccolo*, 22/05.

—. 2011. "Si ricomincia da Vicenza." *Il Piccolo,* 17/1.